FROM TRIBAL CULTURES TO
20TH-CENTURY STATEHOOD

Bred in the frustration of colonial rule and
racked by the nightmare of racial bitterness,
Africa's story is deeply rooted in the past.
AFRICA YESTERDAY AND TODAY offers a
distinguished collection of essays by the
world's foremost geologists, anthropologists
and historians as well as exciting firsthand
accounts by African Nationalists—black
and white. Here is a comprehensive and
moving portrait of Africa's troubled
past and the problems and prospects
of her future.

BANTAM PATHFINDER EDITIONS

Bantam Pathfinder Editions provide the best in fiction and nonfiction in a wide variety of subject areas. They include novels by classic and contemporary writers; vivid, accurate histories and biographies; authoritative works in the sciences; collections of short stories, plays and poetry.

Bantam Pathfinder Editions are carefully selected and approved. They are durably bound, printed on specially selected high-quality paper, and presented in a new and handsome format.

AFRICA
YESTERDAY
AND TODAY

EDITED BY CLARK D. MOORE
AND ANN DUNBAR

THE GEORGE SCHOOL READINGS
ON DEVELOPING LANDS
Clark D. Moore and David W. Miller,
Series Editors

BANTAM BOOKS

BANTAM PATHFINDER EDITIONS

NEW YORK / TORONTO / LONDON

TO STEVEN CURRIER

RLI: VLM 11.0
     IL 9.12

AFRICA YESTERDAY AND TODAY
A Bantam Pathfinder edition / published April 1968
2nd printing
3rd printing

Library of Congress Catalog Card Number: 68-19251

Front- and back-cover photographs courtesy of
Gerald T. Counihan.

CONTENTS

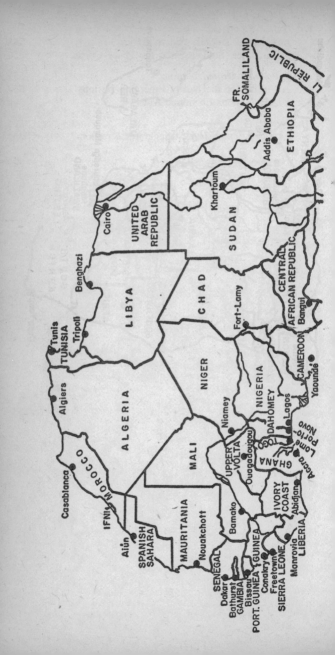

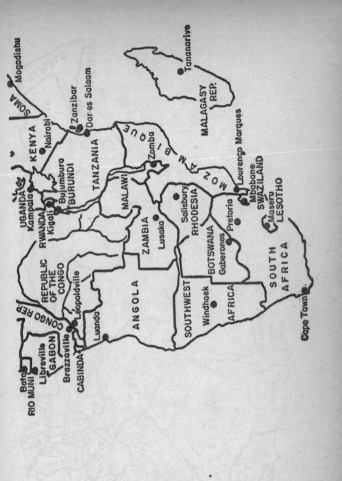

Foreword

Rarely does a reader find himself genuinely in a position to
preface the material from which he would like to teach
a collection of his own stumbling to an occasion which has a
which that is always different to ... the ...
men ...

... their own ...
Chinese, Arabic, and the ...
recent versions have produced that we ... a collection of
appropriate, and readable ... about the econo-
phy culture, but in economics and ancient political development of Africa, with all of its failure. We have rather
concerning questions to ... families and continuity to
the whole. These seems to be the author myself desired
throughout the book.

Our objective has been to give the reader a general
understanding of Africa that will give him a rough copy
prehension of tomorrow's headlines. I'm one thing that
can be said with certainty about Africa first, is that it
will produce headlines. It's plans can at such a rate that
any book on Africa becomes out of date while its type is
being set. And so this book should be read in conjunction

Foreword

Rarely does a teacher have the opportunity to produce precisely the materials from which he would like to teach a course of his own planning. But a private grant has enabled the teachers of the George School's history department to assemble and shape teaching materials to fit the needs of their new Afro–Asian Studies Program. Research, consultation with experts, classroom trials at the George School and neighboring public schools, and frequent revisions have produced this book, a collection of authoritative and readable selections about the geography, culture, history, economics, and modern political development of Africa south of the Sahara. We have written connecting passages to give structure and continuity to the whole. These comments by the editors appear indented throughout the book.

Our objective has been to give the student a general understanding of Africa that will give him a greater comprehension of tomorrow's headlines. The one thing that can be said with certainty about Africa's future is that it will produce headlines. It is doing this at such a rate that any book on Africa becomes outdated while its type is being set. And so this book should be read in conjunction with the daily newspaper for all of the up-to-the-minute facts.

Many people have contributed to the development of this book: the members of the history department who have been in and out of the project over the years; cooperating teachers from neighboring public schools; and especially Dr. Hugh Smythe and Dr. William Hovett, who provided expert evaluation and guidance. Most particularly, this book owes its existence to the vision and the encouragement provided by the former Principal of the George School, the late Richard H. McFeely.

CLARK D. MOORE
George School, Pennsylvania

PART I

A Geographical View of the African Continent

Africa is usually portrayed as a "dark continent," historically and physically isolated from the rest of the world. Although geographic conditions have inhibited communication within Africa, recent scholars know that there was in the past widespread exchange between different sections of Africa and between Africa and the outside world. Before we study in detail the geography which made and still makes economic and political development in modern Africa difficult, let us make a broad survey of Africa's past contacts with the outside world.

While Asia may be the homeland of civilization, Africa is most probably the homeland of man himself. The earliest evidence of man, the tool-making primate, has been found in Olduvai Gorge in Tanzania. Although the shift from hunting and food-gathering to settled agriculture has been most frequently associated with southwest Asia, there is some evidence to suggest that the systematic raising of cereals developed independently in the upper Niger river basin during the agricultural revolution about 5000–4000 B.C.

By the twelfth century B.C., Phoenicians were trading in the western Mediterranean. By the ninth century

B.C., they had founded Carthage, a trading state whose contacts extended far down the west coast of Africa. Hanno, a Phoenician sailor, wrote the best extant record of this trade. His *Periplus* is the account of a trip which extended perhaps as far as the Guinea Coast in the fifth century B.C.

In Carthaginian times the Sahara was not the great desert wasteland we know today, although profound climatic changes were making it increasingly drier. Extensive contact between the Carthaginian and Berber peoples in the interior of North Africa is recorded in stories of Carthaginian libraries given to African princes. The early Christian theologian, St. Augustine, himself a Berber, mentions several Carthaginian books in his writings.

The Carthaginian state was destroyed in 146 B.C. by the expanding Roman Empire. Roman occupation of North Africa never extended far inland, but Roman explorers did investigate the land to the south. One of these expeditions in the first century A.D. traveled as far as the oasis of Asben, or Tibesti, almost a thousand miles from the coast.

The camel, introduced from southwest Asia during the Greco–Roman period (500 B.C. to A.D. 400), made the desert tribes more independent from whatever power happened to be occupying the North African coast. The camel also provided a means of transportation for the trans-Saharan traders who operated continuously, and with increasing penetration to the south, from that time to the present day. The Sahara has been an open sea to some Africans for at least fifteen hundred years.

The earliest record of life on the East African coast is the *Periplus of the Erythrean Sea,* a Greek commercial handbook of the second century A.D. It records a flourishing trade between the East African coast, southern Arabia, and India. Between the sixth and ninth centuries, Persians replaced the Yemenite Arabs in domination of the Indian Ocean trade. Trade was not confined to the shores of Persia, Arabia, and India. Chinese coins of the eighth century have been found in East Africa, and Far Eastern records report African slaves in China and Java as early as the ninth century. Arabs again dominated the East African trade between the tenth century and the establishment of trading posts by the Portuguese in the early sixteenth century. Contact between the East African coast and China continued throughout Europe's Middle Ages, as indicated by pieces of Ming Dynasty porcelain found in the ruins of the ancient coastal trading cities.

The greatest revolutionary feature of the Indian Ocean trade was the introduction to Africa, probably during the first century of the Christian era, of Malaysian food crops such as the yam, cacao, banana, coconut palm, and rice. This was accompanied by migrations of the people who became the ancestors of the Malagasy peoples. Certain types of Indonesian boats and musical instruments have been found as far away as the Guinea Coast. Currently, scholars are not able to determine whether they were introduced to West Africa by Indonesian sailors, or whether their use was passed from one group to another across the continent.

The "isolation" of Africa, about which so much has been written by European and American authorities, is a reflection not so much of the real isolation of the African continent as it is of the Western world's ignorance of it. In spite of all the earlier contacts, little information was circulated. Much of Africa was unknown until the wave of exploration by Europeans in the nineteenth century. The source of the Nile was not discovered until 1863. Our records are, as one writer has put it, "absurdly recent."

Let us now look at Africa's geography. The success with which African states exploit the advantages of their geography and overcome its natural handicaps will determine, to a large extent, the future development of the continent.

Topography

Africa is the world's second-largest continent, with 80 per cent of its area in the tropics. It has more distinctively different ethnic and cultural groups and a lower overall figure of population density (20 to 22 people per square mile) than any other continent.

Only a few African countries such as Nigeria (which

with 55 million people has one fourth of the continent's total), South Africa, and the Congo (Kinshasa) have populations of more than ten million.

Geologically, Africa can be described as a vast block of rock that was thrust above the ocean's surface with comparatively little folding and wrinkling. Therefore, except for the Atlas Mountains in the north, there are few ranges which compare to the Alps or the Rockies. The blocklike nature of the continent has resulted in very narrow coastal plains backed by steep scarps which rise to generally level plateaus.

RIVERS AND VALLEYS

From George P. Murdock, *Africa: Its Peoples and Their Culture*, 1959.

The chief exception to topographic monotony is presented by the great extinct volcanoes and spectacular rift valleys of East Africa. Among the former, Mounts Elgon, Kenya, and Ruwenzori average about 17,000 feet in elevation, and majestic Kilimanjaro lifts its glacier-tipped cone 19,400 feet above sea level. The rift valleys, like the volcanoes, resulted from a series of stupendous north–south fractures which occurred during the uplifting of the continent and produced giant trenches often thousands of feet in depth. . . . The principal rift valley starts at the mouth of the Zambesi River and runs northward via Lake Nyasa and the great interior drainage basin of Tanganyika and western Kenya and thence northeastward across Ethiopia to the coast, after which it forms the floors of the Red Sea, the Gulf of Aqaba, and the Dead Sea, and terminates in Syria. A second rift valley, later in origin, is marked by a chain of lakes to the west of the first— Lakes Tanganyika, Kivu, Edward, and Albert—of which the first has a bottom several thousand feet below sea level.

The geological history of Africa accounts for some of the peculiarities of its drainage system. Its great rivers, like the Congo, Niger, Nile, and Zambesi, are navigable for great distances on the interior plateaus but invariably plunge over impassable rapids or cataracts as they approach the coastal plain. The most spectacular of these, Victoria Falls on the Zambesi, has a drop of 343 feet, or more than twice that of Niagara. Rivers enter the ocean, not through navigable estuaries but through deltas, often obstructed by shifting sand bars. Because of uplift, other harbors are extraordinarily few, except along the western Mediterranean coast. The irregular elevation of the continental mass also isolated a series of interior drainage basins which filled with shallow, brackish lakes, most of which have long since found outlets or, in arid regions, have dwindled to salt marshes. Curiously enough, the largest survivor, Lake Chad, contains fresh rather than brackish water, presumably through underground seepage into other basins.

EFFECT OF TOPOGRAPHY ON TRANSPORTATION IN MODERN AFRICA

We are interested in geography primarily because of its effects on Africa's development. For this assessment we have drawn on Dr. William Hance, an authority on the economic geography of Africa.

From William A. Hance, *African Economic Development*, 1958.

Topographically, Africa is the "plateau continent." The scarp zones which lie behind the narrow coastal plains have presented a formidable barrier to penetration. Streams which are characterized by high seasonal variation of flow, by the presence of rapids in their lower courses, and by mouths where entry is impeded by shifting river and offshore bars, have further contributed to the problem of gaining access to interior areas. Away from the coasts, movement overland is often further obstructed by scarps, and, in East Africa, the two great rift zones are barriers of immense proportions.

The landform disadvantages should not be exaggerated, however. They were more significant as obstructive forces in early penetration. . . . [Today] new roads and rail lines and improved port facilities reduce to a very considerable degree the dimensions of the topographic problems.

Among the physical elements, climate probably has the greatest influence in retarding economic advance. About two-fifths of tropical Africa is steppe or desert where inadequate or unreliable precipitation condemns the area to low productivity. At least a third is savanna country, with adequate rainfall in the high-sun period but with violent seasonality and, again, undependability. . . .

Ports

Africa has the shortest coastline in relation to its area of any of the continents. The tropical area is notoriously poor in good natural harbors. . . . River mouths and estuaries have all too frequently been plagued by shifting sand bars or by the presence of offshore sand bars. Lighterage ports and surf ports are still important. Some are situated in protected waters, but many have been completely open roadsteads, and their piers have more than once been partially or entirely destroyed by storms. In any case, surf loading is slow, expensive, inefficient, and dangerous. . . .

Great progress has been made, however, in improving the port situation of tropical Africa. . . . It is no longer sound to make general statements that African development is hampered by the absence of ports, though . . . many areas continue to suffer from more or less chronic congestion in the ports which handle their traffic. . . .

Port delays do not, of course, reflect only inadequate port capacity. Frequently the feeding rail lines are more responsible for congestion than the ports themselves. An important feature of postwar traffic should also be noted —the much greater increase in goods landed than in goods embarked from African ports. The tremendous variety of import packages makes them much more difficult to handle than most export cargoes, which typically contain a large proportion of homogeneous produce such as sisal, cocoa, cotton, or palm oil. . . .

Waterways

The plateau character of Africa and the high seasonality of precipitation away from the equatorial core have meant that navigable waterways have only limited importance in most African areas.

In West Africa, the Niger continues to be significant, especially for bulk shipments of forest products, palm oil, peanuts, and imported petroleum products. The lower Niger is navigable for 537 miles from Burutu to Jebba, but shallow-draft barges are required seasonally for most of this distance. Its major eastern affluent, the Benue, is navigable for six months in the lower stretches and for several months to Garoua in French Cameroon. The varying regimes on the lower Niger and the Benue require an intricate timing of river operations:

The river fleets with power-craft and barges must concentrate their efforts on the short Benue season, then switch to the Niger between Lokoja and Jebba, and then retreat to the lower reaches from Lokoja southward. This series of operations, which follows an annual rhythm, must be delicately handled by those in charge of river organizations. If they let the craft stay up the Benue a day too long, the vessels will be stuck on sandbanks for ten months! Yet if through caution or misinformation they withdraw the fleet too soon, much valuable merchandise is left behind and can only be evacuated by land at much greater cost. . . .

The Congo system is the most important inland waterway of tropical Africa and the natural feeding system of the Matadi–Leopoldville axis. Generally speaking, water routes are used in the Belgian Congo wherever possible and rail lines have been constructed only as accessories to the rivers, either to go around rapids or to link the waterways with areas lacking navigable streams. . . . The most important stretches are on the main river from Leopoldville to Stanleyville, a distance of 1,082 miles, and from Leopoldville to Port Francqui. . . . Leopoldville, with a total river traffic of 1.4 million tons in 1955, ranks as one of the leading ports of Africa, though it is hundreds of feet above sea level. . . .

The East African Lakes are of some importance in inland navigation. Shipping on Lake Victoria, about as large as Ireland, permits low-cost movement of goods to and from the railheads of Kisumu in the north and Mwanza in the south. . . . The value of the long, narrow, rift-valley lakes can easily be exaggerated for they are, to a considerable degree, barriers to movement rather than aids. Lake Tanganyika, for example, is now the only break in a transcontinental rail route from Lobito to Dar es Salaam.

A few of the rivers flowing into the Indian Ocean, such as the Zambesi, the Rufiji, and the Tana, are navigable for short stretches, but none are important routeways. Lastly, the middle Nile is used in the Sudan. . . .

Overland transportation

Africa is the "plateau continent," and the word "plateau" immediately suggests some of the major problems besetting transport by road, rail, and inland waterway. Almost everywhere the coastal plain, which averages for the continent only 20 miles in width, is backed by more or less formidable scarps, or, more accurately, by scarp zones. This fact is perhaps the single most important physical explanation for the isolation that characterized Africa until so late a period in its history, for the difficulty of surmounting the scarps is often very considerable. It was a high-cost proposition to build roads and rail lines up these steep slopes; it is difficult to maintain the lines, and expensive to operate on them. On the Benguela Railway [in Angola], for example, the powerful . . . locomotives have their maximum load capacity reduced from the 1,-720 metric tons prevailing on the coastal stretch from Lobito to Benguela to 520 metric tons on the scarp route.

The profile of many African railroads shows the difficulties involved. The Djibouti–Addis Ababa line requires 475 miles to cover a distance of 360 miles. . . . It is said to cost as much to ship an automobile from Djibouti to

Addis Ababa as it does to ship from Detroit to Djibouti.
So steep were the gradients on the Benguela line that it
was built originally with a five-mile rack-and-pinion section, which was not converted to normal track until
1958. . . .

West African roads and rail lines do not face quite
such difficult terrain problems. The plateau is lower than
in east and central Africa, though the French Guinea and
Sierra Leone railways both have extremely difficult trajec-
tories. In French Cameroon the great Adamoua Massif
stands as a barrier of considerable dimensions to north–
south routeways, while remaining lines and the few roads
penetrating from the west coast do so with very great difficulty.

In East Africa there is not only a coastal scarp but a
series of scarps with antithetic slopes, so that much of the
altitude gained on each difficult scarp is lost on the gen-
tler plateau slopes. This area also has, in the rift zones,
some of the most awesome landforms in the world. The
term "rift valley," which is often applied to these zones, is
misleadingly simple, as there are usually mountain masses
on each side of the rifts, while scattered volcanic peaks
complicate the pattern. The fact that the most productive
parts of this region are frequently in the topographically
more difficult areas does not ease the transportation problems.

Additional topographic difficulties in constructing land
transport lines in Africa are occasioned by the fact that
major routes of access and egress frequently run against
the grain of the country. For example, a road or rail line
across the Belgian Congo from west to east must cross innumerable valleys which follow a general north–south or
northwest direction. This greatly handicaps that portion
of the area south of the Congo which is not accessible to
river transport, and has thus far precluded the building of
roads and rail lines. Somewhat similarly in East Africa,
the grain of the rift zones and of the many scarps runs
north–south, in opposition to the major east–west routeways.

A problem of some dimensions in scattered areas is the

absence of material suitable for ballast. This lack is particularly characteristic of the areas which require it the most because of climatic conditions. Cuttings and embankments in unstable soil have been troublesome and costly in certain areas. . . .

Size and distance must not be forgotten in an analysis of the physical difficulties facing African transport. The continent is 3¾ times the size of the United States; tropical Africa alone is about 2¾ times as large. To provide an integrated transport system for so vast a region is obviously a staggering task. Many of the productive areas are far from the coast; to meet their needs long lines traversing low-productive regions with poor traffic potential must be constructed. For example, on the western Nigerian line there is practically no freight traffic between Oshogbo, 180 miles from Lagos, and Zaria, at 618 miles. On the eastern line little traffic develops between Enugu, 151 miles from Port Harcourt, and the Kafanchan Junction at 459 miles. . . .

Distance also means time. Therefore, perishable crops cannot be grown for export in some favored areas. Sometimes air transport can meet this problem. Considerable quantities of meat are shipped from steppe areas to the protein-deficient cities of the rain forest such as Douala, Brazzaville, and Leopoldville. But air freight, although it has grown tremendously in postwar years, cannot be more than a limited solution. . . .

CLIMATE

Climate is of tremendous direct and indirect importance in creating problems for African transport. Altogether, climate is more significant as a limiting factor than landforms. High temperatures make for a high consumption of water [by steam locomotives], and lines in steppe areas often have great problems in securing an adequate supply. . . . In Kenya a 65-mile pipeline is under construction to carry water from the slopes of Kilimanjaro to points on the Mombasa–Nairobi line. . . . High temperatures combined with high humidity create problems of oxidation and deterioration that are not easily solved. These help to account for the high maintenance costs characteristic of most African lines.

Precipitation—another climatic element—is even more important. In the rain forest belt, heavy year-round precipitation makes construction of roads and railways very costly. One mile of road with a high tonnage capacity in equatorial Africa costs up to $184,000. I have seen new roadbeds seriously eroded before it was possible to surface them. Laterite roads in rain forest areas fortunately tend to harden on exposure, but they cannot stand up to heavy truck traffic under the climatic conditions that prevail. . . .

In savanna and steppe areas, the marked seasonal distribution of precipitation together with its character—often torrential downpours—has meant that only the most important routeways are kept open on a year-round basis. For large parts of the rainy season most routes are utterly impassable. Wadis which are bone dry in winter become raging torrents, but building bridges across them is often not justified at the present level of economic development. . . .

The third element of climate, wind, is troublesome only in steppe and desert areas, where sand drift becomes a problem. It combines with temperature to make crossing the Sahara a hazardous experience, especially in the summer months.

Weather and climate are, of course, also important in ocean transport. Monsoons have for centuries permitted contact between East Africa and Arabia by ocean-going dhows. Less beneficial are the cyclones which affect portions of that coast, and the frequently wind-tossed seas, which interfere with lighterage and surfboat operations. . . .

The vegetation and animal life of Africa also influence transportation. From the standpoint of transport the most difficult vegetation zones in Africa have been the rain forest areas. Original [railroad] lines were often cut through the forest areas without adequate mapping, these regions being in any case very difficult to chart. The Ivory Coast line was placed where it is because the forest belt, the densest in West Africa, was narrowest at that point. The great tangle of vegetation along river valleys also helps to account for the selection of routes up the steeper scarp instead of along rivers descending from the high plateaus.

River transport on the upper Nile is handicapped by floating vegetation known as "sudd," and although the main course is now kept open, vessels must be careful in tying up not to become enclosed in an impenetrable mass of growth. Recent reports tell of a new menace on the Congo, the water hyacinth, which was introduced as an attractive flowering plant, but which is now multiplying with such speed that it threatens to become a major impediment to river traffic. Low-hanging vegetation is a hazard to navigation on minor Congo waterways.

Sometimes large game interfere with transport. The voracity of the man-eating lions of Tsavo was responsible for delays in construction of the Kenya rail line. Giraffe were constantly cutting telegraph lines on the Southern Tanganyika line. Hippopotami forced abandonment of a Sierra Leone waterway. But insects are today more important causes of transport difficulties. For example, the Southern Railway in Tanganyika, undertaken in haste to serve the postwar Groundnuts Scheme, was forced to use wooden sleepers because steel was not then available. These sleepers were soon so weakened by termites that it was necessary to re-lay the track with steel ties at considerable expense. Termites have also been responsible for closing some of the minor airfields in northern Nigeria by creating mounds that impede runways.

NATURAL RESOURCES

Most people picture Africa as a lush tropical land covered with a variety of vegetation and needing only the application of man's agricultural skills to harness this fertility efficiently. Such is not the case. The continent has a wide variety of soils and climates and many problems related to their utilization which are unique to Africa and not understood fully by temperate-zone agricultural experts.

The preponderant vegetation in Africa is grassland

or savanna, not jungle. Where there is sufficient rainfall on the savanna, scattered trees grow; where rain is scarce, there is thorn bush. On the higher plateaus the savanna gives way to grasslands. Semiarid desert steppes and dry forest also occupy large areas. All of these areas are actual or potential grazing lands and serve to explain why Africa is host to such an exceptional number of wild and domestic animals.

The rain forests or jungle occupy only relatively small areas and are relatively poor sustainers of animal life.

Since any country's most basic resource is the fertility of its soil—"Poor land means poor people"—it is essential that we have some insight into this aspect of the continent's economy. The following paragraphs are from a Food and Agriculture Organization (FAO) report for the United Nations.

From FAO, The State of Food and Agriculture, *1958.*

Africa South of the Sahara contains about 15 percent of the total land surface (including inland water) of the earth and only about 5 percent of the total population. Its share of the world's total of arable land and land under tree crops is also about 15 percent, of the forested land 17 percent, and of pasture 18 percent. . . .

Purely on the basis of these figures the region would appear to have a very great agricultural potential, but it is already clear : . . that there are many limitations on the realization of this potential. In addition, further limitations are imposed by the primitive techniques of production at present practiced in most of the region. Different forms of shifting cultivation are widespread; not only are they destructive of forest resources but they require very extensive areas of land and, with increasing population pressure, are thus inadequate to maintain the fertility of the soil. In the climatic, soil, and social conditions of Africa South of the Sahara, however, these methods cannot simply be replaced by those found successful in other regions. Much further study is needed of African agricultural techniques and of the ways in which they are adapted to local conditions. A further obstacle to increased agricultural production is the tribal systems of land tenure, ill adapted to the production of surpluses for sale and to improved techniques, that still prevail over most of the region. The inadequacy of marketing and transport facilities also hamper agricultural development in many areas. Two-thirds of the forests are inaccessible and less than half of the accessible ones are at present exploited; their heterogeneous nature is a major difficulty in commercial exploitation. . . .

Shifting cultivation

While the greatest single factor dominating changes in the vegetation cover has been the use of fire to provide grazing in the more arid areas, shifting cultivation has also had serious effects in both humid tropical forests and in drier bush country. Shifting cultivation requires a long period to restore fertility and is thus satisfactory only when there is no severe pressure of population on land resources. With the extension of settlement and an enforced stabilization of population, the fallow period is not long enough to restore the fertility of the soil. . . .

Settlement schemes

In some areas of comparatively high fertility, as in parts of the tropical forest of West Africa and around the great lakes in East Africa, a tradition of settled agriculture has long been established. Here, however, increasing pressure of population has led to fragmentation of holdings, which have often fallen well below an economic minimum. Various measures for consolidation are being gradually introduced, but this may not always provide for surplus population and parallel settlement or resettlement schemes are necessary, involving the taking in of new land for cultivation. . . .

Water control

The great hydrological basins, such as the Niger, Congo, and Zambezi, provide considerable reservoirs of untouched fertility. A number of settlement schemes based on flood control and irrigation works have been undertaken or are planned. . . . On several of these rivers, hydroelectric schemes are planned or are under construction, while the valleys themselves contain large stretches of at present uninhabited, but potentially fertile, land. The development of these basins underlines the urgency of watershed management. In areas of intense tropical rainfall, especially where the climax vegetation has been destroyed or modified by fire, the watershed is particularly vulnerable. While conservation measures are necessary to conserve soil and soil fertility, they are even more necessary to preserve water resources and protect the river basin areas from progressive deterioration.

Efficient watershed management affects also the regime of springs and streams in semiarid regions. The introduction of improved and rotational grazing for the large livestock populations of the tropical savanna belt depends largely on the provision of increased watering points, which in turn depend on the maintenance of ground water recharge. The vegetation cover on semiarid areas, once destroyed, is much more difficult to restore than that of the humid tropics, and the coordination of land and water development in these areas must, therefore, proceed on the basis of scientific resource surveys to enable the delicate balance between natural resources and their utilization to be maintained. . . .

Irrigation farming is still in its initial stages in Africa South of the Sahara, although over the greater part of the region rainfall is inadequate for sustained crop production. In particular in areas of unimodal rainfall, the long dry season cannot be utilized for any form of crop production, and underemployment, poverty, and malnutrition result. . . .

Soil fertility

In spite of extensive research activities, which have accumulated an important body of scientific data, it remains true that, from the point of view of management and the maintenance and increase of fertility, much still remains to be learned regarding suitable practices for tropical and subtropical soils. Soil science was developed in the temperate regions and soil management practices cannot necessarily be transferred from temperate to tropical climates. . . .

Here again suitable systems have to be evolved which are acceptable to the African farmer and which will scientifically transform his present cultivation practices. Such a transformation is not only limited by lack of knowledge of suitable soil management techniques and of the plant/soil/water relationship of these climatic regions, but by other factors as well. For example, no perennial herbage legume has yet been found which can be successfully introduced into rotations in tropical Africa for the improvement of soil conditions. . . .

The building up or even the maintenance of organic matter in cultivated soils always presents difficulties, especially in the tropics and subtropics. For instance, in the southern Transvaal and other areas no distinct residual effect of manure can be shown, nor is the carbon content of the soil increased by repeated dressings. In some areas this is readily explained by the quick consumption by termites of all the cellulose in the manure and in others probably by the rapid decomposition of organic matter that takes place under conditions of high temperature with alternating dry and moist spells. . . .

Forestry production

The paramount importance of adequate forest cover for the conservation of basic soil and water resources has already been emphasized. . . . One of the chief reasons for the ruthlessness of forest destruction is that the tropical forest consists largely of species of little or no known commercial value, so that its clearance for crop production is an economic necessity which can be reduced only by enhancing the economic value of the forest itself. In order to attain this objective, a great deal of attention is being devoted to improvement of the silvicultural, logging, and wood-utilization aspects of tropical forestry.

Plant protection

Many plant pests and diseases still take a very heavy toll in the region, especially where extensive areas of cash crops have been established under virtual monoculture. A few examples are quoted below.

Locust infestation covers a larger area than any other insect pest in the region. . . .

Attacks by weaver birds on grain crops also cause severe losses, especially in East and Central Africa, and no effective control measures have yet been devised.

A recent study assembles some striking estimates of the damage caused by plant diseases in certain areas. In 1947/48 about 46 million cacao trees were estimated to be affected by Swollen Shoot disease in Ghana, where the annual loss from this disease was believed to be about 80,000 tons, while Black Pod was estimated to reduce yields by another 24–40,000 tons. These losses were more than 10 per cent of the present world crop. The cutting-out campaign, the only possible control measure against Swollen Shoot, caused further dislocation. In the last few years, however, good progress has been made in West Africa in the control of Black Pod and Capsid by spraying.

It was also estimated that in 1948 at least half the mature clove trees on Zanzibar Island had died from Sudden Death disease during the previous 10–12 years. Diseases and pests of cotton have caused severe losses in Uganda and give rise to serious difficulties in its establishment in some other areas. . . .

Apart from the availability of water supplies . . . the greatest single factor affecting livestock is the tsetse fly, which is the vector of the organism causing sleeping sickness in man and "nagana" or trypanosomiasis in cattle. The area of [tsetse] fly infestation runs roughly in a broad belt across the middle of Africa, depending on certain densities of vegetation, and excludes cattle from approximately half of the region. Over the last 30 years there have been important extensions of infestation, especially in Central Africa. In spite of much research, there is still no generally effective control method. . . .

POWER RESOURCES

One necessary ingredient in the economy of any modern state is some sort of power resource—a source of energy to drive machinery: coal, oil, waterpower, etc. Here is Dr. Hance's assessment of Africa's potential in this important aspect of its development.

From William A. Hance, *African Economic Development*, 1958.

The outstanding facts about power resources are the relative poverty of good-grade coal and of petroleum, and the wealth of water power and fissionable or fusionable raw materials.

There is some coal of coking quality now mined at Wankie in . . . Rhodesia . . . and low-grade coal is mined [elsewhere], but the general shortage of coal must be listed as a major handicap to transportation and industrialization.

Oil has been discovered in the Sahara, the Niger basin in Nigeria, [and] the Gabon basin. . . . Of these, only the Sahara find is likely to be a major one. . . . Recently a methane gas deposit with heat-producing potential equal to 50 million metric tons of coal was reported beneath Lake Kivu. . . . But most of the continent is composed of basement rock where petroleum and natural gas will not be found. . . .

One of the redeeming features with regard to energy is Africa's possession of the greatest water-power potential in the world. Tropical Africa is estimated to have about three-eighths of the total world potential at ordinary minimum flow, or as much as Europe, the Americas, and

Australia combined. The Belgian Congo alone has 21.6 per cent of the world total. At present, there are very few hydroelectric developments, the installed capacity being less than 1 per cent of the world total. . . .

The tremendous reserves of hydro power in tropical Africa are bound to stimulate the introduction of industries using electrical processes, particularly the production of aluminum from either domestic or imported bauxite and alumina. They may also attract the pulp and paper industry and lead to the electrification of the railways in favored areas.

Possession of some of the world's greatest known reserves of uranium ore may give significant leverage in decades ahead to assure a relatively early introduction of nuclear-electric plants. In addition to the tremendous deposit at Shinkolobwe, Belgian Congo, there are known reserves of fissionable raw materials in many tropical African countries. . . .

The energy position, then, shows exciting possibilities, but the great variation from place to place, the unfortunate location of many of the reserves, and the shortage of coal and oil are restrictive factors. The general absence of coking coal will inhibit the introduction of the iron and steel industry, which is still the foundation of a modern, integrated, industrial complex. . . .

One of the serious physical problems for African railways and inland waterways has been the general lack of suitable local fuels. . . . [The] poor quality [of coal] has led to higher maintenance costs of steam locomotives so that it is now planned gradually to dieselize these services. . . .

Many railways and water carriers have consumed large quantities of wood for fuel and continue to do so. This is an expensive business, however, and in places the forests have been denuded to such a degree that adequate supplies within reasonable distances of routeways are no longer available. . . . The use of wood is also a time-consuming affair. For example, refueling on the Vicicongo Railway requires a stop of 30 minutes every 36 miles. . . . Wood also occupies far more space than coal or oil, space that could be devoted to paying traffic. . . .

The cost of fuel, then, whether it be domestically produced or imported, remains one of the factors accounting for the high operating expenses of many African lines and transport services and discourages the adoption of more efficient modes of transport.

PART II

The Structure of African Cultures

The Africans: A Racially and Linguistically Diverse People

The only common racial denominator which the people of Africa south of the Sahara share is a dark skin. Yet within that very general characteristic there are wider differences among Africans than can be found among Europeans. Any racial classification of Africans shows vast variations; to assume that all Africans are alike is to make a mistake.

Authorities differ radically on just how African people should be classified racially. In fact, the most modern among the anthropologists are beginning to shy away from the idea of "race" as a general term, and talk instead about differences in special physical characteristics among people.

The following selections give us some idea of the diversity and distribution of African peoples.

DESCRIPTION OF PHYSICAL CHARACTERISTICS

From Simon and Phoebe Ottenberg, *Cultures and Societies in Africa,* 1960.

The general features of the physical types of Africa are known, though few accurate studies and analyses have been made. No precise classification exists; the relationship between the various African physical types is obscure; and the origin of most of them is unknown. In line with a trend in anthropology, research is turning from the measurement and observation of external bodily features to the analysis of genetic factors, particularly those associated with blood types and conditions. . . .

Past classifications of African physical types have included many inaccuracies and misconceptions, fostered not only by travelers and popular writers, but also by scholars. A common error has been to confuse linguistic with racial categories; these do not coincide in Africa and refer to quite different things in the first place. For example, the term "Bantu race" is sometimes employed, although the word Bantu actually refers to a linguistic grouping and not to a physical type. Furthermore, the literature on Africa is full of statements such as that the skin color of a certain group shows Mongoloid influence, or the thin straight lips of another indicate Caucasoid features. Single traits such as these are poor indicators of origins and contacts and are as likely to be due to local variation within a population as they are to past contacts. In short, most of our knowledge of African physical types is inaccurate; it is clear that all peoples in Africa are Homo sapiens; beyond this all that we can do is to indicate some of the readily observable gross physical differences among Africans and to suggest the direction of current genetic research on African populations.

Numerically, the major physical type in Africa is the Negro, sometimes called the "true" Negro. Although the Negroes are often divided into numerous subcategories, they can be classed together. They are located in the Sudanic Zone south of the Sahara (and even to some extent in that desert), along the Guinea Coast, through central Africa and most of East Africa, and in southeastern Africa and Madagascar. African Negroes have dark pigmentation of the hair, eyes, and skin; woolly hair; broad, flat noses; everted lips; and some prognathism (projecting jaw). They vary considerably in height and in many other characteristics.

Scattered about the forest areas of central Africa are small groups of Pygmies, who are essentially Negro in their physical characteristics but differ mainly in height, averaging about 57 inches for males and about 54 inches for females. There is some evidence that the Pygmies were once more widespread in central Africa than they are today, and that they may even have lived on the island of Madagascar. The evolutionary relationship of Pygmy and Negro is unknown, and it has not been established which is earlier in development.

In East Africa, particularly in Ruanda-Urundi, Uganda, and the eastern Sudan, are found unusually tall, slender, and long-headed Negroes, the Nilotes, who seem to form a distinct subgrouping. Some authors feel that they show Caucasoid features, indicating North African influence, but present evidence suggests that they are simply a localized variant of the Negro. Other Negro groups are also found throughout this Nilotic area.

In North Africa and Egypt, and south into the desert area and the Sudanic climate zone, most people are of the Caucasoid physical type. Wide variation occurs, and some authorities would distinguish those in the eastern parts of northern Africa from those in the western. However, they generally belong to a Caucasoid subgroup living all along the shores of the Mediterranean with brown hair and eyes, hair ranging from wavy to straight, skin color of light olive to dark brown, fairly thin lips, and high-bridged narrow noses. There is considerable intermixture of Mediterranean Caucasoid and Negro in the Sudan and in Ethiopia and other parts of the East Horn; and some mixture along almost the whole length of the East African coast as well, mainly as a result of Arab–African contact. The Mediterranean Caucasoid population of Africa seems clearly related to the Caucasoid groups of Europe and the Near and Middle East, though its origin, if it had a single origin, is unknown.

In South-West Africa are two groups closely related physically to each other, the Bushmen and the Hottentots, who, despite past efforts of scholars to classify them, are difficult to place within any other major racial typology and must be considered as a distinct physical type. The Bushmen are short—but not as short as the Pygmies —averaging perhaps five feet tall. Their yellow-brown to yellowish skin is wrinkly. Their hair is "peppercorn" [tight spiral curls] in form and dark in color, and they have broad cheekbones, flattish noses, and fairly pointed chins. They also exhibit steatopygia, a condition in which the buttocks are enlarged by fatty deposits. The Hottentots, slightly taller and somewhat more long-headed, are otherwise very similar to the Bushmen in physical type, though differing in culture. The origin of the Bushman–Hottentot physical type is unknown, and its relation to other forms of Homo sapiens uncertain. Archaeological and other evidence indicates that it is of considerable antiquity and was once more widespread in southern Africa, possibly even in central Africa, having been driven into its present inhospitable region by Negroes moving into South Africa.

Through intermarriage and interbreeding between Hottentots and European settlers (particularly the Dutch), with some Negro intermixture as well, in the Cape area of South Africa, a mixed physical type has developed. These Cape Coloured are almost all urban dwellers who have lost most elements of Hottentot culture. They now number more than a million and form a distinct population group in South Africa.

There are also East Indians, several hundred thousand in southeast Africa, and smaller numbers in East Africa, who have migrated to Africa chiefly within the past hundred years. They are generally considered by anthropologists to be a distinct subgrouping of the Caucasoid physical type.

The presence of approximately five million Europeans, who are mainly Western European Caucasoid in physical type has already been mentioned.

Thus the African continent is peopled by three distinct physical types—Negro, Caucasoid, and Bushman–Hottentot—the first two being large in number and the third fairly small. The Negro type subdivides into the "true" Negro, the Pygmy, and the Nilote; the Caucasoid, into a Mediterranean Caucasoid of considerable antiquity in Africa, a Western European Caucasoid of a later period, and an Indian Caucasoid of even more recent date. The Bushman–Hottentot type, of course, has two subgroups representing these two peoples.

It has often been suggested that differences in physical type involve some environmental adaptation, but precisely how has been difficult to explain in terms of the physical characteristics used in traditional racial classifications. For example, dark skin color may be adaptive to hot and relatively humid tropical climates, or tall, slender body build to hot desert conditions. Both of these occur in Africa. Yet there are groups of slender Africans who do not live in desert conditions, and Negroes who live in relatively cool highland areas. If such features do represent adaptations they occur very slowly, only after many generations. But because the genetics of such physical features are not fully known it is difficult to understand the exact nature of such adaptations. . . .

RACIAL "SUPERIORITY"

In view of the deeply rooted ideas of racial superiority which exist not only in Africa but all over the world, it is necessary that we introduce at this point an authoritative scientific statement on the subject.

From Adamson E. Hoebel, *Man in the Primitive World,* 1958.

In summary, the evidence from psychology is largely negative. It demonstrates that (1) so-called "intelligence tests" measure innate skill plus cultural experience. No test has yet been evolved that can eliminate the cultural factor, and differential ratings of the various races in intelligence tests must be critically evaluated; (2) aptitude tests do reveal racial differentials in visual, motor, and vocal skills, but these too are subject to cultural influences that have not been eliminated in tests and measurements; and (3) many skills of intelligence and aptitude definitely change when the cultural environment changes.

The whole result of scientific race psychology is to throw the explanation of significant behavior as between people of different races over into the field of cultural experience. The findings of psychology harmonize with those of anthropology and history. . . .

It is the opinion of anthropologists that all races, except, perhaps, the Australian aborigines are equally capable of cultural development and that culture operates independently of racial heredity.

> It is therefore *culture,* not race, which accounts for the significant differences among peoples.
>
> Culture is defined as the sum total of man's learned behavior. It is not inherited like eye color or bone structure, but is learned from the environment into which one is born.

LANGUAGE GROUPS

One of the first and most basic cultural characteristics any individual acquires is his language. For our purpose, it is practical to look briefly at the language classifications of Africa to determine how complex can be the problem of intergroup communication and hence how extensive the political organization.

A language family is a group of languages stemming originally from a single source. English is a member of the Indo–European family of languages. Among the other members of that family are German and the other Teutonic languages, French and the other Romance languages, Russian and other Slavic languages, Latin, Greek, and Sanskrit. Scholars estimate that it has taken about 6000 years for the Indo–European family to reach its present stage of differentiation.

There are over 800 indigenous languages spoken on the African continent, in addition to English, French, Spanish, Portuguese, and Italian. The African languages can be grouped into four major language families: Congo–Kordofanian, Nilo–Saharan, Afro–Asiatic, and Khoisan. "Bantu," a term frequently associated with African languages, can legitimately be applied only to a subdivision of one of the branches of the Congo–Kordofanian family. This and other linguistic designations are often misused, however, to refer to racial rather than language groups. The Bantu languages are widely dispersed, extending from parts of northwestern Cameroon to east, central, and southern Africa. Swahili, spoken as both a first and second language by people in East Africa and parts of the Congo, is a Bantu language.

Another interesting type of language to be found in Africa is Pidgin, which is spoken only as a second language. In West African coastal areas Pidgin developed as the result of trading between Europeans and Africans. It appears to be a blend of a simplified form of the grammar of some African languages and English vocabulary. Currently in some areas it is the common language between neighboring villages which speak different languages, and in cities between speakers of different languages who do not have English in common.

There are frequently many different languages within the boundaries of a modern African state. Nigeria in West Africa contains over 200 languages representing three of the major African language families. Hausa, an Afro–Asiatic language, is spoken in the northern region. Because many Hausa have been traders for hundreds of years, that language can be heard in many other parts of West Africa as well. The other two major languages of Nigeria—Yoruba and Ibo—are both Congo–Kordofanian languages. Each of these three languages is used in major newspapers, on the radio, and in novels, plays, and poems in its respective region.

Since language is a vehicle for the transmission of culture, the choice of a national language has crucial implications for the development of education and the mass media. This decision is often one of the most important political acts of a newly independent nation.

Language diversity is one of the most interesting and challenging features in the development of modern African countries.

The Units of African Society

THE FAMILY

From George H. T. Kimble, *Tropical Africa*, 1960.

The heart of any society is the family and the strength of its beat is the measure of that society's vitality. In the African body social, the heart has always been strong; for it is sustained by devotion and service, and it is the creator and upholder of almost all things. . . .

In its simplest expression the family consists of husband and wife, or wives, with their children.

> They form an economic unit in so far as they cooperate in the maintenance of their common household. This cooperation is not necessarily complete, for very often husband, wife, and even half-grown children have their own individual property, to which they devote part of their work. On the other hand, the family unit is not only economic, for the members, by sharing common work, care, and experiences, grow into a real living community in which love and self-sacrifice are not unknown. (D. Westermann, *The African Today and Tomorrow*. London: Oxford University Press, 1949)

This is not to say that the family is conceived in Western terms. On the contrary, the differences are very considerable, especially in matriarchal (matrilineal) groups, those in which the children belong to the mother's group and descent is reckoned through the mother. Here it is the mother's brother rather than the father that is the guardian of her children. Then, too, African family ties are more often thought of as categorical than individual. Indeed, most terms of relationship are applied not to the individual but to a group of persons. Thus, all members of the same generation within a group of relations, or group regarded as relations, may call each other brothers and sisters; those belonging to the preceding generation they may call fathers and mothers (it is not uncommon for an African to speak of "my fathers and mothers"), and those of the following generation—sons and daughters, nephews and nieces of the first and second degree— their children. And since

> relationship in the male or female line is distinguished, and there is also a graduation between elder and younger, the relationship terms are in this respect even more definite and detailed than ours. The father's elder and younger brother and sister, and likewise the mother's elder and younger brother and sister, and their respective children, have each their own respective designation. The child has to learn and to use correctly all these names and the corresponding behavior to his relatives. This makes him conscious of the fact that he is a member not only of his family but of a larger group which influences his existence on all sides. (*Ibid.*)

The fact is that most Africans take a broader view of family relationship and responsibility than most Westerners. Frequently a family will consist of several households in which live the head of the family, his wife or wives, their unmarried sons and daughters and the husbands and children of their married daughters. These extended or enlarged families, as they are called, are likely to be disposed around a compound or group of compounds. Although such a group is not an economic entity, its younger members have an obligation to help or make presents to the older members, especially to the ranking member, who in turn carries the moral responsibility for their welfare.

Nor does the family tie end here. We have always to keep in mind that the primitive, pagan African family includes both the living and the dead.

> The living are constantly passing into the ranks of the so-called dead; the so-called dead are as constantly re-

turning to the ranks of the living by reincarnation. They return . . . in orderly manner through the legitimatized union of two members of the living section of the community.

To insure this regular return the living section ordains who shall be, and who shall not be, the parents; they signify their approval and seek the approval of the invisible members; and they take steps to secure the well-being of the child, both before and after its birth. (Edwin W. Smith, *Knowing the African*. London: Butterworth Press, 1946)

Marriage

It follows that marriage is not so much the affair of two individuals as the concern of the groups to which they belong. As everywhere else in the world, physical attraction plays a part, but in many tribes this, and the sexual intercourse that often follows from it does not ordinarily lead to matrimony. Among the exceptions to this rule are the Chagga (of Mt. Kilimanjaro), who consider it unseemly for a father to choose his daughter's husband, and the Kikuyu, whose womenfolk boast that they marry only those they want to marry. However, it is probably true to say that even among such liberal-minded people, things are often so arranged that the man a woman wants to marry is one the family wants her to marry. (For that matter, such arrangements are not unknown in Western society!) Among the less liberal-minded groups, questions of happiness, compatibility and mutual attraction are ordinarily subordinated to the wishes of both elders and ancestors, sometimes with satisfactory results but often at the cost of misery and tragedy. In general, marriage is conceived as a civil contract in which both parties commit themselves to certain obligations in regard to each other, but in which they both also maintain a considerable degree of economic autonomy.

Almost everywhere the contract calls for the transfer of goods or money, or both, from the bridegroom's family to the bride's family—the so-called "bride wealth." The exact significance of this custom is still debated by anthropologists. But whatever else it is, it is not to be thought of as the "price" of a bride, for Africans do not buy their wives. Rather it is to be thought of in such terms—to mention only a few of those used—as "a gift to seal the contract," "a recompense to the bride's parents for the loss of her services," "a pledge that the family line shall be continued," "guarantee that the woman shall be fairly treated," "a validation of the legality of the union"; or simply as a help in setting up a new household. In pastoral country, the usual medium of the transfer is cattle, sheep, or goats. Elsewhere the medium may be money, foodstuffs, copper bracelets, iron hoe blades, or even a man's labor. However much may be said against the custom, it makes for stability of the union, and for respect, since the greater the wealth transferred, the greater is the respect in which the woman will be held by her husband and his family. (Significantly, very many Christianized and Moslemized Africans feel that "a marriage concluded without bride-wealth means a humiliation and even dishonor to the wife.")

But "wealth" is by no means the sole criterion of a good marriage. Those who have a say in the matter are also concerned with the abilities and character of the two parties. Courage and skill in hunting (formerly, too, in fighting) are looked for in a man; in a woman, skill in firing clay and in raising and preparing food—and industry: she must look well in the ways of her household and not eat the bread of idleness. Looks, too, have their place in the reckoning. But let no one suppose that the eye of the African beholder sees what the Western eye sees; the vision is different.

As important is the marital eligibility of the parties. No persons in whose veins the same blood runs may on any account marry. And most Africans have very decided views about what constitutes sameness of blood. In many groups marriage is prohibited between the children of fathers who have entered into a covenant of brotherhood by mingling their blood. In parts of Africa the same applies to the children of families who have had direct arm-to-arm inoculation against smallpox. Marriages are customarily prohibited between persons having the same totem, that is, the same protective and therefore sacred animal, plant, or other object, because a consanguineous relation is believed to exist between the totem animal and all the members of the group which bears the totem name. Among such persons the eating of flesh and sexual commerce are equally a mingling of substance. Consequently, neither is permitted when an animal is the totem and the woman's totem is also the man's.

To protect themselves against the destructive consequences of inbreeding, most groups practice exogamy, that is, marriage between parties not belonging to the same kin or clan. Such groups allow a man to marry his mother's brother's or father's sister's child, but not his mother's sister's or father's brother's child. In other words, cross-cousins are eligible for marriage but not parallel cousins. Such marriages cannot be harmful to the group, because "blood" is considered to be inherited only through the mother. And where endogamy is practiced, care is taken to see that the parties are not of "the same blood."

The breaking of the tables of kinship and affinity, "wherein whosoever are related are forbidden . . . to marry together," is everywhere treated as a grave offense. Among many groups incest ranks with witchcraft, both being punishable by death.

In the eyes of the primitive African, the unity and sanctity of the family tie are not forfeit by resort to polygamy [any multiple marriage]. Whatever the evils of polygyny [more than one wife], a divided, dissolute home is rarely one of them. There are jealousies, of course, especially in households where one or more of the wives is barren; but these are seldom fierce enough to blind a woman to the advantages of living in a polygynous household. For the first wife, it means an improvement in her status, as in this way she becomes the chief wife and mistress of the house. For the others, and for her, it means a relief from work, since this is now divided, and more time is available for each wife's own affairs, including, in many cases, petty trading. She is free to come and go among her kin, to per-

orm the family rites prescribed by tribal custom, such as
he death vigil, and to bear and wean her children among
er own people (thus ensuring that the very general taboo
gainst intercourse at such times be not broken). Polygyny also means that the sick are seldom left uncared for
or the young orphaned and undisciplined, and that African society is saved from shouldering "the incubus of
numbers of frustrated single women claiming for themselves a recognition of [the] right to bear children." In
most pre-European, or "untouched," societies there were
next to no surplus women. Prostitution was accordingly
are. And on the whole there was very little divorce—notwithstanding the fact that in most groups divorce could,
and still can, be had for a large variety of reasons, including drunkenness, sexual and temperamental incompatibili-
ty, unharmonious relationship with a mother-in-law, the
discovery that the marriage has broken the tables of kinship and affinity, as well as adultery, barrenness, and impotence. For the man of the house, polygyny means
wealth, prestige and, unless venereal disease is present, an
assured succession. With several wives and many children
he can till much land, and keep a table that will allow him
to live well and provide the hospitality expected of him.

The status of women

The chief end of African marriage is the begetting of children. Because of this, the standing of a woman with her
husband and his people, and often with her own people,
is governed by her childbearing ability. If she is barren,
she is not only of all women most miserable, but also
most undesirable. To be the mother of many children is
to win life's highest prize—and most durable security, for
in a polygynous world, it is to the children rather than to
the husband that a woman looks for support in her de-
clining years.

From the day of her birth she has lived in intimate association with the facts of sex, seeing and hearing things
which in our Western world are studiously kept from a
child's attention. And from the time she could understand

her mother's words she has known that the first and grea
commandment is "Be fruitful and multiply." In spite o
this—or perhaps because of it—she has to undergo a rig
orous apprenticeship, part of it commonly taking plac
at an initiation school run by the older women. Asid
from their direct, practical value, which few students o
the subject would underrate, these schools serve as a re
minder to the initiate that, although she is graduating
from adolescence into womanhood, she is still subordi
nate in status to her elders—a subordination which sh
must at no time in her life fail to show in her conduct
Within a couple of years of leaving the school she wil
normally have become both wife and mother, inured t
hard labor, weariness, and pain.

Not even the death of her husband is likely to bring th
woman respite from her strenuous round, since, in many
tribes, she ranks as property and passes to his brother o
other heirs, to whom she is expected to give such service
as she is capable of until the day of her death.

If the chief end of African marriage is to raise a fam
ily, the chief concern of the contracting parties is to rais
it in conformity with the custom of the group, there bein
no greater crime in African society than nonconformity
From infancy the male, like the female, lives in a tradi
tion-encrusted environment to the preserving of which hi
energies are systematically directed by his elders. Thi
does not mean that the man's role in family life is charac
teristically as hard as that of the woman, for it most cer
tainly is not; but it does mean that nobody has to remine
him of his duties, or the penalty of forgetting them. Fo
the man, as for the woman, who does forget, African so
ciety has penalties in plenty.

The community

The English language is none too rich in words signifyin
hierarchies of social order and organization. Most o
those it does have have been debased by loose usage o
taken over by the specialists and given an esoteric mean
ing. "Community" is such a word. Yet probably no othe

better expresses the web of associations, intimate and casual, constant and infrequent, vertical and horizontal, political, social, and economic, in which the family is "caught." In primitive Africa, the major strands in this web are spun by the clan, the village, the age set, and the tribe (or ethnic group).

THE CLAN

If the family may be called the heart of primitive African society, the clan is its circulation system. Away from his clan or kinship group, the individual has little if any status and not much security. At best he is a tolerated "outsider"; at worst he is a nameless stranger, for whom no pity is felt and toward whom no mercy need be shown. Among his own kin he moves with assurance; with them he is "at home," knowing what is expected of him under all circumstances, knowing also what he can expect, and proud of the associations and prestige which his relationship confers.

The exact connotation of "clan" varies. Basically, however, a clan consists of a group of people claiming common descent, the descent being reckoned by the social relationship of parents and children, which is to say that the relationship may be established by adoption as well as by birth. The "commonness" may be regarded as deriving from either the male or the female side of the group, or from both sides. Where it is regarded as deriving from the male side, the major responsibility for the upbringing of children is vested in the father and his family, to whom the children belong. Here descent is reckoned patrilineally and the woman is likely to spend much of her time in the husband's village. To begin with, she will probably live with her father-in-law; indeed, she may leave her own home even before she is married if her future husband is working at a distance. Where the common tie is regarded as deriving from the female side, the major responsibility is vested in the mother and her family (most notably in her brother), to whom the children belong. Here descent is reckoned matrilineally and the woman is likely to reside in her own village. Where clans recognize both mother-rights and father-rights, questions of family responsibility, residence, property ownership and descent tend to be more complicated. For example, among the Ewe of Ghana and Togo the children are considered as belonging to the father's clan, and so are entitled to inherit their father's real estate. His movable property, on the other hand, is inherited by his sister's children, as in a matrilineal society; and even his own children cannot be married without the assent of their mother's brother.

This feeling of "commonness" is fortified in different ways, as, for instance, by the possession of a common totem and common land, both of which tend to be thought of as evidence of relatedness. Totemism is widely held in west Africa. As mentioned earlier, those who hold it suppose that a blood relationship exists between the totem animal or other object and all members of the clan which bears its name. All who have the same totem are to be treated as brothers. As the totem is inherited, usually from father to son (even in communities which in other respects may be considered matrilineal), and as intermarriage of families having the same totem is comparatively uncommon, in the course of several generations representatives of a given totem group are likely to spread over a wide area, often well beyond their tribal borders. But wherever and however far they go, the freemasonry of the totem goes with them.

> For instance, a Mossi of the Pima clan, animist and savage, who had never left his native country before, finds himself suddenly at St. Louis [Senegal] and meets there a Wolof of the Noliaye clan, who is a Moslem or a Christian and is relatively civilized, who on his part has never been in the Mossi country; the Pima does not understand one word of Wolof, nor the Noliaye one word of Mossi; after some moments, by signs which only they note, this Mossi and this Wolof recognise each other as members of one clan, and immediately the Wolof takes this Mossi, whose home is 2,000 kilometers away from his, under his protection. (M. Delafosse, *Haut-Sénégal-Niger,* Vol. III)

THE VILLAGE

Whereas the clan is an expression of common origins, the village is more an expression of common needs. "It forms," in Westermann's words, "the natural grouping in the daily life of its inhabitants in their work and their recreative activities. It is also the base and center of the many other associations which claim the individual as their member, such as play-groups of children, work-groups of the young people, age classes, drum and dancing clubs, religious cults, guilds of trades." At its simplest, the village consists of the compounds of the families, or extended families, of a single clan or section of a clan. But in most areas it consists of the compounds of several clans, brought together through intermarriage. The larger the village, the greater the amount of interclan marrying, and so the smaller the significance of clan in its corporate life. In the large village, it is the age sets and associations rather than the clans that give polarity to social life.

Age sets and associations tend to arise in any society where there is a call for the cooperation of equals. The symbol of cooperation may be a baseball bat or a football, a jet plane or a battleship, a hunting spear or a garden hoe, an axe or a drum. And while equality of age does not signify equality of skill or stamina, nobody is likely to deny that, over the long haul, it makes for greater compatibility of outlook, better teamwork and more fun. Not every tropical African group has developed age sets or associations, but it is fair to say that most groups have and that in organization many of them are almost as institutionalized as most Western clubs, lodges and other fraternal orders. Indeed, no Western association requires its prospective members to undergo anything quite as institutionalized—or as rigorous—as the puberty rites to which most African boys and girls have traditionally been subject. Numerous functions are served by age sets and associations. Some age sets are primarily concerned with economic affairs. Others are more concerned with religious and military matters, or with recreation. Some have managed to keep their real purpose secret. A good many serve more than one purpose. Thus, among the Nupe of Nigeria age sets have both a recreational and an economic function, the latter being concerned with the execution of cooperative tasks such as tilling and weeding, building or roofing a chief's house, and repairing a bush bridge. Almost all age sets have to do, in some way or other, with the regulation of behavior and status. How this used to work among the Kpe group of the Cameroons, who are by no means exceptional in this respect, is shown in the following age set table:

Age Set	Status
"Young men" (up to 35–40 years of age)	Not considered able to speak in important matters.
"Middle-aged persons" (about 40–50 years of age)	Opinions carry weight.
"Elderly persons" (from 50 to about 65 years of age)	Form the active government of the village and play the important roles in ritual.
"Very old persons" (more than about 65 years of age)	Greatly respected and even reverenced, but too old to take an active role in society.

THE TRIBE

Like "community," "tribe" means different things to different people—so many things that there is a school (tribe?) of thought that favors excision of the term from the body anthropological. And there is much to be said for the avoidance of a word to which even small dictionaries attribute half a dozen technical meanings. However, it may be a long time before anybody thinks of a word which is less liable to misinterpretation by the general reader. For our present purpose, we take "tribe" to mean . . . "an agglomeration of groups and individuals, not necessarily related, [forming] a cultural and political unity through living in a common territory, having a common leader, one language, and similar customs and usages." This definition is not above criticism, but it will serve to identify for us a further strand in the web of associations we have called the community. Of all the strands that go to the making of the web, the tribe is certainly the hardest to analyze, because it is most variable in strength and character. Here it is strong, there weak; in some places it dominates the pattern, in others it is, in a manner of speaking, invisible to the naked eye. Its main function, however, is almost everywhere the same: the maintenance of law and order.

In its most rudimentary form, the tribe consists of no more than a few families or family groups "who live independently by themselves and recognize either the father of the family, the priest, the rain maker, or the magician as their chief, or regulate their communal affairs by means of a council of elders." Small-scale organization of this kind was characteristic of the Bushmen of the Kalahari Desert and adjacent areas, the pygmies of the Congo basin forests, and many tribes in the back country of west Africa and the upper Nile valley.

At the other extreme are tribes with populations running into hundreds of thousands, owing allegiance to a single chief or king whose domain covers an area the size of Massachusetts. But such large units were the exception rather than the rule and should be thought of as supratribal, for more often than not they came into existence through the conquest of one tribe by another. If the members of the winning tribe liked the look of the country, they settled in it, becoming its dominating caste, and running it, feudal-fashion, with the help of regents, governors, soldiers, and labor levies. Given enough time and good treatment, the conquered people would get accustomed to their position as "colonists"; and both conquered and conquerors would tend to absorb the other's culture. Even so, the entente was seldom notable for its cordiality. Such tribal organizations were, accordingly, inclined to be unstable. It took a ruler with a strong personality to keep them from disintegrating. Not even the strongest of personalities could prevent his subject peoples from keeping alive their language, beliefs, and practices, and maintaining a "shadow cabinet" of priests, magicians, and clan and family heads. It was only very rarely that a large unit came into being because men who felt themselves one desired to be one. "Nationalism" and the nation-state are exotic growths.

Each tribal unit, large, medium, or small, in its pristine form, is ruled by a chief or paramount chief, elected or hereditary, and each component group by a subchief owing allegiance to the chief. Not withstanding his "paramountcy," the chief is himself a man under authority: at all times he must act in conformity with the custom of his people, living and dead. For failure to do so he can be censured, fined, and in cases of serious deviation, deposed. His power is still further restricted, paradoxically, by the fact that his person is considered to be in some degree sacred. To preserve the implied sense of distance between the chief and his subjects, various taboos may be imposed upon him. These may necessitate his not being seen eating in public—even not being seen at all, in which case the person chosen to represent him may wield the greater influence. The chief's power is often still further curbed by the secret societies, from whose inquisitorial eyes no man's life is hidden.

In the absence or near-absence of material sources of power, such power as the chief has is largely derived from ability to carry his people with him and from the regard they have for his custodianship of their traditions. While moral qualities are not unesteemed in a chief, they are generally not held to be as important as physical, intellectual and religious ones. What matters most is that he should know how to handle the magic powers inherited from his predecessors. It is these powers that make the tribe truly strong, united, and proud.

But the chief is much more than a symbol and a receptacle of power. He is also its embodiment. One of his most important functions, in conjunction with his councilors and deputies, is to administer the law: to see that injuries to person and property are compensated for, that the young of the tribe are properly instructed in its custom, and that the tribe is kept free from the taint of those who do not hallow that custom—if need be, by the passing of new decrees. Since the scope of African tribal custom is equaled only by the litigiousness of those who offend against it, chieftainship is no sinecure.

To the great cultural value of chieftainship almost all missionaries, anthropologists and government administrators who have had the opportunity of observing it in its pristine form bear witness. True, its excesses, such as trial by ordeal, the "smelling out" of witches, and the arbitrary killing of persons at burials, were barbarous, though probably not more so than many of those committed in more enlightened parts of the world. It was, however, a powerful instrument for the forging of political unity, an apt tool for the shaping of public opinion, a ready-made channel for directing community enterprise, and an unfailing reservoir for the nurture of religious sentiment. And in most parts of Africa it has provided the bridgehead from which men of alien ways are striving to establish a wider social and political order.

The Land, the People: A Way of Life

In an industrialized, urbanized, and highly specialized culture such as ours, we tend to lose sight of the fact that the most basic activity of any group of humans is the procuring of food. In African society, food production is the activity which absorbs the energies of the majority of the population most of the time.

We need to be reminded that for most Africans the economic pattern is one of subsistence rather than profit and exchange. We should also be aware that the practices which developed have social as well as economic significance. And thirdly, we must appreciate that Africans, working against a harsh environment, have often learned to extract the maximum from the land with the means at their disposal.

From George H. T. Kimble, *Tropical Africa*, 1960.

FOOD GATHERING

Before the present century, almost every sub-Saharan African earned his living by gathering food (including hunting and fishing), by cultivating crops or by herding, or by a combination of these activities. We have no means of knowing exactly how many Africans followed a given livelihood, but it is clear that some livelihoods were more common than others.

Contrary to the still popular belief, almost no tribal groups lived exclusively by hunting. Possibly the Bushmen of the Kalahari Desert and bordering areas, the Ruanda-Urundi-Tanganyika borderlands, the Bwamba of Ruwenzori, and the Dorobo of the Kenya Highlands came as near to doing so as any, but their womenfolk spent a good deal of time grubbing for insects and their eggs, and for honeycombs, and collecting edible roots, berries, nuts and other plant foods. Similarly, not many groups lived entirely by collecting foodstuffs. Thus, the Babinga and other food gatherers of the deep forests of equatorial Africa seem to have divided their attention between catching elephants, monkeys and fish, and seeking out wild honey and edible roots.

By far the great majority of the aboriginal peoples were either cultivators or pastoralists, or partly one and partly the other. Indeed, they still are. And, though times are changing, many African peoples still work their land and keep their animals the way their pre-European forefathers did. Much of what follows could as well speak for the present as for the 1890's.

CROP CULTIVATION

All told there are more than four million square miles of tropical Africa where crop cultivation, if not the sole economic activity, has long been the main one, and where the role of the food gatherer, hunter and herder has been secondary at best. Significantly, in a number of African tongues spoken within this area the same expression is ιsed for "to work" and "to cultivate the field." The ρoundaries of the area coincide roughly with those of the distribution of sleeping sickness and tsetse fly infestation.

The cultivation was of two main types, bush-fallowing ιnd permanent. The first of these, bush-fallowing—more ιsually though not always correctly called shifting cultivaτion—was the more common of the two, largely because τhe areas which lent themselves to it were more numerɔus. The forgotten generations who pioneered agriculture in tropical Africa were faced with a situation in which land was plentiful and the soils, with few exceptions, difficult. Left to his own devices, the African cultivator's response to these conditions was basically the same whether it was worked out in the steaming rain forest of Liberia, the open parklands of Northern Rhodesia or the grassy slopes of Ruwenzori. . . .

He felled the trees and piled the brushwood in heaps, or distributed it evenly over the cleared area. Big trees were usually left in place, both because of the labor involved in felling them and because their root systems served to keep the soil anchored against the forces of erosion. Smaller trees were customarily cut off about four feet above the ground. The cleared land had anything but a tamed and tidy look, but in a virtually plowless world this mattered little. The aim of the tree-feller was to collect the maximum amount of readily inflammable material, not to remove every obstruction from the path of the sowers and hoers who came after him.

In the forest zones the disposing of this brushwood was normally done toward the end of the dry season. At any other time of the year, the ground would have been too wet to set fire easily. Even in the dry season the relative humidity of the duff layer remained so high that fire did less damage to the animal and vegetable life of the subsurface layers of the soil than would be the case with a forest fire in, say, the western Sierras. Forest wind velocities being typically low, the risk of a fire getting out of control was not very great. In the drier, better-ventilated bush and parkland zones, it was different. On the plateaus of east Africa, for instance, it is still not uncommon

to see bush fires that started innocently enough in a two
to-three-acre clearing eating up land the size of a Texas
county. . . . The aim of the savanna burner was not just
to get wood ash for fertilizer but also to obtain a finely
powdered seedbed for the ensuing crop. He might get a
meal or two of small game and vermin as well, a much
appreciated bonus in the predominantly vegetarian so
ciety.

As a rule, sowing amounted to nothing more than the
placing of seeds or tubers in holes made by a digging
stick, the holes then being filled in with a kick of the foot.
In some areas, as in the Bemba country of Northern
Rhodesia, only one crop was planted in a given clearing
at a time, but it was more customary to sow a mixture of
seeds and tubers. In this way the cultivator was able to
safeguard himself to some extent against the vagaries of
the weather and the ever-present threat of erosion, the
combination of crops providing a protective mantle of
vegetation. In this way, too, it was generally possible to
obtain from a single clearing a main crop, such as yam,
millet, manioc or maize, and one or more subsidiary
crops, such as beans, peppers or squash. In these subsidi
ary crops the woman took a special interest. Her success
as a wife and housekeeper could well hinge on her ability
to garnish the staple dish with them, and with the food
stuffs she could find in the surrounding bush. . . .

As with every other phase of the cultivator's work, the
sowing was commonly preceded, accompanied and fol
lowed by prayers and sacrifices. And for compelling rea
sons, some of which a modern-day Mossi peasant ex
pressed when he prayed: "My God, I give you this fowl
in exchange, help me to get millet. Making the millet
grow, harvesting and eating it are the three things which
keep the world going. God I give you this fowl so that
you may help me in these three things."

Often it was the intruders that made most work for the
cultivator. The primeval bush abounded in herbivorous
animals that had either to be frightened away or kept out
side the palings laboriously erected season by season.
Herbivorous birds, not so amenable to discipline, had to

be kept at bay with stones, verbal volleys or hand-operated clappers. As the harvest approached, it was sometimes necessary to take up temporary residence at the crop patch. None of these stratagems availed anything against hungry elephants.

The harvesting of the crops was highly responsible work, since an error of judgment could have serious consequences for the family. Unripe grain is wasteful. Overripe grain blows too much dust into the eyes and is partially lost in the gathering. Damp heads of grain hang down and are hard to cut. An educated Bamba once told Audrey Richards that a field sufficient to fill three fourths of a granary would fill only half of it if the grain (millet in this case) were reaped at the wrong time.

The productive life of a clearing depended on several factors. Where the land was fertile, as around the flanks of volcanic mountains, it might be as much as fifteen to twenty years, the same staple being grown year after year. Over most of the not so fertile forested and savanna-covered lowlands, three to four sowings of the same crop in quick succession could easily reduce a field to impotence. And there were places, as, for example, in the Ilorin Province of Nigeria, where it was imprudent to use a field for more than one year at a time.

Practically the only staple crop that did not have to be kept "on the move" was the banana (plantain). Provided the ground was heavily composted with decaying leaves and other handy vegetable matter, and the cultivator regularly replaced the worn-out stems with new suckers, his banana patch could be maintained almost in perpetuity.

The permanent farming of a tract of land is nowhere the easiest of undertakings. In tropical Africa it must be reckoned among the hardest. Seasonally flooded alluvial plains, valleys capable of irrigation by simple lifting devices, and rock outcrops that weather into rich, easily worked and durable soils are scarce. Even scarcer in pre-European times was knowledge of the agronomic virtues of crop rotation, which, in the absence of rich soils and fertilizing floods, alone can keep cultivated land in good heart. Most cultivators believe it is simpler, and better, to

keep planting a patch of ground with their favorite food
until the soil is exhausted than to grow a succession of
fertility-renewing crops, some of which they do not like
or cannot eat, and others of which they have trouble in
storing because of mildew, fermentation, and depreda-
tions by animals and insects. . . .

PASTORALISM

How and where cattle-keeping got its first foothold and
how it spread until it embraced no less than one third of
tropical Africa is beyond the scope of this inquiry. For
that matter, it is probably beyond the scope of present
knowledge. What is fairly certain is that the chief pastoral
peoples came from the Nile valley and brought with them
a derivative of the giant-horned wild ox found in upper
Egypt, similar to the present-day long-horned cattle of the
Ankole and other east African pastoralists. And it is clear
that the chief cattle-raising peoples, such as the Fulani of
west Africa and the Tusi, Masai, Suk, Samburu, Turkana
and Kamasia of east Africa, are quite distinct in physical
as well as in other ways from the main crop-raising peoples.

The major ends served by the cattle were social rather
than economic. A man was known by the company of
cattle he kept. If he had a large herd, he was a wealthy
man. The physical condition of the individual animals
was not very important; generally it did not affect the reckoning of a man's wealth any more than the physical condition of dollar bills affects their purchasing power. In a
sense, cattle was currency. In another sense, they were
also "invested capital at a high rate of interest." With the
"interest" a man could make friends and influence people. Without it he was a nonentity. With cattle he could
get wives and keep his kraal swarming with children who
would work for him, and, if need be, fight for him and so
enhance his social standing. Without cattle a man might
well find himself childless, servantless, and statusless, un-
worthy to rank as an elder among his own people. If,
through misfortune, a Tusi was forced to abandon stock

raising and become a crop raiser instead, he ceased to regard himself as a Tusi.

Above all else, cattle signified "bride wealth." If a man had four sons, he must take care to acquire enough cows and bulls to enable his sons to marry four wives, or more. If he had four daughters, it was his hope that they would bring him a corresponding number of cattle when they married. On no account must his "capital" become depleted. It had been entrusted to him by his ancestors, and he must pass it to his descendants intact—better still, augmented.

For the pastoralist, there was no pleasanter occupation than to be among his animals, admiring them, grooming them, and inventing pet names for those he liked best. Almost from the time they could walk, a cattle keeper's sons "grew up" with the herds, and all their lives they lived in a world where the everyday talk turned on the number, kind, color and horns of their animals. Among the Shilluk and some other pastoral groups, the size and form of the horns were of such moment that a man was set aside for the purpose of shaping the horns of young oxen to their owners' desires. To men reared in this world, separation from a favorite animal was a hardship scarcely more tolerable than separation from a wife.

Not all the pastoralists were cattle keepers, however. In the more arid parts of the Republic of Sudan, the Republic of Chad and west Africa, the horse and the camel occupied important roles, frequently superseding cattle as the basis of the economy. Scattered all over east and central Africa were societies that made substantial use of smaller animals, such as sheep, goats, and donkeys. This was especially true of the areas infested by the cattle-killing tsetse fly. Among the Masai, for instance, sheep, notwithstanding their lower social significance, were almost as numerous as cattle.

For the most part, these pastoral societies were self-sufficing, usually of necessity, but sometimes from choice, for surpluses were not unknown. The Masai often had more animals than they could conceivably use, or maintain on the grass and water available, but it does not seem to have occurred to them that they might have traded the surplus off to their crop-raising neighbors. If it did occur to them, they must either have decided that there was nothing they wanted in exchange, or that anything they could have obtained would have been a poor exchange for the pleasure and prestige they derived from owning a large herd.

Like the Bedouin, and for the same reasons, the herdsmen of eastern Africa were wanderers. To keep animals within reach of grass and water was a clever trick in the best of seasons; in bad seasons it was genius. To do so, the herder must be able to smell water and scent grass without seeing it; to outwit wild animals with the same needs but not with the same scruples about what is edible; and to shake off the attention of other herders, not all of whom were accustomed to settling their grazing disputes as peacefully as Abraham and Lot. Tribes living on the arid fringe of east Africa thought nothing of spending eight months out of every twelve traveling to and fro with their herds, in the wake of the solstitial rains. In periods of subnormal rains they might be kept "on the hoof" the year around and walk twenty-five hundred miles in the course of it.

To such men there was but one great commandment: to maintain the herd. To keep it they could covet their neighbors' animals, steal them, kill them. They could kill their neighbors, if need be. Indeed, they could do almost anything except deny their birthright.

A PASTORAL ATTITUDE ILLUSTRATED

Pastoralism, providing as it does a livelihood for so many Africans, must be seen as a way of life as well as a way of earning a living. Animals are such a vital part of pastoral people's existence that they attach much more than just economic significance to them. Pastoralists' beliefs bind them to their animals beyond any logical economic consideration. Cattle sustain their owners by providing their chief foods—milk, and blood, the latter being tapped only in safe amounts. But with changing times and circumstances, these practices often clash with economic reality.

Such attitudes, of course, also tend to clash with European views. The next selection, from a novel, illustrates this clash and dramatizes the important place of cattle in the thinking of the Masai, a pastoral people of East Africa. The reading is a dialogue between an English lawyer, Mr. Hobbes, and an educated Masai who has taken the European name of Jim. They are awaiting the outcome of a trial in which one of Jim's friends is being tried for the murder of a European who failed to understand that the white cow was the African's sister.

From Richard Llewellyn, *A Man in a Mirror*, 1961.

"Tradition and feeling have very little to do with a breach of the law," Mr. Hobbes said. "Important though they might be, the fact of murder is not to be explained away. A Judge may be the kindest-hearted chap you could wish for. They often are. But they have a duty. Where do you think I failed?"

Jim sat up, watching the car turn into the courtyard.

"I don't think you failed as a European," he said, "but your law is not our law."

"You mean to say that murder of an unarmed man is not a crime among the Masai?" Mr. Hobbes asked, in the same gentle voice. "No penalty at all?"

"It would not occur," Jim said.

"Yes, but it did occur, and the man's in the cells and the jury's deciding a verdict," Mr. Hobbes said. "What would have happened under your law?"

"He might have been exiled, without family or cattle," Jim said. "His cattle might have been paid to the family of the dead man. Or the Council might give him to the women."

"Might not be as attractive as it sounds," Mr. Hobbes said. "I don't think I've seen any Masai women."

"Old women," Jim said. "Very old women. They know many things. In everyday sickness, they are our physicians and surgeons. They are adept with a knife. It is a strong punishment."

"I can well imagine it," Mr. Hobbes said. "I think I'd prefer the sudden drop. But if strong punishment's the rule, why do you object to this trial?"

"Well, I think he was guilty only of protecting his sister," Jim said.

Mr. Hobbes pulled the lobe of his ear, and watched the ants taking his cigarette to pieces.

"I'm not sure that his sister made an appearance in the evidence," he said, gently as ever.

"The white cow was his sister," Jim said.

"Ah, yes," Mr. Hobbes said, and looked up without a smile. "Your suggestion is that the white cow, taken to fulfill a contract which had been paid for, shouldn't have been chosen or listed?"

"We believe so," Jim said. "There were tens of thousands of other animals to choose from."

"Would all of them have been somebody's brother or sister?" Mr. Hobbes asked.

"It would not be likely because they have to be born at the same moment," Jim said. "That cow was driven by accident into the herd. It was only chance which led the owner there. When he claimed her, he was refused. But that cow's mother was born with him. I was brought up with a black bull calf on the same milk. His son is still with me. If somebody tried to take him, I would also kill."

"Your own mother suckled the first calf?" Mr. Hobbes asked.

"As a sign, after feeding me," Jim said. "After that, the calf's mother fed me. Quite fair?"

"Oh, quite," Mr. Hobbes said. "If I understand you, this calf becomes your brother, and when it dies, one of its progeny takes its place? Still as your brother?"

"Exactly," Jim said. "So you see, we have a duty. The white cow's mother was brought up with him. She took the mother's place. He told the officer. But the officer didn't understand. He told his men to take the cow because it was paid for."

"The cow was part of a quota sold by the chiefs of your people for an over-all price to the Government," Mr. Hobbes said. "A cattle train was waiting at the railhead. A ship or ships waited at the port. Your friend objected to the choice of his—ah—sister. The officer, you feel, was inclined to ride roughshod over any consideration of family ties. And therefore, in finding your remonstration or offer of exchange were alike futile, your friend was justified in putting a spear through an unarmed Government agent?"

Jim shook his head.

"He was not justified," he said. "He was only angry."

"Is anger sufficient excuse?" Mr. Hobbes asked. "Is the crime made any less deserving of punishment?"

Jim stared across at the courthouse steps. The question made him want to shout an answer. But the voice was always quiet, and gentle.

"No," he said. "But this is not a usual crime. Not one of my people has ever been in a court before this. It has taught us that we must look to men of another nation to help us. We don't know how to defend ourselves. To us, cattle are just as important as people. That is an absolute fact. If it isn't understood, then neither are we. That's why we must have our own lawyers. We must, because every day we come closer to Europeans and their laws. Every day we are in more danger. Every day, less defense, more helpless. The man who died made contemptuous remarks about our beliefs. He was contemptuous, also, of a man with a spear. He had no time to find out his mistake. But his death has caused very much more respect for us."

A YOUNG PASTORALIST EXPRESSES HIS GOALS

A somewhat more cheerful expression of the African pastoral attitudes can be seen in the following "pen pal" exchange.

The school children of Petoa (Cameroons) began an exchange of letters a few years ago with the school children of Costes-Gozon, a small village in southern France. In the following letter an African boy explains his plans for the future and reveals a good deal about his attitude toward his way of life.

From UNESCO *Courier,* September, 1960.

[When I grow up] I shall raise cows, sheep and goats.

I won't grow any crops, but with the milk from my cows I shall buy a big gourd of millet.

With the meat of a goat or a ram killed each month we shall eat well.

Clothes will be no problem. I shall take a six-year-old bull to market and with what it brings I shall buy fine clothes.

My son will guard my sheep, my daughter will look after the goats, and I shall take the cows out to the pasture. There I may have to endure rain and storms, but the delicious, creamy milk will soon make me forget these discomforts.

When I grow old I shall employ paid shepherds. In the shadow of the "danki" I shall stretch myself on my sleeping mat, a glass of coffee by my side. "Bouba has more than a hundred head of livestock; he is one of the richest among us" the villagers will say.

When I am 80 years old I shall sell some of my animals and I shall spend the money on a pilgrimage to Mecca.

[signed]
Bouba

SYSTEMS OF LAND TENURE

The land is, of course, inextricably related to making a living. Therefore, the mores which a group has concerning the land—its uses and rights to it—are very close to the heart of its culture.

Because African mores about land differ so from ours, they were and are the source of many misunderstandings and hostilities between Africans and Europeans. Also, African land holding mores have a bearing on the ease with which Africans can move from a subsistence economy to a more complex one.

From George H. T. Kimble, *Tropical Africa*, 1960.

The ideas men hold about the land they live on depend largely on how much there is of it and the uses to which it can be put. There being in the tropical Africa of pre-European days plenty of land but few ways of using it, the basic ideas concerning the ownership and use of land were everywhere much the same.

The most widespread of these ideas was that of communal ownership. Land was not thought of as belonging to persons, but to people; and the people could be the members of a clan, a village, a tribe or a kingdom. One Nigerian chief spoke for many millions of his fellow Africans when he said, "I conceive that land belongs to a vast family of which many are dead, few are living, and countless members are still unborn." Although a person could have the use of a particular piece of land, his rights over it and what he could do with it were limited by other rights over the same piece of land held by the other members of his "family." These rights were limited both as to the period of effective occupation and as to transfer and succession. So long as a man worked a piece of land or members of his community worked it for him, it remained in his possession and no one might encroach on it. Should he leave it temporarily, he could, as a rule, take possession of it again on his return. If he did not wish to retain the use of it he might negotiate its transfer to another, receiving in exchange goods or services of some kind. But usually he could not treat it as either a salable or a rentable commodity. There was, accordingly, no opportunity for land speculation and no incentive to acquire large holdings from which a return might be derived in the form of purchase money or rent. There were no rentiers, and no tenants in the American sense of the term; but a landowner always had plenty of relatives and friends to whom he could loan land in return for help given him in cultivating and reaping crops on his "home farm."

In many areas, customary law limited the extent of land that anyone might hold to the amount he required for the support of himself and his family. The absentee owner was therefore a rarity. So, too, was the compact lot, since in most areas either bush-fallowing or shifting cultivation was the rule and, by the laws of inheritance, good and bad land had to be divided equitably. This almost always meant that a man's holdings consisted of a series of patches scattered over a wide area.

The ideas entertained about useful trees were in several respects similar to those entertained about the land on which they stood. Thus, the fruit of a wild palm tree was generally anybody's, but the moment the tree was tapped for wine it became the tapper's. He retained possession of it even though he neglected the land on which it stood— even though he did not own the land on which it stood. Similarly, if a person planted a palm tree, or any other tree of economic importance, the tree belonged to him no matter on whose ground it was planted. To make sure that its ownership was accepted, the planter would be likely to summon the village elders to witness the planting, more particularly if the ground did not belong to him. In a sense, a tree was more of a property than land, for if a man who owned both a tree and the land on which it stood should leave his village, he would not automatically lose his rights over the tree. If he wished, he could even rent out his tree.

Land and trees, then, were regarded in the same light as sunshine and air: as plentiful and necessary, and as things to be enjoyed by all members of the community according to their requirements. In themselves they had little or no value; it was the work which a man, a family or a community put into a piece of land or a tree that gave it value. Consequently, when a piece of land was transferred from one owner to another, its value was adjudged to be the value of the standing crop, if any, and of the work which had gone into clearing and breaking the ground for the crop.

Departures from this generalized pattern of land tenure were frequent, especially among pastoral societies. Where cattle-keepers were accustomed to range freely in search of grass and water, as in the semi-arid country of the northern savannas, close delimitation of land rights was impracticable. For one thing, there were few landmarks; for another, there were not enough people to guard them; and, for a third, hungry animals do not bother about the laws of trespass. Where pastoralists were restricted in their movements, more definite rights arose, though they were seldom as definite as cultivators' rights. Thus, in the

Sukuma country of western Tanganyika individuals were able to establish rights over grazing areas and demand rents from cattle owners for their use. This was reasonable enough since the conversion of bush lands into well-demarcated grazing grounds involved much labor. Rights of ownership arose in many areas in respect of salt licks, water holes and the like. But the granting of such rights was attended by all manner of possibilities for the litigious possessor of them and his less fortunate neighbor, particularly where individuals sought to reserve areas with a view to producing short, sweet herbage. Even today wherever personal rights in grazing grounds are recognized law suits are frequent, since the grounds often form a patchwork lacking easily distinguished boundaries.

MARKET SYSTEMS

The following selection is a description of trading activities in Agbaja in the eastern region of Nigeria. It illustrates the complexity of the market system among the Ibo people, and its importance in their daily lives.

From M. M. Green, *Ibo Village Affairs*, 1964.

If agriculture is the basic occupation of these Ibo people, trading is a close second. One might almost say that whereas they farm of necessity, they trade not only of necessity but also for pleasure. Their markets are one of the main features in their lives. They provide a meeting point for the discussion of common business and the dissemination of news; they are a social event where the spice of gossip, the recreation of dancing and the zest of a bargain relieve the almost continuous toil of hoeing, planting, weeding and harvesting throughout the year. Trading is the breath of life, particularly to the women among the Ibo, and the vigor with which bargaining and haggling are conducted is evidence of the prestige attached to successful commercial enterprise.

In this densely populated part of Ibo country each market is normally held once in eight days, and there is a market somewhere within a few miles' radius from Umueke every day. This does not mean that every individual goes to market every day, but it was considered obligatory for the whole village to turn out for its own market. . . . The distances people walk with a heavy head load tend to be less here than in some parts of Ibo country, but now and then individuals go for many miles. A stranger going round to a number of Ibo markets is apt to have the impression that thousands of people are buying and selling minute quantities of the same things. Rows of women seem to have trays or baskets with more or less the same miscellaneous collection of small objects—little leaf packets of mashed oil bean, a few red peppers, half a dozen matches, some sliced cassava. But in fact the markets are to a certain extent specialized in the sense that one is reputed good for meat or livestock, another for pots, another for yams and so on. There is a constant flow of foodstuffs such as yams from the less densely populated areas into those with a heavy population, the return being partly in palm oil. There are, moreover, trade secrets or small specializations in such matters as mashed bean oil. One village will possess the art, the next-door village will not.

The women are the great petty traders, spending much time and energy for what must often be a very small profit. But even a few heads of cowries are worth having as a profit when life is on a modest scale, particularly when the gaining of them involves the pleasures of the market. But the time and energy involved are considerable, and already the women have much arduous work with their farming, cooking and palm oil making. It is small wonder that they are thin as rakes and often show signs of physical strain, and their frequent references to the amount of work they have to do are amply justified.

Men trade in rather a larger way than the women and in certain different classes of goods. But everything here was on a small scale compared with a trading center such as, for example, Onitsha. No one here had a bicycle, far less a lorry with which to carry oil to distant collecting centers. It was sold by the potful usually at the nearby markets, and therefore at a lower price than it would ave fetched nearer to the European depots. Young men would sometimes go as far as Umuahia to buy stockfish which they could then sell retail.

Markets are arranged according to well-recognized customary rules. Some of the more important goods such as livestock will be displayed in special places, but the women with their small wares sit according to geographical principles. The women from each village sit along the path which leads from the market place back to the village from which they have come. Thus, as they say, if there is fighting in the market they can escape easily to their own homes.

A number of small objects are made in the village in people's spare time either for use or for sale locally. Men would often bring to some gathering the climbing ropes they were making and get on with them in the intervals of discussion or other business: mats, baskets and wooden spoons, chairs and bed-frames of so-called bamboo were made by the men and boys. A few women very occasionally made a small number of pots.

Religion and the Role of the Supernatural

Religion anywhere provides a human community with an explanation of forces it cannot comprehend or control. In most African traditional religions there is one supreme God, who is approached through lesser forces; and whether these be ancestors or animistic spirits embodied in a tree, a river, or an animal, their power to influence man's destiny is unquestioned. Since such spirits or fetishes are believed to affect men's behavior, their advice is sought frequently in the settlement of questions and disputes. Special offerings are made to the particular spirit or fetish believed to be the mediator between a community and God.

Ever since the first Europeans witnessed the ceremonies of African religions they have been baffled and sometimes frightened by examples of what in their eyes could only be a malevolent magic or bewitchment of one person by another. A few came to know certain communities well enough to appreciate the mysterious forces at work. One of these was Geoffrey Gorer, the author of the following selections. Traveling in French West Africa in the 1930s he kept careful notes of the experiences he and his companion, Benga, shared as they moved from place to place studying traditional dances.

The first selection illustrates the powerful use of psychological suggestion in apprehending criminals in a community near Abomey, Dahomey. Once the community has come to believe in certain remedies for wrongdoing, tremendous pressure is put upon a guilty person to comply with tradition. The second selection describes an initiation ceremony for a panther fetish and certain other phenomena observed by Gorer.

A FETISHER CATCHES A THIEF

From Geoffrey Gorer, *Africa Dances,* 1962.

A man called Epiphane had had a silver bracelet stolen. Instead of going to the police about his loss he called in a fetisher. The fetisher took up a position just off the main road a little way out of Abomey (where the bracelet had been stolen) and had a chicken brought to him. He held the chicken by the claws in his left hand above his head, so that the bird's beak was level with his mouth, and started talking to it quietly. He was telling it about the theft, repeating the same words over and over again. After some little time the chicken began to bleed from the mouth, a drop every few minutes. The fetisher went on talking quietly. This had been going on for more than half an hour when a man suddenly arrived desperately out of breath and with his pagne torn; he fell panting on the ground by the fetisher. The fetisher went on talking to the bird which suddenly gave a sort of strangled squawk, at which the exhausted man confessed that he had stolen the bracelet and explained how he had taken it and where it was. The fetisher put the chicken on the ground; it started pecking rather uncertainly.

Prince Aho explained that this was the usual method of dealing with stolen property. When the chicken started to bleed the thief was forced to come to where the fetisher

was, wherever he might be and whatever he was doing. . . .

A FETISH INITIATION

Benga and I were made, as it were, honorary members
of the Agassou (panther) fetish, on the ground that I was
certainly and he probably harboring the spirit of a dead
fetisher. But before our initiation we were made to swear
that we would neither write nor speak about anything we
might see or experience, and we had to leave cameras,
pencils, and notebooks behind. For the greater part I am
going rather regretfully to keep my word—regretfully, for
a number of very curious things occurred. . . . Concerning three incidents, however, I am going to break my
vow; they are none of them fundamental but all to my
mind interesting.

The first occurred before we were admitted into the
convent. A sacrifice was being made at which we could
not be present, and we both stood outside the courtyard
on the grass in the moonlight holding a piece of dried
grass in our left hands (this grass played a considerable
role later) probably looking ridiculous and feeling very
silly and rather alarmed. Our sponsor and interpreter was
with the priest. After a time he came out and said to me,
"You live in a white house on a hill surrounded by trees;
you have a mother and two brothers who are walking
under the trees" (a quite adequate description of my
home and family; and it was very probable that on June
25th they would have been walking in the garden in the
evening). Then he turned to Benga and said, "You have
no home. In the place you think of as home there are
many people. Your two sisters are well, but your dead
mother's husband was taken very ill two days ago; he will
recover, however, before you see him again." This was
exact in every particular; on June 23rd Benga's stepfather
had had a severe attack, as we verified on our return to
Dakar, and he was quite convalescent before we returned.
We were more than a thousand miles from Dakar at the

time, and had received no communications from there for the better part of a month.

After a night spent in the convent we were considered to be fetishers. Fairly early in the morning we went with the priest and the other fetishers into the open country, among maize fields. A chicken was killed . . . and the priest started to sing in a low voice. The rest of us stood about, smoking or chewing cola. After about half an hour a full-grown panther walked out of the maize and started moving among the people; it was quickly followed by another, and in a short time there were fifteen panthers among us. They arrived from every direction. We had been told most earnestly on no account to touch them, and not be afraid of them for they would only harm wicked men (i.e., sorcerers). I was scared so that I felt my legs shaking but I was able to keep quiet. When the fetisher stopped singing they went away again. The first animal had eaten the chicken. This was the only time in Africa that I saw any of the fiercer mammals alive and in freedom. There were a number of villages within an hour's walk. It was about fifteen miles from Abomey.

It was a particularly fine and cloudless afternoon when we visited the convent of the worshipers of Héviosso, the thunder fetish. After the usual sacrifice three men went into a trance inside the hut, while we stood in what shade we could find in the courtyard. Suddenly against the blue sky there was a flash of lightning followed shortly by a loud peal of thunder. The flashes and thunder got more frequent and louder, till they seemed simultaneous, and the thunder gave that peculiarly unpleasant crack which it does in the tropics when the storm is nearly directly overhead. Gradually the thunder and lightning got fainter and finally died in a rumble. It had been exactly like a quick tropical thunderstorm, except that there had been no rain and no clouds; the sun was shining all the time.

MAGIC IN PUBLIC LIFE

With such beliefs and practices so widespread, it is inevitable that they play a part in the public and political life of Africa's new states.

From Robert Coughlan, "Black Magic: Vital Force in Africa's New Nations," *Reader's Digest,* September 1961.

When a whale beached itself and died on the African coast near Accra, why did Ghana's President Kwame Nkrumah and members of his cabinet leave their offices and attend a funeral for it? . . .

[The] answer: "Magic." The details go this way.

Among the coastal villagers of Ghana the whale is considered the semidivine king of the sea, and its body must be enshrined with high honors. Properly flattered and placated, the spirit of the whale will help the local fishing fleets. . . .

There are, of course, a number of African leaders to whom this does not apply. Men such as Julius Nyerere of Tanganyika [Tanzania], Tom Mboya of Kenya, Leopold Senghor of Senegal and Sir Abubakar Tafawa Balewa of Nigeria are sophisticates who can hold their own in any intellectual company. But even in the most advanced countries of Africa only a tiny fraction of the population has had any sort of higher education. And the amount of superstition that sometimes remains even within this minority can be inferred from certain spectacular examples:

The Liberian Department of Justice officially investigated charges that Edwin Barclay, the defeated candidate in the 1955 presidential election there, had imported a sorcerer from Nigeria to put a fatal juju curse on President William Tubman.

Bradford Phiri, organizing secretary of the Nyasaland branch of the moderate Central African Party, resigned because he believed that a curse had been put on him by members of Dr. Hastings Banda's all-out-nationalist Congress Party.

One of the leading intellectuals of Ghana, a seemingly Westernized graduate of a famous English university, fled the country in terror to escape a juju curse put on him by some of President Nkrumah's lieutenants.

As for the African masses, there is no doubt that magic plays an important part in their lives. Even the professing Christian more often than not holds to some of his older beliefs, mixing the white man's magic with the black man's, according to his personal needs and tastes. The African churches represent some influence toward literacy and usually some identification with Christian ethic, but Christianity of any sort, including the most bizarre local sects, accounts for at most 20 per cent of the black population. Perhaps another 18 percent are Moslems. The remaining 62 percent are wholly involved with local gods and primordial desires and fears.

Consequently, the educated African leader, like politicians everywhere, works within the framework of popular convictions. In some cases, the old superstitions are put to extraordinarily cynical use. When Dr. Banda, after 40 years abroad, flew into Nyasaland to take care of the independence movement, tribal delegations asked if he were the One prophesied in the old lore who would descend from the sky to deliver the Nyasas from foreign domination. Dr. Banda, formerly of the universities of Chicago and Edinburgh, solemnly assured them that he was indeed the selfsame "Great Kamuza" and must be obeyed. . . .

It is easy, of course, for the white nations, forgetting their own frequently irrational beliefs, to say that all this indicates racial retardation. Yet African beliefs actually possess a good deal of internal logic. Indeed, as Freud once pointed out, they compose a wonderfully satisfying faith, because they supply an apparently reasonable answer to everything.

Animism, as the basic African belief is often called (from the Latin word *anima,* meaning soul), holds that all things alive or lifeless—a stone, a tree, an animal—have invisible inner selves that make them what they are. These inner selves are conscious; they have feelings, and they can take revenge if disturbed. If a man moves a boulder, he had better do something to propitiate the spirit that lives in it, or it will cause him bad luck. The bigger the boulder, the worse the curse—and so it goes for rivers, trees, forests, thunderclouds.

Believing in this universal inner reality, the African naturally takes human immortality for granted. After physical death, the human soul goes to heaven for awhile, but then it returns to reside in or near the family hut to await reincarnation within the family as a baby. In African society, the new child does not "take after" his late relative; he *is* that relative.

The African stands in the midst of this spiritual multitude with mixed hope and dread. Since he believes that the behavior of the spirits can be influenced by human actions, it follows that, if he can enlist them in his favor, he will get what he wants and can even destroy his enemies. Conversely, an enemy who gains control over them can confound and destroy him. Hence the African does not simply get sick; instead, a spirit or some occult force, usually at the behest of a human, causes the sickness to happen to him. Death itself, far from being inevitable, is sometimes not even normal. One dies because someone else has arranged that one should. It is through magic that these invisible forces are manipulated. . . .

Both black and white magic often actually do produce effects on human behavior and health. How can this be accounted for logically? The witch doctor's kit does contain some items of medical value, just as the sorcerer's contains some real poisons. But mainly, of course, the effects are due to human suggestibility. If the victim knows of the curse—and the person responsible always tries to see to it that the news reaches him—and if he believes in its power, it is bound to affect him unless he receives belief in his power to recover. This he gets from the witch doctor's "white" medicine. The psychological mechanism involved is the same as that which accounts for the spectacular "cures" associated with hypnosis and faith healing in other societies.

Progress in Africa comes slowly—but it does come. Thirty years ago, when the British proposed to drain the filthy Korle Lagoon at Accra and turn it into a wholesome port, the people living along the lagoon's edge rebelled and the harbor project took place instead far up the coast at Takoradi. The Accra populace rebelled because they feared that the spirit of the lagoon would curse them for disturbing its domain. Yet last spring when the government (now Ghanaian and black, of course) announced plans to do the same thing, there was very little objection—even from the priest who serves the lagoon spirit.

Undoubtedly magic will continue to have an important part in shaping the attitudes of Africans toward Americans and Europeans. What does this mean in terms of our attitude toward this peculiar power in Africa?

The best slogan for the long run would seem to be: "Wait and educate." As for the years directly ahead, the most useful thing is simply to realize fully that in our relations with the nations of Black Africa we may often find ourselves dealing at first hand with the forces of superstition. We had better face that fact—and keep our fingers crossed.

The Nuer and the Ashanti—Two Representative Tribes

Now that we have looked at some of the basic ingredients of African culture, let us see how these generalizations actually apply to two specific groups of Africans.

The following case studies deal with two groups separated by almost the entire width of the continent, living in very different environments, and making a living in different ways. You should look for contrasts and similarities in their cultures as you compare them in terms of the earlier discussions.

THE NUER OF THE UPPER NILE

From Elman R. Service, *A Profile of Primitive Culture*, 1958.

From the southern margins of the Sahara Desert and continuing southward into East Africa is a long belt of tropical grasslands inhabited by tall, long-limbed, narrow-headed peoples who represent varying blends of Mediterranean whites and African forest Negroes. Most of them speak related languages which have been recently classified as Eastern Sudanic. These tribes are cattle pastoralists, most typically represented in the northern part of East Africa and becoming more and more mixed with the Bantu-speaking horticulturalists farther south into Uganda, whom they apparently conquered. Of the purely pastoral peoples, the Masai of southern Kenya and northern Tanganyika are the best known, though they are not the most typical. The Nuer farther to the north are more representative of the widely dispersed group of pastoral Sudanic tribes.

The south-central part of the Anglo–Egyptian Sudan, the homeland of the Nuer, is a great open grassland traversed by the upper Nile River and its several tributaries. The climate is tropical, and the year is divided almost equally between a very dry season and a very wet one. From December to June the rivers are low and the blazing landscape is parched and bare. From June to December the rainfall is heavy and the rivers overflow their banks and nourish a heavy growth of high grasses.

To a European the vista from horizon to horizon is a desolate wasteland, no more inviting as a swamp in one part of the year than as a desert [during] the other. From the point of view of either modern agriculture or animal husbandry, there seems to be always either an excess or an insufficiency of water. Insects of various kinds are constant pests. In the wet season, mosquitoes swarm so thickly that repose for men or beasts is impossible except in the midst of the choking smudge of the dung fire. In the dry season, ticks and many kinds of biting flies harass all animal life.

The Nuer believe that this dreary land is the finest country on earth. Only a few of them have even been as far away as Khartoum, the provincial capital, however, so it is no wonder that they remain assured of nature's bounty to themselves. The Nuer people are nearly as inhospitable as their land. The neighboring tribes fear them, and civilized nations have shown very little interest in occupying the land or putting the natives to work. Consequently, the Nuer today are one of the tribes of primitives most purely aboriginal in their social customs and organization. . . .

The Nuer total about 300,000 people, but there is no political unity of the whole group. Nuer refers not to a nation or kingdom, but to contiguous tribes who are similar culturally and linguistically and who sense this likeness to the degree that they feel distinct as a group from neighboring peoples. Generally, the character of the relations of the Nuer to any of their neighbors is hostile.

The Nuer are essentially pastoral, although, like many of the other herding peoples of the world, they grow a few crops when poverty demands and where soil and climate permit. But to the Nuer, and to all the East African pastoralists, horticulture is degrading toil, while cattle raising is viewed with great pride. Cattle represent the main source of food in the forms of milk, meat, and blood; the skins are used for beds, bags, trays, cord, drums, and shields; the bones and horns are made into a wide variety of tools and utensils; and the dung is used as a plaster and as fuel. Cattle are by far the most cherished possession and the Nuer seem to be interested in them nearly to the exclusion of anything else. Professor Evans-Pritchard writes: "They are always talking about their beasts. I used sometimes to despair that I never discussed anything with the young men but livestock and girls, and even the subject of girls led inevitably to that of cattle.". . .

Milk is the staple food of the Nuer all of the year. It is drunk fresh, mixed with millet as a porridge, allowed to sour for a particularly relished dish, and churned into cheese. Milking is done twice daily by women and children; initiated men are forbidden to milk cows unless for some reason there are no women present to do it. During the dry season, when food is scarce and when cows are running dry, the Nuer bleed their cattle from a small cut in a neck vein. Blood is boiled until thick or is allowed to stand until it is coagulated into a solid block, after which it is roasted and eaten.

Cattle are not raised expressly for the meat; but when

they become barren, injured, or too old for breeding, they are butchered and eaten under festive and ritualized conditions. The Nuer men are devoted to their cattle. After the women have milked the cows, the owner escorts the herd to pasture and to water, oversees them all day, and brings them back at night, meanwhile singing songs he has composed describing their virtues. In the evening he goes among his favorites, cleaning ticks from them, rubbing their backs with ashes, and decorating the horns with long tassels. The Nuer wash their hands and faces in the urine of cattle and cover their bodies, dress their hair, and even clean their teeth with ashes made from cattle dung.

The crops cultivated by the Nuer are millet (sorghum) and some maize. Next to milk, millet is the most important food. It is made into a boiled porridge and also brewed into a weakly alcoholic but nutritious beer. A little maize is eaten, but it does not grow nearly as well as millet under the wet conditions. Goats and sheep are interspersed among the cattle, but are not considered important. Fish is the other significant source of food. At the onset of the dry season the lagoons and small rivers begin to drop and fish are easily speared in the dammed pools. The territory is rich in game, but the Nuer do not hunt intensively. Many kinds of antelope, buffalo, elephant, and hippopotamus are plentiful, but the Nuer feel that only a man poor in cattle will bother to hunt for food. Lions and leopards are a threat to the herds in the dry season and the Nuer hunt them in self-protection, relying on dogs and the spear. The Nuer do not keep domesticated fowl, and regard the eating of the plentiful wild birds or their eggs with repugnance.

During the rainy season, the Nuer live in villages located on the areas of higher ground and cultivate their small gardens. So rare are these spots and uninhabitable are the extensive flooded areas that anywhere from five to twenty miles separate one village from another. The size of the village is determined by the extent of the habitable and cultivable ground and one village may contain from fifty to several hundred persons. At the end of the rainy season, after the ground has dried off, the villagers set fire to the grass to make new pasture and set off to camp near streams and rivers for the next six months. Frequent movements during this season are necessary as the pasturage becomes more and more sparse.

There are no permanent land rights among the Nuer. A village selects its site with the idea that land for all should be available. Cattle are individually owned—in fact, they are almost members of the family, so carefully are they tended—and some families are somewhat richer in cattle than others. This variation is closely related to the prestige of the owner, but it does not result in significant differences in the standard of living. The degree of sharing in a community, and even among neighboring communities, is such that a whole group seems to be partaking of a common stock of food. Anyone is privileged who, through luck or the possession of more or better cattle than others, is better enabled to provide for the less fortunate. There is no trade, the technology is poorly developed, and at certain times of the year, especially late in the dry season, there is a real shortage of food. The Nuer community is thus required to act as a corporate economic body. As a quick survey of the primitive world clearly shows, it is scarcity and not wealth which makes people generous.

The minimal economic unit is the household, or "homestead," which is a hut or a small group of huts and a cattle barn, both of wattle-and-daub construction. The homestead may be a single nuclear family, or it may be an extended family composed of a patriarch and several sons with their families. In the dry season the temporary camps of simple wind screens and flimsy beehive huts may consist of related families surrounding a common cattle corral, or of single families strung out over a wide area, depending on the conditions of the land, the proximity of pasture and good fishing sites. Usually the economic activities are individualized by homesteads during the time of residence in villages, whereas in the dry season the cattle of the associated families are herded together and, in general, there are more communal activities.

All of the members of a village or camp are kindred, as indeed, at least by fiction, are all people with whom a Nuer associates. All rights, privileges, obligations, in all of the customs of interpersonal association, are regulated by kinship patterns; there is no other form of friendly associations—one is a kinsman or an enemy. Genealogies are lengthy and well remembered, so that a Nuer can place nearly any individual with whom he is likely to have contact into the proper category. . . .

Relative age is of great importance in Nuer interpersonal relations, and seems to have overridden other genealogical considerations to a considerable degree. Every person in Nuer society is categorized explicitly in terms of an age-set system. All males are divided into age grades so that each one is a senior, equal, or junior to any other male. One is deferential to a senior, informal with an equal, superior to a junior. Women belong in the system as mothers, wives, sisters, or daughters of the particular males. The relativity of age, therefore, rather than genealogical relationship, frequently governs the use of kin terms in address. Anyone of an older age-set is addressed as "father" or "mother," and the younger as "son" or "daughter." Very old people are called "grandfather" or "grandmother." Men of the same age-set, if they are well acquainted, call each other by personal "ox names"—i.e., the name of a prize ox is applied to the owner. . . .

Villages commonly have members of two or more different lineages within them, and a given lineage has members in different villages. The lineage thus plays, in a sense, a political role. All of the people in a village naturally have a strong feeling toward their village—it is in some ways a corporate entity whose members share many economic and social activities. . . . The lineages do not permit marriage with a fellow member, but members of the same village frequently marry. Lineage membership thus cross-cuts these village units and creates larger entities out of segments of otherwise independent villages.

Related lineages form a still larger, more amorphous group, the clan. A person knows the precise genealogical position of each member of his lineage, but clans are viewed as composed of lineages, not of individuals; the genealogical-like relationship of each lineage to another in the clan is known, but the individuals are known only as fellow clan members, all descended from a common ancestor.

Villages are units of common residence. Several villages together occupy a territory which they feel to be theirs by custom and occupation. There is a tendency for this felt relationship of villages to be signified by a common name, a district name, which is at the same time a name of the group of people in it. Several of these districts feel a kinship to others in a larger territory, and again these to another, and finally the ever more attenuated recognition of unity peters out. This final area of recognition of communality is the tribe. The Nuer, as a whole people, are divided into eight or nine large tribes, averaging about 5000 people each, and several much smaller ones. But the tribe is the largest unit of people who defend a common territory, who are a named group, and who act together, manifesting a sense of patriotism or "belongingness." Among the Nuer tribes there is only anarchy; they are a nation in the sense of sharing a language, culture, and territory, but not a nation in the political sense.

Each Nuer tribe consists of several clans, but always there is one which is felt to be the oldest and most distinguished. It is sometimes, but not always, the largest as well. A clan tends to have at least some members in each of the many villages of the tribe, but always one particular clan is felt to be the most important in each village, another in each district, and so on, so that one may speak of the dominant clan in each of the areas as well as for the tribe as a whole. In the above sense, some social differentiation of families is therefore present everywhere. It is a matter of prestige, however, and not of privilege. There are no economic classes based on inherited wealth differences or standards of living.

Nuer tribes have no true government or regularized authority, no laws or lawgivers. There are, to be sure, influential men, but these men have a degree of authority which rests on their individual abilities to command respect rather than on inherited status or function. Usually, a prominent leader comes from the dominant clan, but he must be of strong character and of impressive wisdom in order to attract a following. The Nuer are strongly egalitarian and do not readily accept authority except in familial ways implicit in the age and sex categories of the kinship system.

The position most closely resembling political office is that of the "leopard-skin chief," so called because he is entitled to wear a leopard-skin wrap. His main function, in addition to certain ritual duties, is to mediate feuds. The most serious social disturbance in Nuer life occurs when one man kills another. As in other primitive societies without governmental institutions, this act inevitably brings retaliation from the bereaved kinsmen, and is frequently the beginning of a true feud. Nuer communities do not let this situation go uncontrolled for the society is not wholly anarchic, yet no judgment or force of a legal or governmental sort is involved in the settlement.

When a homicide has been committed, the killer goes to the local leopard-skin chief, and if he fears vengeance at that time he may remain with the chief, whose home is a sanctuary. The role of the chief is then to go to the family of the slayer and elicit from it a promise to pay a certain number of cattle to the aggrieved, after which he attempts to persuade the family of the dead man to accept this compensation. He is only a mediator, however, and he has no authority to judge or to force either a payment or its acceptance. On the surface, there seems to be a governmental-like characteristic involved—a restitution rather than retribution is provided—but it is not a payment to the state or society as such, or in any sense a fine or sentence.

Occasionally the leopard-skin chief acts as a mediator in other kinds of disputes, such as cases involving a disputed ownership of cattle. He, and perhaps some respected elders of the community, may express their opinions on the merits of the case, and attempt to argue the two sides into a settlement. But again, he has no official power. He does not summon the defendants, and he has no means of enforcing compliance with his opinion.

At certain times, men perhaps best called "prophets" have had some political influence. These men are most usually shamans or healers, believed to be possessed by one of the powerful sky spirits. A few times certain of these have been able to unite more groups in a war campaign than could have been possible to this otherwise loosely bound society. The most notable occurrences of "prophets'" influence were in rallying opposition to Arab and European incursions in the last century, but British rule has effectively halted their activity. Warfare consists normally of small-scale raids, and only rarely in the past have several communities united in conducting wars.

It seems to the Nuer that peaceful relations should obtain between kinsmen and that kinsmen must defend each other; and the closer the relationship, the more necessary it is that peace should prevail. In general, the Nuer marry within their own tribe, so that relationship ties do not transcend the tribal boundary. On the other hand, kinship extends, in one way or another, far beyond the local villages, as a consequence of the Nuer conception of incest, which includes an extraordinarily wide range of people in its prohibition. First of all, one cannot marry within one's own lineage or clan. Inasmuch as clans may be very large, a wide segment of the population is thus prohibited from intermarriage. The rule also prohibits marriage with any of the mother's lineage, though not with other lineages in her clan, and even with those considered kindred by a fiction or analogy, as, for example, in the case of a boy and girl whose fathers are in the same age-set. There is no exogamy explicitly by locality, but a village is such a network of various kinds of kinship ties, real or fictional, that usually a mate must be sought outside one's own village. Ideally a marriage should take place between persons whose families are of villages within visiting distance.

Marriage, a home, and children are the goal in Nuer life for both males and females from early childhood.

After puberty, boys and girls have a good deal of free-dom in experimental lovemaking, and usually find their lovers without any particular interference from the re-spective families, but marriage is the purpose behind every romance. In the final choice, however, the girl's family must approve of the suitor's family. They should be steady, agreeable people with a sufficiency of cattle.

The actual marriage is made by a payment of several head of cattle from the groom's family to the bride's fam-ily. Normally, three periods of payment and associated rit-ual are involved, which could be considered betrothal, wedding, and consummation. At the time of the betrothal ceremony at the bride's home, the groom's family makes a token gift of a few cattle and the groom's friend, a sort of "best man" acting as negotiator, reaches an agreement with the bride's family on the number of cattle to be given later, and the dates for the subsequent ceremonies. Then singing, dancing, and a feast of a fine ox follow. A few weeks later, after prolonged discussions and even ap-parent arguments have resulted in an agreement on the complexities of how many cattle will be presented and what proportions will go to particular kinsmen of the girl, the marriage feast is held, again at the girl's home, with great numbers of relatives of both families present.

The "true marriage" occurs when a third feast is held, this time at the home of the groom. This ceremony is the significant one; it celebrates the final binding of the union of families, and not until this occasion does the husband have full conjugal rights over his wife; that is, he cannot punish or sue in case of the wife's adultery, for example, or prevent her from going to the dances held by unmar-ried people. High points in the ceremony are the first night, when the bride and groom presumably have their first sexual encounter; and in the morning, when an ox is sacrificed and a great feast is held, shared by the two families except for the bride, who is not allowed to eat in the home of her mother-in-law. On this occasion the bride is anointed with butter and her head is shaved to signalize her change in status.

Nevertheless, the married couple do not actually live

together until a child is born. The girl is given a special hut in her own family's homestead and the husband remains with his own family, making overnight visits to his wife whenever he can. After a child is born, the husband is fully accepted as a member of the girl's family. They stay with her family, however, only until the child is weaned, and then go to live in the husband's village.

Husband, wife, and all of their respective kinsmen are most anxious for a child to be born. This is not only because they love children but also because the marriage is not stable until a child is born. Should the marriage break up because of infertility, all of the cattle have to be returned; consequently, none of the cattle may be disposed of in other bride prices or gifts in all this time. . . . It should be apparent that, over time, nobody loses in the payment of bride wealth. The group receiving cattle at any particular time divides them among relatives, and when one of these later makes a bride payment all the relatives contribute.

The payment of cattle is therefore not literally the purchase of a bride; cattle go out of a settlement and cattle come in. The most significant aspect of these movements of cattle in one direction and women in another is that a stabilizing function is created. It is very complicated and difficult to dissolve a marriage, inasmuch as all of the cattle, now widely dispersed, must be returned. Thus the wife's family uses all its influence to make her remain with the husband. It is in order to avoid such difficulties that so much time and so many discreet stages are involved in the making of a marriage. People want to be as certain as possible that the marriage will be stable before they fully commit themselves.

A young man must be exceptionally deferential to his in-laws, but after the birth and weaning of the first child, his status changes and he tends to become accepted as a relative rather than a mere suitor. The girl's parents now call him "father of ————" (the child's name) and social relations become structured in kinship terms. The boy does not avoid his mother-in-law any longer. They can now converse openly, though not informally, and he may visit her from time to time. Only two stringent prohibitions still obtain: the husband may not eat in his in-laws' home, and he must never appear naked before them.

A form of levirate is practiced among the Nuer in the event that the death of a man leaves a wife and children surviving. Normally, a younger brother of the deceased takes over the responsibility for the wife and her children; "he provides a hut for her." He becomes the guardian of the children primarily, for this is not, strictly speaking, a marriage. No ceremony is performed and the widow retains her original name as the wife of the dead man.

Occasionally a man has more than one wife. The first wife has no special status; the Nuer believe all the wives should be treated equally. It is, of course, a situation which contains many possibilities of friction between the wives, and the Nuer know this well, for the word for the condition of being "co-wife" is also the word for a condition of jealousy. A common cause of polygynous marriages, in addition to the levirate, arises when a man dies without male heirs. A man's name should continue in his lineage, and it is believed that his ghost will be angry should this fail to occur. Such a situation is commonly remedied by a sort of "ghost marriage" whereby the dead man's younger brother or close kinsman takes a wife in his name. The dead man's ghost is regarded as the legal husband and the children take his name. . . .

Children live with their mothers in the small huts which surround the cattle barn. When boys are about 7 or 8 they are taken from the mother and come to sleep, eat, and spend their leisure hours in the barn, which, although it shelters cattle in the rainy periods, is essentially a men's club, as is a particular windbreak in the dry-season camp. The huts go with the gardens, the barn goes with the cattle; the economic division of labor—woman's gardening, man's cattle-tending—is thus manifested in the separation of quarters. But women do not have a degraded status in Nuer society. They take an active part in the daily life of the community, mixing freely with men and delivering opinions with an easy assurance.

A Nuer child's experience is not confined closely to his own family. All of the people who share the adjacent homesteads take an interest in the child's upbringing, and lactating women in any part of the locality may nurse it. It falls to the mother, and to a lesser extent to other female relatives, particularly older sisters, to correct or chastise the child. Nuer fathers indulge their children and spend a great deal of time playing with them, but never really punish them.

The first-born child, especially if it is a boy, is treated in a special manner. As previously noted, he is born in his mother's family's house, and is taken to his father's household after weaning. If his maternal grandmother is alive, he might remain under her care, and never live in his father's village during his childhood. If not, he stays with his father and mother until he is 6 or 7 and then goes back to his mother's home to live with his maternal uncle until initiation time, when he comes back to his father's home again.

For a Nuer boy, the most important event occurring before his marriage is his initiation into his age-set. This, like initiation or puberty rites in many primitive societies, involves a series of severe ordeals and complicated rituals which move him from childhood into the grade of manhood. Boys between the ages of 14 and 16 are put through these rituals together whenever there is a sufficient number of them in a village. After successive groups of boys are initiated over a six-year period, a four-year interval is kept free, after which initiations may begin again. From four to ten years in age thus separates the members of any one age-set from the adjacent one. Boys who have been initiated together have a lifelong comradeship and all the groups of a particular age-set are set off in behavior from each of the others.

The most notable ordeal in the initiation is an operation which consists of six long cuts made from ear to ear across the forehead. After the operation the boys live in partial seclusion and observe various taboos. The operation, rituals, and festivities are attended only by the fathers and their age mates. The opening and closing of the initiation period is simultaneous over the whole tribe and is signalized by a ritual performed by a specialist called Man of the Cattle.

Boys who have been initiated are eager to engage in a raid in order to prove their manhood and valor, but the age-set organization is actually not a warriors' organization, as it is among some of the other African herding societies, nor are there any other corporate activities. Even in the initiation rites themselves there is no educative or moral training; they seem to have no other meaning than to stratify the society into groups which will explicitly structure the behavior of men to each other in terms of relative age. It is chiefly in local domestic relations that the initiation of a youth into his age-set is of great importance. At this time a boy's father or uncle gives him his first spear, which elevates him to warrior status, and his first ox. At this time he takes his "ox name"; i.e., he is called by the name of his ox. From this time until he marries and becomes a father—a "true man"— he is heavily engaged in proving his worth as a potential head of a family, and in dancing and lovemaking in quest of his wife-to-be.

The Nuer are meticulous about showing proper deference to older people, but except for this kind of social stratification there is no pattern of subordination or superordination; the society is eminently egalitarian, as is manifest in nearly all actions. The people are generous to each other always, but any request which has an overtone of an order quickly angers them. They are inclined to be reticent and dour with any strangers, who are always potential enemies. The presence of a stranger, even as wildly strange as a modern European, does not appear to frighten them or arouse either their curiosity or hospitality: the Nuer "strut about like lords of the earth, which indeed, they consider themselves to be."

The Nuer have not particularly developed any of the arts except the singing of poetry, a trait they share, for some reason, with most other pastoral peoples of the world. When a Nuer boy feels happy he sings, when he guards the cattle he sings, when he courts a girl he sings.

Some songs are traditional, others may be composed at the whim of the singer. Some are always by individual soloists, others are sung by groups. As might be expected, praise of cattle figures in a great many of them.

There is a great fear of the ghosts of the dead. Shortly after a death, the corpse is buried in the fetal position in a grave about four feet deep. A cowhide is wrapped around the body, but no possessions are placed in the grave. Relatives and age mates then allow their hair to grow and put aside their body ornaments. The most important ceremony takes place at the end of the mourning period, some six months after the death of a man and three months after the death of a woman. Bullocks are killed for a feast and the assemblage is ritually sprinkled with milk. After the feast, the mourners shave their heads and resume wearing their customary ornaments. The main purpose of the ceremony is to placate the spirit of the deceased so that it will make no attempt to take its wife or husband, children, and cattle.

If a person is struck by lightning or dies suddenly without a previous illness, it is believed that the Sky God has removed the spirit and taken it into the sky. A mourning period is not held, inasmuch as the spirit has not lingered in the vicinity during the usual period; the sacrifice of cattle is made immediately after the burial. The Nuer do not betray great sorrow because of a death. It is the will of the Sky God if a person is taken, and to show emotion would be to complain against the action.

There are several Sky Gods or spirits. The most powerful is Deng, who is associated with sickness. Certain others are gods of war, hunting, thunder and lightning, and so on. There are also certain earth spirits, many of which are related to species of birds or animals and which function as totems of lineages. Birds are particularly sacred totems of the Nuer, which is apparently the reason why the people will not eat the flesh or eggs of birds.

Certain men claim special powers of healing and prognostication due to having possession of one of the totemic spirits. Particular healers are known for their specialties; one is good at divining, another at curing constipation or headache. Divining is accomplished by reading signs, most typically by interpreting the pattern in the fall of mussel shells thrown against the side of a gourd rattle. Curing involves the world-wide technique of massage and the extraction of a foreign object from the patient's afflicted part. Some shamans have acquired wide influence and are known as "prophets," being possessed of mightier spirit helpers than the ordinary diviner. Some of these men function as rainmakers, conducting ceremonies which involve the sacrifice of animals to the thunder spirit. Rainmakers are very important ritual functionaries among the neighboring Dinks and Shilluk, but less so among the Nuer.

The Nuer sometimes raise pyramids of considerable size in honor of a particular god-spirit. One of these is about 50 feet high and 300 feet in circumference. These monuments are built of baked earth and ashes and ringed around with upright elephant tusks. The idea of pyramids may have diffused in ancient times from Egypt; but the Nuer pyramids, in contrast to those of the Egyptians, are not burial mausoleums, nor are they built with conscripted or forced labor.

The Nuer also have a conception of "evil eye"—a person of some supernatural power who will commit malicious damage to people by looking at them. Allied to this is the notion of witches, particularly a kind of ghoul who secretly performs rites over the bodies of the newly dead in order to gain control over the souls of the surviving relatives. As is so common in human society, people who are disliked or who commit antisocial acts which arouse fear are sometimes accused of witchcraft, and it is said that in the past such witches were killed with the consent of the community. . . .

The time perspective of the Nuer is limited to a very short span—in a sense they are a "timeless people," as are most primitive tribes. The year is seen merely in terms of the cycle of events created by the two distinct seasons. "Moons," which are roughly months marked by the lunar cycle, are sometimes used to demark time, as are numbers of days and segments of a day. But essentially, time is marked by reference to activities. The Nuer have no word for "time" in the European sense. They have no conception of time as an abstract thing which can be wasted, or saved, or which passes. Activities are not coordinated with the passage of time, therefore, because the temporal points of reference are generally the activities themselves, which are conducted in a leisurely, habitual pattern.

In reckoning past events, the Nuer are not as likely to attempt to count years as they are to cite a remembered action which occurred before or after the event which is being located in time. Among the most frequent markers are the age-sets. Such and such a thing happened just after a particular age-set began, or a person may say, for example, that the event occurred three sets before his own initiation (roughly thirty years). History, then, does not last long for the Nuer, at the most only about a century. Remembered events, such as famines or wars, of earlier times than that merge into tradition and are all seen in the flat time perspective common among nonliterate peoples. The shallowness of this time view may be judged from the fact that the tree under which they believe mankind was created is still standing.

The outside world has not molested the Nuer to the point of radically altering their culture. Probably the greatest change has been caused by the decimation of the cattle herds in the present century by rinderpest, an infectious disease which attacks cattle, sheep, and goats. In the past, forty to sixty head of cattle might be included in a payment of bride wealth, whereas about half that many are all that could be expected today. The loss in cattle has caused the Nuer to plant millet to a greater extent than before to make up the loss in subsistence. Possibly the increased dependence on horticulture has had an effect on the villages, rendering them more stable.

The dwindling of the herds may, partly at least, explain the aggressiveness of the Nuer. The pastoral Dinks have been raided most persistently by the Nuer in the present century. Other tribes, such as the Shilluk, are not raided by the Nuer because "we only raid people who possess cattle. If they had cattle we would raid them and take their cattle. . . ."

Arab slavers and ivory traders, who conquered many of the Sudanic tribes in the past, had little effect on the Nuer. The Egyptian government and the later Mahdist government (the famous "dervishes"), which attempted to govern the Sudan between 1821 and the end of the last century had no control over the Nuer, nor did any other agency until the Anglo–Egyptian government of the Sudan finally established firm administrative posts in Nuerland after 1928. These posts are remote from everyday Nuer life, however, and the only general effect was to diminish the amount of raiding. Some effect on the religion has been caused by the government's pursuit of "prophets," whom they consider responsible for uprisings; but inasmuch as the phenomenon of prophets leading war parties was a consequence of a foreign threat rather than the cause, the basis of native religion is little altered.

The area contains no resources desired by foreigners, hence the Nuer have not been pushed from their homeland. The Nuer, on the other hand, have not shown any desire for modern innovations. Their fixation on cattle and their simple way of life permit them to remain aloof and self-sufficient in their infrequent relations with Europeans. . . .

THE ASHANTI OF WEST AFRICA

The great Negro African kingdoms are among the most interesting and complex civilizations ever attained by nonliterate peoples. Particularly along the west coast, militaristic monarchies with large capital cities grew to dominate trade and industry over wide dependent areas. All of the essential characteristics of government are present in these states: they collect taxes, make censuses, conscript armies; they even have constitutions and courts of law. The history of the relations of these states with the modern nations of Europe shows the strength of their native institutions; for they have stood the test of conquest, colonization, and acculturation without loss of national unity, and today some are entering the world stage as independent nation-states with modernized political institutions.

The former British Crown Colony of the Gold Coast contained as its most centrally located and most powerful native kingdom the proud Ashanti people. The history of the course of empire in this region makes particularly inspiring reading to Negro nationalists in other parts of Africa today; for despite the surrender of Ashanti sovereignty to the British after the Ashanti war of 1873–1874, and the final incorporation of the Ashanti into the British colonial system after the so-called War of the Golden Stool in 1900–1901, the Ashanti nation and most of its governmental institutions remained intact. Finally in 1957, in confederation with the neighboring Fanti peoples, the Gold Coast nation now called Ghana was formed as a modern sovereign state. . . .

In common with other West African kingdoms, the Ashanti state was established in its historically known location only shortly before the Europeans first encountered it. Some of the militaristic and economic features of the state were directly related to the wars and dislocations caused by the Europeans, who avidly sought the famous gold deposits which gave that portion of the coast its name, and later by the competitions involved in the slave trade. During the sixteenth century, when the Portuguese were the most active Europeans in West Africa, the Ashanti were a series of small independent tribal units, each with its own capital town and inchoate political institutions. By the early part of the eighteenth century, the general pressure and competition along the Gold Coast had caused a series of wars which finally unified the independent Ashanti tribal divisions. The leader who accomplished this, Osai Tutu, and his head priest and adviser, Okomfo Anokye, are now revered heroes of the Ashanti. One of the political inventions of this period was a symbol of nationalism which was needed to help unify the various Ashanti tribes and to demonstrate the "divine right" by which the new dynasty was to rule over them all. This was the Golden Stool which Okomfo Anokye is said to have brought down from the sky. It represented the ancestors of all the Ashanti. This state grew in power, territory, and internal strength until it was defeated by the British in 1874. But by then the Ashanti as a whole were consolidated as a people and have remained firmly united to this day.

The Gold Coast consists of a highly variable terrain; there are coasts and mountains, forests and grasslands, fertile agricultural areas and near-deserts. The territory of the Ashanti, inland and centrally located in the Gold Coast, is mostly fertile and partly mountainous. Rainfall is plentiful during the rainy season from April to November, and the land is well drained by many streams. The dry season, however, is very dry. It is depressingly hot all the year. It is probably a somewhat more healthful area than the coastal strip, but, like the west coast in general, it apparently deserves its reputation as an unhealthy climate. Malaria is the greatest scourge, but there are also many other kinds of fevers: blackwater, yellow, relapsing, typhoid, typhus, cholera, and others. Leprosy, elephantiasis, and sleeping sickness are some of the more spectacular diseases, but intestinal and skin parasites are a greater problem because of their higher frequency.

The Ashanti number 200,000 people, all speaking a single language, Twi, one of the members of the widely distributed Niger–Congo family. They live in a number of scattered villages and some larger towns, of which a few number over 1000 inhabitants. The houses of the poorer people are of plastered wattle-and-daub construction surmounted with a domed grass-thatched roof, often in the form of compounds—connected buildings arranged around a court. Some of the larger towns have veritable palaces for the families of important chiefs. The walls of the larger houses are of sun-baked clay, enclosing many rooms. Complicated scroll designs adorn the walls and posts, and a sort of wide veranda runs all along the sides of the house. Clay walls are not suitable for such a rainy climate, but the overhanging thatch roof protects them from being washed away. Sometimes leaves are sewn together, shingle fashion, to roof important houses.

Hunting is not an important economic activity of the Ashanti, for the country has been farmed so intensively that large game has become scarce, but fish are frequently obtained by trade from the coastal tribes, some of which are highly specialized as fishermen. Domestic animals include the inevitable dogs, goats, and great numbers of fowl, especially chickens, which are used for sacrifices and divination as well as for food. A few sheep, pigs, and cattle are kept in some districts.

Horticulture is the basic economic activity of the Ashanti. The most important staple plants are plantains, yams, and manioc. Manioc, incidentally, originated in the New World and was introduced, along with maize, into Africa early in the period of white colonization, where they became basic in the economy of many African tribes. Other plants cultivated by the Ashanti are sweet potatoes, millet, beans, onions, peanuts, tomatoes, and many fruits. The oil palm is of great importance. Palm wine, along with maize or millet beer, is a favorite drink, and the oil has many culinary and domestic uses. Many of the vegetable crops can be harvested twice a year, and the manioc, or cassava plant, a very starchy root, can be harvested daily in whatever quantity is needed for the day's use, after it has been allowed about two years of growth. Fields are prepared by burning shortly before the onset of the rainy season and cultivated with an iron hoe. Since fertilizers and crop rotation are unknown, fields must be fallowed for several years after two to four years of continuous cultivation. Most of the villages and towns, however, are permanently located, for the fields are usable again after fallowing.

Like other West Africans, the Ashanti are experts at many handicrafts and have a number of professional specialists. Ironworking by bellows and charcoal fire after the fashion of the village blacksmith is one of the most specialized crafts. Ax and hoe blades, knives, daggers, projectile points, nails, hammers, and many ornaments, bells, and fine chains are made by the smith. Hand-modeling of pottery is also a specialized craft, as is woodcarving. Great attention is lavished on the carving of wooden stools, and beautiful wooden figurines of human beings are also made, so fancifully symbolic and abstract that they have become collectors' items for many Europeans.

The Ashanti formerly made bark cloth for clothing, but sometime in the seventeenth century the art of weaving was learned. Women grow and pick the cotton and spin it into thread, but the weaving of the cloth is man's work alone and is specialized in family lines. . . .

One of the most interesting of Ashanti technological items is the "talking" drums. Messages can be drummed across Ashanti, about 200 miles, as rapidly as a telegraphic communication. The drums very nearly do talk the language. The drummers are very proficient and the people have cultivated a fine ear for the nuances of sound, but the high development of the drum language is made possible because of the nature of the Ashanti language. Ashanti, like several other African languages, is a tonal language; a much greater amount of meaning in a word or phrase is conveyed by its tone than is true of English, for example. Drums can reproduce these tones, punctuation, and the accents of a phrase so that it is nearly like hearing the phrase itself. . . .

The household, which is often polygynous, is the basis of day-to-day economic and social life. The matrilineal lineage, however, is the unit of society of greatest significance in Ashanti ideology and in all practical economic, social, political, and religious matters which are above the level of domestic household affairs. A person, male or female, is seen as related by blood to others only through mothers. Descent in the female line is the principle which determines land rights, inheritance of other property, and offices and titles. Social and political status is derived from this line, and it is the focus of the ancestor cult, the basis of much of the religious activity. Emotional ties between individuals are created by the "blood" they share, and it is mother's blood which creates the child's body.

The father is regarded as the catalyst of the conception and the provider of the spirit (ntoro) to the infant. A child receives from his father his life force, "a small bit of the creator," and also his distinctive personality and disposition. . . .

The land belongs to the abusua [matrilineal] ancestors who are buried in it. No individual Ashanti owns land; he only occupies a portion of it which has come from his clan ancestors. He does own the products of his labor on the land and can dispose of them as he pleases, but he may not be removed from the land, nor has he any right to sell it or to determine which of his descendants would get the major share. All this is prescribed by rigid traditional rules of inheritance. Because the abusua is matrilineal, a man's goods are passed on to his brother, if the incumbent dies fairly young, or to his sister's sons. . . .

Both men and women possess individual property that they have made or acquired by their own efforts. All other possessions are family and lineage property, consisting chiefly of carved stools which symbolize the kindred household and lineage gods and fetishes, and various heirlooms, none of which can be disposed of by individuals. Trade in Ashanti is of two kinds, an import-export business which is run bureaucratically as a state enterprise, and the more petty local trade which takes place in town markets. Various handicrafts and food products are exchanged here. This minor trade is conducted individually by women, but usually in the interests of the household. Some things are bartered directly, with much haggling, but frequently a sort of "money" of cowrie shells intermediates in the exchange. Local representatives of the state regulate the market, settle disputes about prices and quality of goods, and exact a transaction tax.

Slaves are also bought and sold, but this occurs as a personal transaction rather than in the market. Usually these unfortunates are prisoners of war, but sometimes they are actually sold by their own tribes as punishment for some criminal action. Sometimes natives of Ashanti are placed in a condition of servitude because their relatives "pawn" them to secure a debt. The work done by a pawn is considered as interest on the loan. Pawns are usually redeemed, and in any case retain their clan affiliation and their offspring suffer no stigma. Slaves are not cruelly used; in the opinion of the public, a person who mistreats a slave is contemptible. Slaves are allowed to marry and their children belong to the master. Frequently, the master takes a female slave as a wife, in preference to a usual marriage, and often enough her children inherit some of the father's property and status. This preference is a result of the conflict between the matrilineal system and the desires of a husband and father. In a normal marriage, the wife has considerable status, but many husbands prefer a slave or pawn wife who has no powerful abusua to intercede on her behalf every time the married couple have an argument. A husband also has more control over his children if the mother is thus isolated from her own kin, and he can pass some of his property to his own sons. . . .

Status differentiation among families is largely a political matter. The most important of all is the royal family. Next in importance are those families whose heads are chiefs of territorial subdivisions of the kingdom. In each of the chiefdoms, a particular matrilineal lineage provides the chief, but he is chosen by the lineage from among several men who are eligible for the post.

"Elections" take place in the following manner. The senior female of the chiefly lineage is asked to nominate a chief from among the eligible males of the lineage. She, in turn, consults all of the elders (male and female) of the lineage, and together they make the selection. This nomination is sent to a council of elders, who represent other lineages in the town or district. They in turn present the nomination, with appropriate arguments, to an assemblage of the people. If they do not approve, the whole process is begun again to nominate a different man. The new chief is "enstooled" by the elders, who admonish him with the list of expectations they have of him. He, in turn, takes a solemn oath to the Earth Goddess and to his ancestors to fulfill his duties.

The chief is surrounded by a great deal of pomp and ceremony, and theoretically he has considerable despotic power, including the ability to make judgments of life or death on his subjects. When he sits upon the stool he is sacred, as the holy intermediary between his people and the ancestors. But his power is more apparent than real. He must listen to the Council of the Elders, govern justly and bravely, and behave circumspectly. Should the Elders and public opinion turn against him, he can be impeached —destooled—and then he becomes merely another ordinary man, except that he is derided for his failure.

The chiefs of the tribal divisions, as well as village and subdivisional chiefs are elected in the same way, and each swears fealty to the one above him. The Ashantihene (King of all Ashanti) is chief of the division of Kumasi, the nation's capital, and is appointed in the same way as the others, but the other tribal chiefs are subject to him. His power, too, is circumscribed by the elders and by public opinion in his own division, and the chiefs of the other areas have a considerable constitutional check over him. As a symbol of the nation, his importance is testified by the extraordinary deference ritually accorded to him, but the context is religious—he sits for the sacred ancestors. The land, for example, is said to belong to the king, but the phrase means actually that it belongs to the tribal ancestors whom he represents. He cannot alienate land or, in fact, indulge in any act of arbitrary power not agreed upon by the people.

The presence of aristocratic clans and the power of elders would seem to be evidence of a sort of oligarchical tendency in Ashanti political life. But there is an additional feature of the society which in considerable measure assures a kind of democratization of the governmental process. In modern urban civilization, it tends to be the poor and the illiterate who need special machinery or organization in order to have a hearing, but in primitive life older men typically monopolize political power and young men are relatively helpless. The Ashanti have elaborated a peculiar institution called the mmerante, an organization of young men. At their meetings they select a representative to argue their views, and he adds his opinion at all meetings of the Council of Elders and chiefs. No action can be undertaken without consulting the representative of the "Young Men."

The Ashanti state addresses itself to the problems of internal order by evoking religious rather than secular-legal postulates. The state is, after all, a theocracy, hence crimes are viewed as sins. Acts which are antisocial with respect to the body politic are seen as offenses against the ancestors first, and only derivatively and secondarily are they defined as harmful to the community. If the chief or king failed to punish a crime, the ancestors would be angry with the whole Ashanti people. The penalty for all crimes is death. Only the king has the power to exact this penalty. But the king also has the power to commute the sentence, which lays the way open for bribes and ransom. These are not so regulated as to be considered fines, properly speaking, but they are a considerable source of revenue to the state, which consequently welcomes quarrels and litigation. Such commutations were actually more frequent than execution. . . .

Ordinarily disputes between individuals are settled by the families or lineages concerned, but it is possible to bring disputes to a trial if one of the disputants utters a tabooed oath of a chief or of the king. The case will then be tried in the court of the district chief whose oath has been used. In the end, the king's court is the sentencing court, however, for only the king can order the death penalty. In the trial, the two litigants state their cases in long orations directed to the chief and his court and the Council of the Elders. Cross-examination of the testimony can be made by anyone present, but eventually, if the proceedings do not lead to a verdict, a special witness is called and his testimony decides the case. Strangely, there is only one witness; the two litigants do not each have their own witnesses. It is assumed by everyone that the oaths the witness must swear insure his telling the truth. The idea that he might be friendly or hostile to one of the disputants is unthinkable, even if he is a kinsman. Sometimes, particularly in cases such as witchcraft or adultery, which would have no witnesses, questions of fact are decided by ordeals. The ordeal is requested by the accused, rather than imposed by the court, and frequently takes the form of drinking poison.

The character of the judicial system emphasizes that the Ashanti conception of rectitude and good behavior favors harmony among the people. One must act always in terms of the rules made by the gods and the ancestors. Ancestor worship is fundamental to the Ashanti moral system, and lies at the base of the governmental sanctions. The link between mother and child is the relationship that is the basis of the whole network, which includes ancestors and fellow men as well. The rituals and beliefs associated with conception, pregnancy, and birth reflect the main assumptions on which the unity of the kingdom is founded. . . .

Childhood is a happy time, a "play time," and Ashanti parents are very indulgent. A child is not considered responsible for any of its actions, for it has no power to do good or evil until after puberty. The death of a child does not require funeral rites; the body is merely buried in the refuse dump. Such children are called "pot children," after the receptacle in which the body is placed for burial. The absence of funeral rites is not caused by lack of sentiment, but because a child is harmless; hence there is no worry about controlling the soul, which is the original purpose of all funeral rites.

Puberty rituals are held only for girls. Boys are given instruction by their fathers, but no public observance of the change in state from child to man is made. As a girl nears the time when her first menstruation is expected, she goes to her mother's home. When she discloses the fact of her menstruation, the mother goes into the village beating an iron hoe with a stone to arouse the populace and make known the good news. All of the old women come out and sing bara (menstrual) songs. The mother spills a libation of palm wine on the earth and recites the following prayer:

> Supreme Sky God, who is alone great, upon whom men lean and do not fall, receive this wine and drink.

Earth Goddess, whose day of worship is a Thursday, receive this wine and drink.

Spirit of our ancestors, receive this wine and drink.

This girl child whom God has given to me, today the bara state has come upon her.

O mother who dwells in the land of ghosts, do not come and take her away and do not have permitted her to menstruate only to die.

Five days after the onset of menstruation, the girl is bedecked with finery and displayed publicly. At this time she also engages in ritual bathing and eating, which lift the taboos she has observed. After the ceremony a girl is addressed as "mother" by younger children. Old women regard this change in state with sadness, for they believe that it will cause the death of one of them. Just as each birth in this world is a death in the spirit world, the "birth" of a girl into full womanhood takes one away from the living group. . . .

A man is expected to marry a cross cousin, i.e., either his father's sister's daughter or his mother's brother's daughter. Parallel cousins, of course, are members of the ntoro or abusua groups and hence prohibited as marriage partners. Frequently the marriage has been promised even before the couple are born. If not, a boy is sometimes allowed some initiative, but always the consent of both households is necessary. The only formalities required to make a marriage legal are these consents and an appropriate payment of "bride price," various goods given by the boy's family to the girl's. . . .

Polygyny is legal and very common, but . . . the senior wife must be consulted. Jealousy is apparently not frequent, and a woman likes to have a co-wife, if she is compatible, added to the household—it lightens the work and adds to her husband's status.

A major event in the lives of the Ashanti people is the sickness and death of a close relative. In case of illness, there are two possible causes, and two kinds of practitioners who may be called. One is the ordinary herbalist who by means of divination finds the supernatural cause of the illness and treats it with herbal concoctions. But if pure witchcraft is the cause of the illness, a specialist is called. This specialist, or "witch doctor," is a person possessed by a spirit, and who, after a training period, is able, by the use of the spirit, to combat witchcraft. A witch, as usual, is one who has this same power, but uses it as black magic, that is, for antisocial and malevolent purposes.

If efforts to cure a person are unavailing, the last rites are performed. These consist of pouring a little water down the throat of the dying person just as it is believed the soul is leaving the body and of saying the following prayer: "Your clansmen [naming them] say: Receive this water and drink, and do not permit any evil thing to come whence you are setting out, and permit all the women of the household to bear children." This rite is considered so important that old people are loath to be alone for long without someone available to perform it for them in case of a collapse. After death, the corpse is washed, and the body is dressed in its best clothes and adorned with packets of gold dust ("soul money"), ornaments, and food for the journey "up the hill." The body is generally buried within 24 hours. Until that time a riotous wake is held consisting of dancing, drumming, shooting of guns, and much drunkenness, all accompanied by the wailing of the relatives.

The sixth day after death is the "Day of Rising," when the soul is finally dispatched from the vicinity. The central ritual of this day consists of all the blood relatives shaving their heads and putting the hair into a large pot. A sheep is sacrificed and cooked, and this food, utensils, and the pots of hair are taken to a special part of the cemetery where the ghost will find it and take it for his journey. After these rites, normal life is resumed except for mourning on the eighth, fifteenth, fortieth, and eightieth days, and at one year. . . .

The greatest and most frequent religious ceremonies of the Ashanti are those whose purpose is to recall the spirits of the departed rulers, offer them food and drink, and ask their favor for the good of the tribe. These ceremonies, called the Adae, occur every 21 days. On the day before an Adae ceremony, the talking drums announce it to the people, and the stool treasurer gathers together the sheep and liquor which will be offered. On the day of the Adae, the priest-chief officiates in the stool house where the ancestors come, and offers each stool food and drink. The public ceremony occurs outdoors, where everyone is free to join the dancing. Minstrels chant the tribal traditions and the talking drums keep extolling the chief and the ancestors in traditional phrases everyone understands.

The other large ceremony is an annual event which lasts for a week or two in September. The Odwera, as it is called, is the time for a cleansing of the tribe of sin and defilement, and for the purification of the shrines of the ancestors and gods. After a sacrifice of a black hen, and a ritual feast in which both the living and dead are believed to share, a new year begins and everyone begins it clean, strong, and healthy.

In all ceremonies, the strongest motif is the ever-present concern with the ancestors. But Ashanti religion and cosmology are not simply ancestor worship, for the universe is peopled with many other kinds of spirits as well. The greatest, the Supreme One, is the creator of all things and head of a pantheon of lesser gods, each of whom is in some way a part of or a descendant of the creator. These act as intermediaries between the people and the creator, hence many of them are local patrons of a village, district, or household. Others are gods of a place or geographic feature, the most sacred of these being the gods of rivers. All of these gods, including the Supreme One, are subjects of a great number of myths which explain how they acquired their characteristics.

Each of the important gods has a temporary abode on earth. This shrine may be almost any material object, from a simple stone to an elaborate image. Specially trained priests look after these objects, and part of their knowledge consists of knowing how to call the god to come and to speak, using the priest himself as a medium. There are a great many minor spirits who abide in tiny beads and other small objects which are carried by ordinary people as supernatural charms and fetishes.

In addition, all animals and plants are believed to have souls which can be prayed to or otherwise moved to action, and even earth is seen as a powerful female principle from which plants grow. The Earth Goddess has no priest or fetishes, but important offerings and prayers are made to her. Some spirits are hostile and are found in the forests, and from them black magic and witchcraft may be learned. Nevertheless, all are related; the hostile spirits, the souls of man and his ancestors, of animals and plants, the earth, and all of the ranks of gods are descended from the remote Supreme One.

There are both Christian and Moslem converts in Ashanti in modern times, and in principle, it would seem there would be no intellectual or logical conflicts. All three are hierarchical and involve the conception of a supreme being. There has been a conflict, nevertheless, particularly between Christian converts and the older Ashanti. The Ashanti government is theocratic; at every point religion is an aspect of the king's and chiefs' rule as well as the rationale of all traditional ethical and moral conduct. Some Christians alienate themselves from their communities because they refuse to participate in "fetish observances," even when these are a part of ordinary obedience to their chiefs. As the Christians, in attempting to resolve this conflict, separate ceremonial (religion) observances from secular government—the chief as a ruler from the chief as sacred head—this has, of course, weakened the position of the chief.

PART III

A Survey of the Past

Early African States

Research has only recently begun to piece together a somewhat vague picture of the history of Africa prior to European contact. In studying African history we are rediscovering an Africa known and celebrated in the Middle East and to a limited extent in Europe from the beginning of the Christian era to the coming of the Portuguese in the fifteenth century.

Before the founding in the eleventh century of the earliest known Muslim dynasty south of the Sahara (Kanem in the western Sudan), there was a succession of pagan states such as Ghana in West Africa and Zimbabwe in the east. The Arab invasions of North Africa in the seventh and eleventh centuries brought the ideas and practices of Islam to Africa. Many Berbers of of North Africa who adopted Islam but resisted strict Arab control established empires of their own. At least two of these, the Almoravide and the Almohade dynasties, affected the Negro peoples in the southern desert and Sudanese areas. Islam often provided an already

established dynasty with a means of extending contro
over people beyond the limits of traditional kinshi
ties.

The economy of the African states, both pagan an
Muslim, was based largely on trade, and their technolog
was at a high level compared to that of Europe. At th
site of Kumbi-Saleh, believed to be one of the capita
of ancient Ghana, iron nails, farming tools, knive
scissors, lances, and arrowheads, as well as glass weigh
and pieces of Mediterranean pottery have been foun
Throughout Africa copper, tin, gold, and iron wer
mined. (The western Sudan was a major source of gol
which found its way into Europe's economy throug
trans-Saharan and Mediterranean trade.)

The mysterious ruins of Zimbabwe in Rhodesia testi
fy to a civilization which probably existed between th
eleventh and fourteenth centuries. Since the Portugues
first brought reports of this city to Europe, scholar
have debated its origins. It has been labeled everythin
from a Greek colony to the city of Prester John. Bu
modern archaeological evidence supports the thesis tha
it was the work of indigenous Africans. The architectu
al style of the massive buildings has no counterpa
among other cultures, and the political structure whic
they housed was typically African. The *Monomatap*
was considered to be a divine king. His lesser subject
crawled into his presence and were never allowed t
look at him. Members of the court imitated his sligh
est movement. They coughed if he did, or limped if h
limped. With old age, or if a serious illness occurre
he was supposed to commit suicide so that he migh
not die the natural death of mortals. There was a
elaborate court and hierarchy of chiefs. Within th
court were titled officers of chancellor, court chambe
lain, drummer, military commander, keeper of fetishe
head doorkeeper, and chief cook. The queen mothe
was also an important figure in court life. There was
class of governors who received their authority fror
the royal fire of the king. With the death of each kin
the fire had to be extinguished and a new one set.

Ghana, Zimbabwe, Mali, and the Zenj states—som
Muslim, some not—were all important African king
doms of the Middle Ages. However much their socie
ties may have been influenced by the forces of Islam o

other foreign cultures, their development was essentially indigenous.

Let us now examine two of these African kingdoms in detail—the Zenj Empire in East Africa; and Mali, from which the modern West African state takes its name.

EARLY ARAB CONTACT IN EAST AFRICA: THE ZENJ EMPIRE

From Zoe Marsh and G. W. Kingsnorth, *An Introduction to the History of East Africa,* 1957.

The Persians and the Arabs settled on the east coast of Africa, and the period from 975 ... to 1498, when Vasco da Gama sailed to Mombasa, is often called the time of the Zenj Empire. The word "empire" is used because the state of Kilwa took the lead among the coastal settlements. These were Sofala, Mozambique, Kilwa, Tumbatu, Pemba, Zanzibar, Vumba, and Lamu Archipelago and Mogadishu....

Most of these places were on islands, although some of them, like Mombasa, were only separated from the mainland by a narrow stretch of water. This was because their Arab or Persian settlers were people who were used to making their living as traders on the sea. As their settlements were in a strange land they were also all fortified, and gradually towns grew up behind these defenses. From the ruins left behind by these settlers we know that many of them carried with them memories of their homes in Persia. To Kilwa, for instance, they brought the knowledge of how to build in stone, carve wood and weave cotton. But as the years went on, these settlements became more and more Arab in character. That is why these 500 years of the Zenj Empire are thought of nowadays as the period of Arab settlement....

Decline of Arab trade

From earliest times southern Arabia was the market for goods from the East, and the northeastern monsoon brought Arabian dhows to the coast of East Africa. In

the second century A.D. this trade decreased. First, the irrigation of southwest Arabia was seriously disturbed by
the bursting of a large reservoir which reduced the prosperity of the whole. Second, the Bantu people had begun
to appear on the coast and, as they were fiercer and better armed than the original peoples, the Arab traders were
further discouraged. Trade revived with the rise of Islam
and the arrival of Arab settlers on the coast.

Trade in the Zenj Empire

During the period of the Zenj Empire, southern Arabia
was the center of the valuable maritime trade between the
Far East, Mesopotamia and Persia and the countries bordering the Mediterranean Sea. Chinese silks, Indian cotton cloth, rhubarb from China (valued for its medicinal
properties), precious stones, pepper, nutmeg, mace, ginger and cloves were brought there by sea and sent thence
by caravan across the desert, or transshipped up the Red
Sea by the Arabs, who monopolized its navigation. To the
East went copper from Arabia and horses from Mesopotamia.

As well as being an important market place for the
traffic between East and West, Arabia also annually sent
a fleet of ships down the east coast of Africa to carry on
the trade in ivory, slaves and spices which had originally
attracted the Arabs to the coast. . . . Neither Indian nor
Arab showed any desire to explore the vast continent
which lay behind the coast. They were content to exchange the ambergris, slaves and gold. This exchange involved sending caravans into the interior and sometimes
fighting to keep a trade route open. But unless it served
the interests of trade, the Arabs were not to be found in
the interior.

Life on the coast

On the coast the Arabs intermarried with the Africans.
The result was the birth of the Swahili people, who
shared the faith of Islam and much of the Arab way of

life. This life on the coast was dependent on slaves who had been marched down from the interior. Those who survived this journey to serve Arab masters in their plantations and homes were relatively fortunate, for the Koran taught Muslims that kindness to slaves was a virtue, and many were as well treated as slaves can be. The more unfortunate were those who had still to face the horrors of a sea passage in which they were packed so closely together that they could hardly turn around. These included those who were shipped to Oman (where the slaves made up a large portion of the population), to India and probably to China.

A KINGDOM OF THE OLD SUDAN: MALI

In the Western Sudan and along the Gulf of Guinea there developed a succession of states which drew to varying degrees on the cultural background of the Muslim world. The wealth of the Western Sudan was based on its control of the trans-Saharan trade in salt and gold. This control was much competed for, and one state gave way to another over a period of several centuries.

Whereas Ghana had been a great empire trading in salt and gold, Mali under Kankan Musa achieved control of the sources of both. Reaching its apogee in the fourteenth century, it was followed by the empire of Songhay. When the latter was disrupted in 1591 by the armies of the Moroccan El Mansur, the last of these empires of the western Sudan dwindled away.

From Basil Davidson, *The Lost Cities of Africa*, 1959.

Timbuktu and Djenne, both to become famous throughout the Islamic world for their commerce and learning, seem to have grown into cities by the twelfth century. But their eminence dates from Mandingo supremacy and its empire of Mali. Then it was, in 1307, that the most renowned of all the monarchs of the old Sudan, Mansa (sultan or emperor) Kankan Musa, inherited power over Mali and began to extend its dominion.

After much success in conquest and diplomacy, this remarkable man followed others from the western Sudan on pilgrimage to Mecca, and gave the world a proof of the widespread loyalties of Islam as well as a chance of measuring the wealth of Sudanese civilization.

This realm had grown during Kankan Musa's pilgrimage. In 1325 his army commander, Sagaman-dir, took the Songhay capital of Gao on the middle Niger; and with Gao there fell to the dominion of Mali the whole wide trading area which the Songhay had already captured to the north of them. Thus for size and wealth if not for the number of its people, who were comparatively few when compared with the empires of the East, Mali was one of the greatest states in the world of its time. Kankan Musa returned home by way of Gao, enjoying his general's conquest and receiving the submission of the Songhay king and notables, and went on upstream to Timbuktu.

There in Timbuktu he caused new mosques to be raised, mosques that would long be famous in the whole Sudan. They are said to have followed the design of a poet of Granada in southern Spain, Abu Ishaq es Saheli, whom the emperor had come to know in Mecca and persuaded to return with him. . . . And soon after Kankan Musa's visit, according to tradition, the earliest flat-roofed houses were built in Gao and Timbuktu. In any case the wealth of these cities must greatly have expanded from this time, for Mali had succeeded better than Ghana and now controlled the country to the north as well as the country to the south—many sources of copper, salt, and gold, as well as the caravan trails between.

Centers of commerce and religion, these cities became centers of learning. Scholars sheltered in their relative ease and security. The literate culture of the Western Sudan, already in existence for several hundred years, flowered in Timbuktu during years that saw, in Europe, the ravage of the Hundred Years' War. No one now can say how much it flowered, nor what fruits it bore, for the books that men read or wrote there are lost or not yet found; but Leo Africanus, two centuries later, gives some measure of the city's intellectual life. "In Timbuktu," he says, "there are numerous judges, doctors, clerics, all receiving good salaries from the king. He pays great respect to men of learning. There is a big demand for books in manuscript, imported from Barbary. More profit is made from the book trade than from any other line of business." The king in question was Mohammed Askia of Songhay; but conditions would not have greatly differed in the years of plenitude that came in the wake of Kankan Musa's conquest.

This was a civilization in its own right. . . . Peace reigned over the long caravan trails. Men were free to travel and trade and prosper as they could. There would be interruptions in this security, true enough—Mossi raiders would pillage Timbuktu only eight years after Kankan Musa's visit—but they would remain interruptions, disturbing rarely the everyday peace. . . . And they must have disturbed even less the peasants and pastoralists who dwelt and throve on the banks of the Niger and out across the plains beyond. Many of these remained pagan even at the height of Islamic fame in the cities and gave, with their stolid clinging to the ancient ways, another native and authentic accent to this Sudanese civilization. . . .

With the conquests of Kankan Musa the rulers grew wealthier; and the cities, profiting from their control of the caravan terminals and their increasing monopoly of the more important products, followed suit. Perhaps Djenne was the greatest of them. "It is because of this hallowed town," the author of the *Tarikh es Sudan* [Ibn Battuta] would write some three hundred years later, but the comment will apply to the dominion of Mali as well as to the later dominion of Songhay, "that caravans come to Timbuktu from all points of the horizon." Crossing southward over the Sahara in the mid-nineteenth century, Heinrich Barth could still find potent evidence of the extent and wealth of this far-flung trading system. Though reduced by then to proportions that might be insignificant when compared with the carrying trade of nineteenth-century Europe, it made a still convincing witness to the commercial machinery which had helped to build and maintain states and long-enduring dynasties in this savannah country of the Middle Ages.

In the same thoughtful probing manner he [Barth] looked into the value and the nature of the salt trade, a trans-Saharan staple whose handling would not have greatly changed over the centuries, and has left an admirably detailed account of the means whereby bold and enterprising men could profit from it. During the dominion of Songhay, the second-in-authority at Agades—one of the south Saharan caravan stations—had had to levy tax on all merchandise imported into the town. (It would not have been much different under the earlier dominion of Mali; and the king of Ghana, long before that, had done the same on his narrower frontiers.) This office had been of great importance [not only] in providing royal revenue but also in the means of individual enrichment.

Tales of fabulous kingly wealth had always been common. El Bekri had long before reported the king of Ghana as having a nugget of gold so large and heavy that he could safely tether his horse to it. But with the growth of Mali and its trading network the fables acquired a more statistical shape, and ceased perhaps to be fables after all. Kankan Musa was said to have taken five hundred slaves on the Mecca pilgrimage, each carrying a staff of gold that weighed about six pounds. On his baggage camels there were said to be eighty to one hundred loads of gold, each weighing about three hundred pounds. And anyone who has chanced to see a modern durbar of chiefs and traditional rulers in West Africa, a parade flashing with scores and hundreds of golden staffs—wooden staffs, no doubt, yet covered with beaten gold—will not find this so hard to credit.

Trading links multiplied. By 1400, according to Ibn Khaldun, annual caravans across the Sahara by way of the Hoggar Mountains counted no fewer than twelve thousand camels; and this was only one of half a dozen well-used routes. But the caravans went in many directions as well as to and from the northward and Mediterranean; the whole Sudan was criss-crossed by their patient profit-seeking trails. Thus Bornu—in what is now northeastern Nigeria—brought copper from Wadai, its neighbor to the eastward; and Wadai had this copper in turn from Darfur, again to the eastward.

The Declining African States

What happened to these African empires, the vitality of which we are just beginning to grasp? Furthermore, why was there no greater recognition of them by contemporary Europeans? The answers to these two questions are tied together.

The great states of the old Sudan were inland states. Their wealth came from trading across the interior of Africa, as the continent's inhospitable coastline and general topography prevented the development of shipping. Unlike other continents, the coastal areas of Africa enjoyed few geographical advantages. Hence, economic activity and cultural development in these areas lagged behind that of the interior. It was, of course, coastal people with whom Europeans first made contact.

As Europeans opened up the west coast of Africa to trade, they unwittingly disrupted the economics of the inland states dependent on transcontinental trade. Thus the presence of European traders on the coast siphoned off the vital trade of the interior and hastened the decline of the early empires.

The slave trade, greatly stimulated by Europeans, encouraged intergroup raids, and disrupted trade and communications to a paralyzing degree.

By the time Europeans penetrated the interior of the continent, these deadly factors, plus dynastic difficulties, had done their work, and the great empires of Africa were represented only by dimly remembered legends and decaying ruins.

European Attitudes and Contacts

The Renaissance in Europe ended Africa's isolation by stimulating the revival of trade and exploration. The

explorers of the fifteenth and sixteenth centuries set out
for the Far East; but two land masses blocked the sea
routes. Columbus found the American continents in-
conveniently in the way; and the Portuguese spent most
of the fifteenth century groping their way around Africa to reach the East. For four centuries Africa was
considered primarily in terms of supporting colonial
and commercial development elsewhere. For the
Portuguese and Dutch, with extensive interests in the
Far East, Africa provided way stations and bases for
their commercial activities in the Orient. For the Spanish, French, English, and Portuguese, whose holdings in
the New World required a large labor force to make
them profitable, Africa provided the manpower. As the
following selection suggests, Europeans had considerable respect for the coastal people. Only much later did
the European superiority complex develop.

EARLY EUROPEAN ATTITUDES TOWARD AFRICANS

From Basil Davidson, *Black Mother,* 1961.

One outstanding fact about the old states of Africa, well
understood in earlier times but afterwards forgotten, is
that they were seldom or never conquered from outside
the continent. They resisted invasion. They remained in-
violate. Only here and there along the coast could European men-at-arms gain a foothold even when they tried to
win more. The Moorish states of northern Africa had little luck with their overland invasions of the south, and
were in the end frustrated and forced to withdraw.

Writers of the colonial period have sometimes explained this fact of successful African resistance by reference to the climate and the mosquito. Certainly, malaria
and the sun were grim discouragers of foreign invasion.
Yet the early records indicate another and more persuasive safeguard against conquest. They point to the striking power of African armies. They show that it was
the military factor, time and again, which proved
decisive. . . .

In 1481 [the Portuguese] built their first fort on the

Gold Coast, at a place they named Elmina, "the mine," believing that from here they could best tap the sources of African gold. Yet they built this fort by agreement with the chief of the people of the region, and not conquest. At the close of a long plea by Diego d'Azambuja, who commanded the Portuguese expedition, the chief in question consented to the building of a fort, but only on condition that "peace and truth must be kept." And one of the earliest actions that followed on the building of the castle at Elmina was not a military expedition to "the mines" of the interior, but a diplomatic mission of friendship and alliance. Messengers had come from Mamadu, lord of Mali. King John of Portugal ordered that these messengers should be accompanied back to their country by eight Portuguese emissaries, including two knights of the royal court, "with gifts of horses and mules and arms and other things prized in that country." . . .

Opinion in Europe nonetheless grew common that European power held sway over the interior. "There is no small number of men in Europe," a Dutch factor on the Gold Coast wrote back to his employers in the year 1700, "who believe that the gold mines are in our power; that we . . . have no more to do but to work them by our slaves: though you perfectly know we have no manner of access to these treasures." By this time men in Europe were accustomed to seeing Africans only as men in chains, slaves without power, and they transferred their impressions to Africa and the states from which these slaves had come. The belief in African inferiority was already in full bloom.

Those who traveled in Africa knew better. "With nauseating presumption," complained Father Cavazzi of the states of the Congo in 1687, "these nations think themselves the foremost men in the world, and nothing will persuade them to the contrary. They imagine that Africa is not only the greatest part of the world, but also the happiest and most agreeable." The lords of Congo, he found, were even more arrogant. "Similar opinions are held by the king himself, but in a manner still more remarkable. For he is persuaded that there is no other monarch in the world who is his equal, or exceeds him in power or the abundance of wealth. . . ."

The reasons for this African self-confidence were not really obscure. They were the same reasons as those that had enabled Africans to resist invasions: the steady growth of Iron Age concentrations of power, the evolution of central government, the raising of armies, the swearing-in of vassals, or the elimination of rivals that had accompanied much of African social development for the previous thousand years. They were, in short, the reasons that had enabled African types of feudal rule to emerge and grow strong.

THE EUROPEAN SLAVE TRADE IN WEST AFRICA

> The slave trade played such a large part in both Arab and European interest in Africa that it deserves a closer look. It should be repeated that neither Arabs nor Europeans introduced the institution of slavery to Africa. It was already there, just as serfdom was a part of Europe's social structure during the Middle Ages. The demand created by foreign slave traders, however, increased the value of slaves and thus disrupted the existing pattern of slave–master relationships. Slavery ceased to be a social relationship and became a big business. The results of this change had serious effects on slaves, masters, and traders alike, as will be explained later.

> From Zoe Marsh and G. W. Kingsnorth, *An Introduction to the History of East Africa*, 1957.

Motives for the European slave trade

The first of the European countries to import slaves from Africa was Portugal. In 1441, when Henry the Navigator's seamen searched the West African coast looking for the sea route to India, they captured twelve men, women, and children, and brought them back to Portugal as slaves. Within seven years nearly a thousand slaves had been imported and sold at the Lisbon slave market, where we are told Henry the Navigator looked upon them with great pleasure, thinking that these people would be converted to Christianity. By the end of the fifteenth century the determination of the Portuguese explorers was rewarded. Vasco de Gama had established the route by sea to India, and the Portuguese carracks carried home the immensely profitable spices of the East. In comparison with this cargo slaves were of little value, and interest in them might have been expected to decline. But whereas the discovery of the route to India made the collection of slaves comparatively unprofitable, Columbus's discovery of the West Indies and America made them the most profitable cargo of all. By one of the ironies of history the discovery of the continent which now has the Statue of Liberty standing outside its greatest city was responsible for the greatest increase in the slave trade that the world has known.

During the fifty years after Columbus first landed in the Bahamas in 1492, the Spaniards conquered Mexico, Peru, and the main West Indian islands, while in 1531 the Portuguese began the colonization of Brazil. Not only were extremely rich deposits of gold and silver found, but also plantations of tobacco, indigo, and sugar were laid out. But to mine the silver and gold, and to work the plantations, labor was needed in large quantities. Neither the Spanish nor the Portuguese had the numbers, the inclination, or the stamina to provide this labor in the tropical heat; they turned to the Indians with no success, although a considerable part of the Indian population was wiped out in the attempt. The situation was saved by the importation of slaves from West Africa, the first batch arriving in 1510. The Spanish missionaries, led by Las Casas, the first bishop of Mexico, encouraged this importation. They realized that it would relieve the Indians, whose sufferings they, and the Spanish government, had been trying to prevent. Throughout the sixteenth century the number of slaves imported to America increased. In theory Portugal controlled the area of export in West Africa, and in 1580 the supply of slaves to Spanish colonies was entrusted exclusively to them by the Spanish government under an agreement known as the "Asiento." But in fact other countries took part also, and the voyages of John Hawkins to the region of Sierra Leone were among the earliest.

The slave trade and the West Indies

But so far as Britain was concerned the Atlantic slave trade did not become a matter of supreme importance until the second half of the seventeenth century. Before 1660 the British colonies used slaves, but not on a great scale, and as a result the English Guinea Companies had been small associations maintaining a few insecure African posts, and the number of interlopers was small compared with later years. But in the second half of the seventeenth century the plantation colonies developed rapidly, and as they did so the slave trade on which they depended became a matter of vital importance. The greatest cause of the development of these colonies and the slave trade which it involved was the realization that sugar could be grown in the West Indian islands, and that it brought tremendous profits. It was in 1643 that the sugar industry took root in Barbados, which had previously grown mainly tobacco and cotton, and had supported a population of 18,000 male whites, with comparatively few slaves. By the end of the seventeenth century the exports of Barbados to Britain, which were composed almost entirely of sugar, were worth more than the exports of all the rest of the British American colonies put together. Meanwhile the population had entirely changed. The small plantation had given way to the large; the many small owners had given way to a few fabulously wealthy ones; and the proportion of slaves had increased tremendously.

Where Barbados led the other West Indian islands followed, and in the eighteenth century Jamaica became the greatest British sugar island, with a slave population of 300,000. But slaves were required not only for sugar, nor in the West Indies alone. Tobacco, and later cotton, plantations also needed slave gangs, and by 1760 half of Virginia's population of 400,000 were slaves. North of Maryland the proportion was far smaller, and it was domestic, not plantation, slavery.

The figures for the Spanish, Portuguese, and French colonies were also alarming. By 1800 there were 776,000 African slaves in Spanish America; in the last half of the eighteenth century 642,000 slaves were shipped into Brazil; in 1775 there were over half a million slaves in the French West Indies alone. The total number of slaves carried by the Atlantic slave trade from its beginning until its end has been variously estimated. Probably it was at least fifteen million.

The slave trade in West Africa

The vast majority of these slaves came from West Africa. The remainder came from Angola and a few from Mozambique. In the early days of the Atlantic slave trade the area between Gambia and the Gold Coast was the main source, but before the end of the seventeenth century the huge increase in the demand for slaves resulted in the spread of the trade to the whole Gulf of Guinea. As Zanzibar was the center of the east coast slave trade during the nineteenth century, so Calabar was the chief center of the slave trade on the west coast from 1600 until in the nineteenth century Lagos superseded it as the worst slave depot of the region. Slaving gradually developed from a mere affair of kidnapping to a highly organized trade. During the late seventeenth and eighteenth centuries, when it was at its height, the British, Dutch, French, Danes, Portuguese, Germans, and Swedes had between them nearly fifty forts along the West African coast to which slaves were brought from the interior, and particularly from the area north of the Niger delta. From these fortresses the slaves would be purchased and shipped across the Atlantic.

The extent and organization of the trade

The British took a leading part in this trade from the middle of the seventeenth century, with the development of the plantation colonies. New impetus was given when at the Peace of Utrecht in 1713 [Britain] obtained the Asiento. By 1770 half the total slave trade of the Atlantic was carried by nearly 200 British ships with cargo space for nearly 50,000 slaves. The French came next with 30,000, and the Portuguese third with 10,000. Most of the British trade was managed from Liverpool, and the remainder from Bristol and London.

Some of the slaves were carried by companies, and others by individual traders. For a man, or a group of men, with capital there could be no better investment than to hire a ship and an experienced captain, and to load at Liverpool a cargo of cloth, hardware, or spirits. From Liverpool the ship would sail to one of the forts on the West African coast where the cloth, the beads, and the spirits would be exchanged for slaves and probably some gold and ivory as well. With this new cargo the ship would turn westward across the Atlantic to the West Indies and perhaps some of the mainland colonies also. Here the slaves would be sold, and sugar, cotton, and tobacco would be loaded in their places. Then, with a cargo many times more valuable than the original, the ship would return to England. The whole trip usually took about six months and fell clearly into three stages—the outward passage from England to West Africa, the middle passage across the Atlantic, and the homeward passage from the West Indies or American mainland to England. So great were the profits that if only one ship in three made a successful voyage the enterprise was well worth while.

A comparison of East and West African slave trade

There are interesting similarities and contrasts between the slave trade in East and West Africa. The volume of each was enormous, but while we can make some sort of a guess at the number of slaves taken from West Africa it is extremely difficult to make an estimate for East Africa, because the volume varied and figures can only be obtained for the comparatively few final years. But we do know that the European slave trade across the Atlantic did not begin until the sixteen century, that it did not reach its maximum until the eighteenth century, and that at the start of the nineteenth century it was abolished. But the Arab slave trade across the Indian Ocean began before the Christian era and did not stop until the end of the nineteenth century, so that although its volume in any one year did not reach the highest figure of the European slave trade the total number of Africans exported during two thousand years may well have exceeded fifteen million. The treatment of slaves by those who transported them was dreadful in both cases, but whereas about half those captured as slaves in West Africa reached their destination, we have seen that only about one-fifth of those captured in East Africa survived. Yet those deported from East Africa who reached their destination in the Middle East were usually treated with comparative kindness and were used as domestic slaves, while those who were deported from West Africa to the American or West Indian colonies were used in gangs on plantations. Sugar is perhaps the most exhausting of all crops to harvest, and the overseers were interested in making the greatest profit in the shortest time so that they could return to England. Consequently their treatment of the slaves does not make happy reading. The Spanish alone, among the European countries, made a sincere and effective attempt to treat their slaves with something like kindness. The effects of the slave trade upon Africa went deep, and even when internal warfare ended at the abolition of the slave trade, the population in both the east and the west remained low.

THE ARAB SLAVE TRADE IN EAST AFRICA

Methods and effects of the Arab slave trade

The size of the caravans varied. On the shorter trade routes a caravan might consist of only fifty men, but for long, dangerous journeys inland, parties might join together, making a total of a thousand or more. With the native guide in front carrying his tattered blood-red flag, the sign of Seyyid Said's protection, the file would set off westwards in search of its prey, through the coastal forest, the hated thorn-scrub, and the long grassland, watching for hostile tribes and wild animals by day, and camping by night beside the watch-fires which kept off the marauding hyenas, jackals and lions. Progress was slow. The journey from Tabora to Ujiji, for example, though only about one hundred miles, usually took over three weeks. When the rainy season started, movement became almost impossible, so most of the caravans started in the dry period of April or May after the long rains, and sometimes they remained away from the coast for two years or more. In the interior slaves would either be purchased from chiefs or Arab merchants, or the caravan might raid a village itself. These raids, whether carried out by hostile tribes or by the Arabs themselves, were devastating and merciless. A shot in the night would be followed by a bonfire of blazing huts while the screaming inhabitants rushed into the bush. Those who were fit would be enslaved, and those who were useless would be massacred. Then the raiders would depart leaving the village a smoldering graveyard. Such was the picture Livingston saw. Apart from the human misery involved, the unrest and depopulation caused by these raids were enormous. When the explorer Speke visited the east side of Lake Tanganyika in 1858 he wrote:

> How the shores should be so desolate strikes one with much surprise. Unless in former times this beautiful

country has been harassed by neighboring tribes and despoiled of its men and cattle to satisfy the spoilers and be sold to distant markets, its present state appears quite incomprehensible. In hazarding this conjecture it might be thought that I am taking an extreme view of this case; but when we see everywhere in Africa what one slave-hunt or cattle-lifting party can effect, it is not unreasonable to imagine that this was most probably the cause of such utter desolation here. These war-parties lay waste the land for endless time.

On the return journey of the caravan the guide would be followed by the long, infinitely pathetic, line of slaves yoked together and carrying on their heads elephant tusks, and bundles of cloth, beads, and grain. Beside them marched the exultant Arab traders with ready whips for the weary, and ready swords for those who could march no more. At the rear of the file came the most important of the Arab merchants. When the caravan reached the coast the ivory and the slaves might be sold on the spot or else shipped to the main market at Zanzibar. For this journey they were heaped in tiers on top of one another and many never reached their destination. By the middle of the nineteenth century about 15,000 slaves a year passed through the squalid, sandy square of the Zanzibar slave market, where men and merchants in every variety of costume from mere rags to the brilliant gold and vermilion raiment of the Arab aristocracy gathered each afternoon from five until sundown to purchase the haggard wretches who were ornamented and arrayed for their inspection. Some of their purchases were kept for the merchants' own use, but most were exported under appalling conditions to Arabia and the Persian Gulf. For every five captured in the interior only one reached his or her destination. Most died before they even reached the coast.

Upon the great expansion of the slave trade which took place during his reign Seyyid Said smiled with satisfaction, as well he might considering the increased prosperity of his dominions which it brought. But the results of the trade upon the African interior were catastrophic. Tribe attacked tribe to obtain profit from those they captured and enslaved; whole villages were destroyed and their inhabitants removed or massacred, while the slave routes themselves were strewn with the skeletons of those who perished. Constant internal war and depopulation on a vast scale were the price of the East African slave trade.

THE STORY OF A BEMBA SLAVE BOY

This is a first-person account by a Bemba boy who had been taken by Arab slavers and rescued by British who raided the slave vessels. It was written in 1880 at the school to which he was taken following his rescue.

From Peggy Rutherford, ed., *African Voices*, n.d.

Since I left my own land [west of Lake Nyassa], and, indeed, since I was born, I never saw or knew my mother. I lived with one of my mother's relations. He brought me up, till I was about eight years old, and after a time they said, "Now we are going to travel and join our other people." So we started. It was because there was a war very near us, but we escaped, sir, and got safe to a country, where was a chief and this chief's name was Mweenge. There we lived, in the same place as others of our tribe.

One day, when it was time for us to go home again, we started and traveled for three days, and then slept in a very large hut. Here the Magwangwara came upon the hut. I had gone into the fields to play and look for something to eat with a man whose name was Kipofu, and the older women of the family were left in the hut. Well, in the evening, the Magwangwara came, and we were in the fields, and we heard the cries of the people, and the houses burning with fire. We ran away to get to the village, and found nothing but men's heads. Then we cried till we were tired, and then climbed up into a tree and slept. In the morning we woke up, and considered, and said, "Well, where are we to go now? We have not got a morsel of food." All I had with me was a little basket. Then we went back, and found a garden which had been planted with groundnuts, but they had been dug up. However, we went and picked up a few nuts, about ten apiece. The house to which the garden belonged was on a little hill, and the people saw us, and came down to catch us. My companion heard them coming running down, and he ran away as fast as ever he could, and the people came and caught me. And I thought, "This man will make me his slave." I stayed there thirty-two days, and then he sold me for just seven hoes.

My new master carried me off, and they took me to their town called Malani, and there I stayed a month, and my master got into trouble, because of a man who accused him of witchcraft. They took the omens about him, but the omens did not convict him. Next they carried me away to Bisaland, and there I met Mpunga. I remained there with my mistress, whose name was Namlia Isani. Then some Arabs came there, bringing their cloth, and the people sold me and Mpunga too.

The Arab was a very cruel man, and he had a great many slaves. There were thirty-one. Then we came to Yaoland, to the country of a chief called Makanjila. There we settled, and grew crops of millet and maize, and groundnuts, and food of many kinds, remaining there a great many months. When we had finished eating all our crops, the Arabs made up a very large caravan, and we came to a town called Akasunga. But we did not stay there; we started off and came to Kilwa, and there we stayed. My master sold me to another Arab, me and Mpunga and another, and we were sent by the Arab to carry rice to the encampment. We carried the rice and went off, and when we got there we found a great number of Arabs and others, among them Taisiri. And all the people we were with had a very heavy chain.

There were two dhows there, one smaller than the other, but sailing faster than the one we got into. When we got into the dhow, it was quite night time, perhaps the time we go to evening service—8:30 P.M.—and when we went into the water it came up to our necks. Then we got into the dhow and were arranged in order, and the Arabs weighed the anchor, and we put out to sea, and lay down for three or four days. It was a very large number of people who went on board, with goats, and fowls, and a large stock of food. But the Arabs were very cruel during the voyage, and because we were in a dhow we were told that the Europeans were bad people, but we thought, "Never mind, they can't be worse than you. You torment us for nothing." One night a child in the dhow cried very much, and the Arabs were just going to kill it, but one Arab said, "Never mind; let it alone. We are nearly there." So they let it alone, but when it was four o'clock in the morning we heard a cannonshot over the sail, and the Arabs cried "Oh! ah! the English!" When the English boarded the dhow, everyone said, "I am a slave, sir." For when we were caught by the English, we were glad. But when I thought about my home, I cried.

> This case was unusual. As a rule one of the chief difficulties of an English officer on boarding a dhow suspected of carrying slaves was the unwillingness of the slaves to confess that they were so. This was partly from a vague fear of people they knew nothing about, but mainly because the Arabs used to tell them that all Europeans were cannibals, who only caught slaves in order to fatten and eat them.

THE SLAVE TRADE AND THE DEVELOPMENT OF STATES IN THE GUINEA FOREST

> The slave trade is usually studied in terms of the human destruction it wrought. It is true, however, as the following reading shows, that some African kingdoms adapted their political institutions to the situation of expanded trade and conquest, and thrived.

> *From* J. D. Fage, "States of the Guinea Forest," in Roland Oliver, ed., *The Dawn of African History*, 1961.

Our modern concepts of humanity incline us, when we think of the slave trade today, to stress the word *slave* more than the word *trade*. But for all the great moral and material evil of the slave trade, we must not forget that the sale and export of slaves was only one half of the bargain. In return for the slaves they sold to the European traders, the Africans received not only firearms (and hence, incidentally, the means to build larger empires and to secure more slaves) but also many commodities which were socially more beneficial: cloth, tools, the raw materials for local smithies and workshops, and many other items of equipment needed by virile societies eager to increase their wealth and power under the stimulus of the contact with European culture and its ideas. It is true that West Africa paid for these things by exporting her people in a manner which we today can only regard as inhuman. But it may help to give a better perspective, if we remember that nineteenth-century Britain, while advancing to peaks of wealth and power unparalleled in her history, did so while no less than 19 million of her inhabitants were being forced, basically by economic pressures, to emigrate overseas, incidentally in conditions not so very much better than those in which the African slaves had been transported. It need not therefore cause surprise that the great increase of trade on the Guinea coast in the seventeenth and eighteenth centuries, even though it was occasioned primarily by the great demand for the export of labor to America, could have stimulated the growth of rich and prosperous new empire-states which, unlike their predecessors in the western Sudan, sought the commercial bases for their wealth and power by looking not north, toward the Sahara, but south, toward the Atlantic.

Some Conclusions on Early European Contacts

When the Portuguese and others first made contact with the native states of West Africa, they found a culture there which they felt they could understand and appreciate. The feudal nature of the West African kingdoms was enough like that of fifteenth century Europe for the Europeans to recognize the system and to feel at home in it. True, they oversimplified the comparison, and drew some unwarranted conclusions, but the important idea here is that they accepted the idea that native African states were on an equal footing with European ones. African and European kings considered themselves to be brother monarchs and addressed each other as such.

A radical change in the relationship came about with the development of the large-scale slave trade. This worked in several ways to change the European attitude toward Africans. The European had to justify the trade to himself by assuming the inferiority of the African, thus persuading himself that it was part of God's plan that "lesser breeds" work for the superior races. This became increasingly easy to do as more and more Europeans came into contact with Africans—Africans who had become thoroughly debased and dehumanized by enslavement. Thus, the continent's population came to be judged by Europeans in terms of the uprooted and shattered fragments of humanity which were the stock in trade of the slaving business.

As the slave trade grew in proportion, it destroyed some African political and cultural institutions and created others. In the eighteenth century, for the most part African states held their own in the delicate balance with European traders. The nineteenth century was to witness several new factors—both European and African—which upset that balance.

Africa in the Nineteenth Century: Europe Takes Over

THE ROOTS OF COLONIALISM

Just as changes in Europe produced the first contact between Europe and Africa, so further historical evolution had to take place in Europe before Africa could play more than a supporting part in Europe's economic and imperialist development. The key to this change is

the Industrial Revolution, which created new demands
for raw materials, and produced a vocal working class
and a powerful middle class, particularly in England.
These groups, motivated partly by economic considerations and partly by a newly awakened humanitarian
spirit, waged and won a battle against the slave trade.
In 1807 England declared the trade illegal and was
soon followed in this by most European states—although it was another sixty years before the trade was
stamped out in West Africa.

From Harry R. Rudin, "History of European Relations with Africa," in Calvin W. Stillman, ed., *Africa in the Modern World*,
1955.

This extinction of slavery and of the slave trade removed what had been Europe's greatest economic interest
in Africa. By comparison, other trade was unimportant.
The end of slavery was accompanied by something like a
revival of interest in Africa as a base of operations for
getting at the wealth of the Far East. This renewal of interest can be seen in the efforts of Napoleon to conquer
Egypt and to dig a canal at Suez in order to get at the
wealth of India, which the French had lost to the English
in 1763. This French move had its counterpart in Britain's permanent conquest of South Africa, which was
taken from the Dutch along with Ceylon in 1814–15 to
assure English control of a water route to the Far East,
particularly to India, where Englishmen were deeply involved in the military persuasion of Indians to accept
British control.

French ambitions in Egypt were not checked by Napoleon's defeat. In the 1830's, while the conquest of Algeria
was taking place in the western Mediterranean, the
French gave their support to Mehemet Ali's plans to free
Egypt from Turkish rule and to establish a large empire
in the Near East. The English failed to block the French
conquest of Algeria; but they succeeded in thwarting the
ambitions of Mehemet Ali in Syria and blasted whatever
hopes the French had entertained in his regard. French

interest in Egypt and in that route to the Far East re
mained, however, and assumed tangible form in 1855
when the concession for the Suez Canal was obtained
Despite opposition from England, the canal was com
pleted and opened to traffic in 1869. Disraeli's purchas
of canal shares from the bankrupt khedive in 1875, th
British occupation of Egypt in 1882, and the French rec
ognition in 1904 of special British rights in Egypt re
moved the century-old fears that England had of th
French in this part of the world.

European interest in Africa was greatly intensified as
result of the industrial revolution. Led by England, Euro
pean countries became industrialized and experience
what must be regarded as the most far-reaching revolu
tion in Europe's history. This change was essentially a de
cision to use power and machinery for the manufacture o
articles that were to be traded for the food and the re
sources required by the appetites of men and machines
Farming was virtually abandoned as the number of acre
devoted to the production of grains declined. People lef
the countryside for the factories, where their rapidl
growing numbers expanded villages into towns and cities
With their machines men turned out vast quantities o
manufactured articles which were exported in ever in
creasing amounts to pay for the food and raw material
being imported in larger amounts. Lands overseas expand
ed the production of food and of raw materials to pay fo
rising imports of manufactured goods. Thus, as market
and sources of supply were found in distant parts of th
world, the national economies of Europe became interna
tionalized.

The industrial revolution and the commercial expan
sion that accompanied it gave Europe the greatest eco
nomic security it had ever had. . . . Europe's populatio
doubled in the century at the same time that the per capi
ta consumption of wheat, cotton, iron, wool, sugar, etc
mounted. The famines that had occurred about every te
years for several centuries of European history now vir
tually disappeared. So natural was the flow of manufac

tured articles out of Europe and of food into Europe that governments found it possible to abandon the mercantilist regulations that had operated for many generations and gave men a taste of that economic freedom which Adam Smith had argued for in his *Wealth of Nations*. . . .

It was during this economic crisis in the 1870's and 1880's [when England lost her monopoly of industrial techniques] that men turned their thoughts to Africa as well as to other parts of the world. Trade had been increasing along the coasts of Africa, and competition had become more intense as more Europeans crowded into the ports to get rid of surplus goods. To protect the overseas market, Europeans found it necessary to proclaim their occupation of territories in Africa and elsewhere.

The Scramble for African Real Estate

Not all of Europe's reawakened interest in Africa was economically motivated. The Industrial Revolution and the abolition of the slave trade paved the way for a new relationship between Europe and Africa. Humanitarians were not content with outlawing the slave trade in areas under European control. They were disturbed by the fact that slavery continued to exist in the interior of Africa and a lively trade in human lives was still carried on by the Arabs on the east coast. Many Europeans toward the middle of the nineteenth century felt it their duty to work for the end of these practices.

The scientific spirit of the age also played a part in the changing Afro–European relationship. The eighteenth-century explorations of Mungo Park were followed in the next century by many more efforts to unwrap the secrets of the continent. The Lander brothers completed Mungo Park's work on the Niger by tracing it south to the sea. European knowledge of Africa was greatly enhanced by Heinrich Barth's careful studies of the Sudan. David Livingstone led an expedition into Rhodesia, and Burton and Speke explored Lake Tanganyika about 1858. These scientific expeditions received extensive publicity in Europe.

Enthusiasm for these geographical explorations was undoubtedly stimulated by the growth of missionary societies in the Christian churches. Although the Catholic Church had long been supporting missionary activity in the New World and Africa, new orders were established in the nineteenth century for this purpose. Members of the Congregation of the Holy Ghost worked in West Africa, the Gaboon, Congo, Southwest Africa, and the East African coast. Another group, popularly known as the White Fathers, expanded after 1868 from their base in Algeria to establish missions all over Africa. These groups joined other orders: Benedictines, Franciscans, Dominicans, and Jesuits.

The first Protestant missionary group was founded in England by the Baptists in 1792. The London Missionary Society worked throughout the Pacific and in South Africa. In 1799, with the foundation of the Anglican's Church Missionary Society, one of the most extensive of all the missionary groups began proselytizing.

Financing mission activities and finding personnel willing to undertake the hardships of overseas service was hard, but by the second half of the nineteenth century, European concern for the Christianizing of Africans succeeded in creating a whole new area of European–African contact. Missionary groups took the lead in applying pressure on their governments for action which would further curtail slavery and the slave trade where it still existed.

By the end of the nineteenth century, there was further intellectual support for European exploits in Africa. Charles Darwin's concept of evolution and its corollary, survival of the fittest, buttressed the European conviction of racial superiority. There was a great increase in scientific study of race. Africans, with their societies, customs, and religions that were not only foreign to the European but also threatening to the isolated explorer or missionary, were believed to be in the lower stages of evolution. The European thought that with his superior racial and cultural background he might bring the savages into the modern world, and that, furthermore, it was his responsibility ("the white man's burden") to do so.

Surprisingly, up to the last two decades of the nineteenth century, the growth of European interest in Africa was not accompanied by governmental policies of conquest and empire. In 1879, the deepest penetration on the entire continent was in southern Africa where the two English colonies of the Cape and Natal bordered the Afrikaner republics of the Transvaal and Orange Free State. The British interest in East Africa was restricted to Zanzibar, while the French had only begun the penetration of Madagascar. Portuguese interest by this time was confined to vaguely defined trading spheres in what were to become Portuguese Guinea, Angola, and Mozambique. Although England and France had had commercial dealings in West Africa for four hundred years, their official control was substantial only in the Gold Coast and French Senegal. The British colonies of Gambia, Sierra Leone, and Lagos were small enclaves surrounded by African kingdoms. It is true that some colonialists had earlier tried to press for European expansion. But the cries of men like Faideherbe, the Senegalese governor who urged France to push her claims to the interior, had fallen on deaf ears. Until 1880–1900, European governments, notably England and France, were not interested in undertaking any additional expensive responsibilities.

By 1902, at the conclusion of the Boer War in South Africa, all this had changed. European governments claimed sovereignty over all but six of some forty different political units they had created on the African continent. Certainly, control of the interior was tenuous, even in 1902; but the bitter resistance of a few African leaders like Ahmadu and Samori of the western Sudan, of the African states of Ashanti, Dahomey, Oyo, Benin, and Matabeleland, and of the Arab and Swahili slave traders of East and Central Africa, had failed. The foreseeable future of Africa was in European hands.

The factors which combined to bring this about-face in European policy are legion. It is safe to say, however, that the entrance of Germany into the fields of European power politics and colonialism after 1871 aroused the competitive spirit of both France and Britain. All three great powers were spurred by the creation of the International African Association by Leopold II of Belgium. In 1879 and 1880, the English explorer Stanley, acting as Leopold's agent, had negotiated "treaties" for 900,000 square miles of territory in the Congo basin. Thus was created the Congo Free State with Leopold as its virtual master.

The ensuing tensions among the European powers led to the calling of the Conference of Berlin in 1884, the purpose of which was to draw up the ground rules for the strenuous game of dividing up Africa.

THE BERLIN ACT, 1885

The result of the Conference of Berlin was the Berlin Act, parts of which appear below. It reflects the variety of ambitions which conditioned European interest in Africa. Furthermore, it established the framework for the annexations to come.

Cited in T. Walter Wallbank, *Contemporary Africa: Continent in Transition,* 1956.

ARTICLE I.   The trade of all nations shall enjoy complete freedom. . . .

ARTICLE III.   Wares, of whatever origin, imported into these regions, under whatsoever flag, by sea or river, or overland, shall be subject to no other taxes than such as may be levied as fair compensation for expenditure in the interests of trade, and which for this reason must be equally borne by the subjects themselves and by foreigners of all nationalities.

ARTICLE IV.   Merchandise imported into these regions shall remain free from import and transit dues. . . .

ARTICLE VI. All the Powers exercising sovereign rights or influence in the aforesaid territories bind themselves to watch over the preservation of the native tribes, and to care for the improvement of the conditions of their moral and material well-being, and to help in suppressing slavery, and especially the slave trade. They shall, without distinction of creed or nation, protect and favor all religious, scientific, or charitable institutions, and undertakings created and organized for the above ends, or which aim at instructing the natives and bringing home to them the blessings of civilization. Christian missionaries, scientists, and explorers, with their followers, property, and collections, shall likewise be the objects of especial protection. Freedom of conscience and religious toleration are expressly guaranteed to the natives, no less than to subjects and to foreigners. The free and public exercise of all forms of Divine worship, and the right to build edifices for religious purposes and to organize religious missions belonging to all creeds, shall not be limited or fettered in any way whatsoever. . . .

ARTICLE IX.   Seeing that trading in slaves is forbidden in conformity with the principles of international law as recognized by the Signatory Powers, and seeing also that the operations, which, by sea or land, furnish slaves to trade, ought likewise to be regarded as forbidden, the Powers which do or shall exercise sovereign rights or influence in the territories forming the Conventional basin of the Congo declare that these territories may not serve as a market or means of transit for the trade in slaves, of whatever race they may be. Each of the Powers binds itself to employ all means at its disposal for putting an end to this trade and for punishing those who engage in it. . . .

ARTICLE XXXIV.   Any power which henceforth takes possession of a tract of land on the coasts of the African continent outside of its present possessions or which, hitherto without such possessions, shall acquire them, as well as the Power which assumes a Protectorate there, shall accompany the respective act with a notification thereof, addressed to the other Signatory Powers of the present Act, in order to enable them, if need be, to make good any claims of their own.

ARTICLE XXXV.   The Signatory Powers of the present Act recognize the obligation to insure the establishment of authority in regions occupied by them on the coasts of the African continent sufficient to protect existing rights, and, as the case may be, freedom of trade and of transit under the conditions agreed upon.

THE CONGO ATROCITIES

Despite the pious statements of the Berlin Act, there was another side to European activity in Africa. Many regarded Africa merely as an opportunity to get rich quickly, and considered its native population as either a means to that end or an annoyance to be removed. Joseph Conrad's short story "Heart of Darkness" reveals the conflict between ideals and practice most effectively. The most extreme example of exploitation can be seen in Leopold's Congo Free State, as the following accounts bear witness.

From Ludwig Bauer, *Leopold the Unloved,* 1935.

Lieutenant Tilkens writes [in letters]: "Commandant Verstraeten visited my station and congratulated me warmly. He said his report would depend upon the quantity of rubber which I was able to provide. The quantity increased from 360 kilogrammes in September to 1500 in October, and from January onwards it will amount to 4000 per month, which will bring me in a monthly premium of 500 francs. Am I not a lucky fellow? If I go on like this, within two years I shall have earned premiums of 12,000 Fcs." He continues: "S.S. Van Kerkhoven is coming down the Nile and will demand 1500 Porters. Unlucky niggers! I can hardly bear to think of them. I am asking myself how on earth I shall be able to hunt up so large a number." Then: "Marshes, hunger, exhaustion. How much blood will be shed because of this transport! Three times, already, I have had to make war upon the chiefs who would not help me to get the men I needed. The fellows would rather die in their own forests than as members of a transport train. If a chief refuses, that means war, with modern fire-arms on one side against spears and javelins on the other!" . . .

Senator Picard . . . traveled in the Congo Free State. Here are his impressions: "The inhabitants have disappeared. Their homes have been burned; huge heaps of ashes amid neglected palm-hedges and devastated abandoned fields. Inhuman floggings, murders, plunderings, and carryings-off. . . ." And: "The people flee into the wild or seek protection in French or Portuguese territory." Near Stanley Pool on the caravan road he notices: "A continual succession of blacks, carrying loads upon their heads; worn-out beasts of burden, with projecting joints, wasted features, and staring eyes, perpetually trying to keep afoot despite their exhaustion. By thousands they pass, in the service of the State, handed over by the chiefs, whose slaves they are and who rob them of their wages. They totter along the road, with bent knees and protruding bellies, crawling with vermin, a dreadful procession across hill and dale, dying from exhaustion by the wayside, or often succumbing even should they reach home after their wanderings. . . ."

Here are extracts from the reports of a commission which traveled through the whole State, compiled from the declarations of eye-witnesses. . . . "Within the territories of the Abir, the chief Isekifasu of Bolima was murdered, his wife and children being eaten by the cannibal guards; the houses of the natives were decorated with the intestines, the liver, and the heart of the murdered. . . . The successor of the murdered chief . . . attended by twenty witnesses, comes and lays a hundred and ten twigs upon the table, each of them signifying a murder for rubber. . . . . The soldiers had shown him the corpses of his people saying: 'Now you will bring us rubber!'" So it goes on: "Children have their brains dashed out; murders without ceasing; the bodies of the slain are eaten; soldiers are flogged by the agents' orders if they have been slack in the work of murder; women mutilated because they are true to their husbands. The commission spends many hours, many days, listening to such reports. . . . Behind each who complains, stand hundreds who do not dare to speak, or lie hundreds of slain who will never speak again. The wailings from the Congo are slow and repressed, but, irresistibly, the cry grows."

Reports such as these caused an international scandal. Demands for an investigation of the Congo were met in 1903, and Leopold was forced to turn the Congo Free State over to the Belgian government, which embarked on a new policy designed to make amends for the past.

THE ASHANTI: A CASE OF AFRICAN RESISTANCE TO THE ESTABLISHMENT OF EUROPEAN RULE

The following reading shows some of the turmoil that built up during the nineteenth century between Africans and Europeans. The Ashanti, whose society was described earlier in this volume, fought valiantly against the incursion of British rule.

From Smith Hempstone, *Africa—Angry Young Giant,* 1961.

In 1805 the Ashanti, seeking new conquests among the coastal tribes, became involved in the first of seven wars against the British which were to be the principal feature of nineteenth-century Gold Coast history and eventually were to result in the secular eclipse of the Ashanti state. These Ashanti invasions coupled with the 1807 British interdict against the slave trade completely reversed the political situation on the coast. Raids before had been desirable since they provided the raw material of the slave trade. Now the white traders could only prosper in the traffic of palm oil, timber and gold, and this trade could go on only where peace and order prevailed. In 1821, in an attempt to achieve this, the British revoked the charters of the companies and took over the forts in the name of the Crown. It is worth noting here that, as has happened in our own time, high idealism unbacked by hard thinking can cause more suffering than it alleviates: one of the immediate results of the outlawing of the slave trade was to give a terrific impetus to the practice of large-scale human sacrifice, a custom not unknown to the Ashanti. The blood-bath which followed the end of the slave trade was in part an appeal to the old gods for success against the enemies of the Ashanti; it was also a logical means of relieving society of unwanted mouths to feed which, in the days of the slave trade, had had a commercial value. Slaves and prisoners were sacrificed by the Ashanti on any public occasion and, at the death of one Asantehene [king of Ashanti] 2,600 were slaughtered. When the British finally took Kumasi in 1873, they found a brass bowl five feet in diameter which had been used to collect the human blood necessary to wash the stools of dead kings. In any case, the closing of the coastal market for slaves meant only that more were destined to make the killing trek across the Sahara to the harsher servitude of Asia Minor, many of them after undergoing castration, which increased their commercial value. By outlawing the European slave trade before first being in a position to police the religious customs of Africa and to cut the Arab slave routes, the Western nations relieved their own consciences and condemned thousands of Africans either to ritual murder, death in the desert or lives of misery in the Arab world.

The first governor, Sir Charles Macarthy, soon found himself embroiled in an Ashanti war. Through a series of blunders he managed to get himself cut off from his base by the main Ashanti army at the village of Nsamankow. When his ammunition ran short, Macarthy sent an officer back for reserve supplies. This gentleman arrived at the eleventh hour with four kegs, which were eagerly opened. Three were found to contain macaroni. This not being very lethal stuff unless consumed in quantity, the Ashanti cut up the British column, wounded Macarthy (who committed suicide to avoid capture), and returned to Kumasi bearing the governor's head, which is said to be nicely pickled and a big ju-ju [an object considered to contain a spirit] around Kumasi to this day.

The Ashanti came down again in 1826 under the personal leadership of the Asantehene and at Akantamasu a battle was fought which decided the fate of the Gold Coast. At a crucial moment the British fired a barrage of rockets which completely unmanned the Ashanti. The Asantehene, wounded seven times and depressed by the news that the Golden Stool had been captured, was seating himself on a keg of gunpowder preparatory to giving himself the kind of send-off which such a military disgrace required when news came that the Golden Stool had been recaptured and spirited away. The Asantehene consented to live, paid the British an indemnity of 4,000 ounces of gold and gave hostages.

Weary of its unprofitable responsibility, the British government withdrew from the Gold Coast leaving administration in the hands of the merchants. As their governor the merchants chose a man little known today, although he must rank with Warren Hastings and Cecil Rhodes as one of the great men of the Age of Imperialism. George Maclean, who came to the coast in 1828 and remained there until his death nineteen years later, did more to make possible the Ghana of today than any other man. Armed with little money but much patience, without recourse to arms he virtually ended the slave trade, eradicated human sacrifice and gradually grafted Western culture onto the lives of the people. When the British government returned a few years before his death, Maclean stepped aside and accepted the lesser post of Judicial Adviser. He followed the path of honesty and understanding and when he died, the natives, who are no mean judges of human nature, gave him the funeral of an African king.

In 1844 the British formalized their position in the Gold Coast by signing a bond with the chiefs, who acknowledged their jurisdiction. Six years later they bought from Denmark her five remaining forts and in 1872, 274 years of Dutch rule ended with the sale of Holland's remaining posts to Britain. From that date until 1957 Britain was the boss.

In 1896 another Ashanti war broke out, Kumasi was captured and the British demanded an impossibly high indemnity of £357,000 in gold. When this was not paid, the Asantehene, the Queen Mother and other important chiefs were accommodated in the Seychelles [islands in the Indian Ocean] . . . the palace was looted, and the sacred trees and altars dynamited. Not content with this, Sir Frederick Hodgson, the new governor, in 1900 demanded the surrender of the Golden Stool so that he might sit on it. This was an unimaginable sacrilege. Not even the Asantehene himself may sit upon the stool, which contains the soul of the nation, and always rests on its side atop a stool of its own. . . . For his stupidity Hodgson was besieged in Kumasi for two months before the Ashanti were finally subdued, more chiefs were deported to the Seychelles and the warriors were disarmed. It was the last Ashanti war and the kingdom was formally annexed. In 1924 the Asantehene was allowed to return from exile.

With peace and a solid economy firmly based on cocoa, diamonds, gold, manganese and timber, the Gold Coast made advances in all fields during the first half of this century. When it became obvious at the end of World War II that colonialism was a dead duck, the Gold Coast was the obvious place for the British to begin their "creative abdication" in Africa. In 1946 the Legislative Council, established as early as 1850, was reconstituted and the Gold Coast became the first territory in British Africa with a black majority in its political institutions.

The Rapid Pace of Annexation

After the Conference of Berlin, Britain, France, Germany, and Italy proceeded with their imperialist ambitions. Italy's defeat by the Abyssinian army in 1896 ended her expansionist plans and left her with two East African enclaves: Eritrea and Somaliland. The Germans, after much negotiating with the British in 1886 and 1890, formalized their encroachments in West Africa (Togo and Cameroon) and East Africa (Tanganyika). The British in East Africa had a protectorate over Uganda and the East African Protectorate, later called Kenya.

French and British rivalries in West Africa were intense. The French established control over Dahomey (1892) and the Ivory Coast Protectorate (1893). Nigeria was the only nation in West Africa where the British were able to push inland, and there they succeeded because of the energies of Sir George Goldie and the Royal Niger Company. A series of treaties made between 1890 and 1898 settled the French and British boundary disputes.

The Upper Nile valley was another scene of intense rivalry between these two powers. The French sent Marchand east and the British sent Kitchener south in 1898 to lay claim to the Sudan. After several months of tension following the intersection of the two expeditions at Fashoda, the French gave way.

British rule in East and southern Africa was furthered by the fabulous Cecil Rhodes. Through his powerful South Africa Company, based on the wealth of diamond and gold discoveries in South Africa, he successfully sought increasing government support in pursuit of his dream of a Cape-to-Cairo railroad. Britain took over Bechuanaland; then, through the South Africa Company, treaties were made with Lobengula, the chief of the Matabele, and the settlement of Rhodesia was begun. Central Africa was further brought under British control by the establishment in 1889 of the Protectorate of Nyasaland.

Cecil Rhodes' ambitions in southern Africa drove a deeper wedge between the Boer Republics and the English community in South Africa. The policies of the British High Commissioner, Lord Milner, who wanted to Anglicize the Boers, led eventually to the Boer War in 1899. British victory in 1902 assured control of South Africa and led to the creation of the Union of South Africa in 1911.

The history of the scramble for African colonies is filled with stories of personal courage as well as almost unbelievable ambitions for personal empire. Until recently, historians have concentrated on the European participants and policies. We are only now beginning to learn about the African leaders who attempted to defend their lands from alien invaders.

PART IV

The Development of Colonial Systems Between World War I and World War II

Between the Berlin Act of 1885 and World War I, all of sub-Saharan Africa was partitioned by the European powers. Liberia remained the unimportant exception. After World War I and the readjustment of ex-German territories, the colonial systems of the various European powers in Africa took final shape.

The modern African states are emerging from these colonial foundations. To a large extent their strengths and weaknesses are inherited from the colonial administrations which ushered them into the 20th century. Not only the physical accomplishments of the administrating power, such as transportation systems and development of resources, but their settlement policy, social attitudes, and political philosophy—all have had a direct bearing on a colony's future as an emerging state.

The Influence of World War I

The African situation added to the international tensions that preceded World War I. German territorial ambitions in Africa, as much as anything else, had moved Britain to settle her differences with France and Russia, thus forming the Triple Entente. The most significant change brought about by the peace settlement was the application of the "Mandate System" to ex-German territories.

THE MANDATE SYSTEM

From Walter Fitzgerald, *Africa: A Social, Economic and Political Geography of Its Major Regions*, 1957.

It is claimed that a new principle in colonial government was introduced by the statesmen of the Allied Powers at the Paris Peace Conference [1918] and thereafter applied to the confiscated lands of the dismembered German and Turkish Empires. The case for depriving Germany of every vestige of her colonial domain, which was mainly located in Africa, rested on the traditional usage of penalizing the loser in war and on the argument that Germany had proved herself to be unfitted for the role of colonial administrator.

However, instead of a division of the spoils of war—mainly tropical lands—between the victorious Powers a system of international guardianship and control of the confiscates' territories was devised. All member states of the League of Nations were to cooperate in the new enterprise, though for the sake of convenience a particular member state was to be selected, by reason of its special opportunities or experience, for the actual work of administration, it being understood that the League should always retain the right of surveillance. It was agreed, moreover, that administration by the Mandatory Power should terminate when the indigenous community, having benefited by the training in self-government which the Mandatory Power was expected to confer, showed capacity to accept, without danger to itself, the gift of independent statehood. A Mandatory Power was thus in the position of the trustee of an estate, whose heir had not yet come of age.

This experiment in international cooperation was not without precedent, for it will be remembered that the

Congress of Berlin (1884–85) had initiated the principle of international supervision in respect of the newly discovered regions of tropical Africa, though it is also true that very little had resulted from the attempted application of the principle.

Great Britain, the Union of South Africa, France and Belgium thus received separately mandates to administer, on behalf of the League, the several ex-German colonies of Africa. Italy, though very willing to accept the responsibilities and privileges of a Mandatory Power in either Africa or the former Turkish Empire of Asia, was overlooked in the distribution of territory and later complained strongly against her exclusion. The Mandatory States agreed to permit freedom of trade, within the territories they administered, to member States of the League, and they were expected very definitely to observe certain guarantees relating to the integrity of native society and tribal lands. As from time to time one or other of the Mandatory Powers has been known in its own interests to violate one or more terms of its charter of government there were critics who claimed, with considerable evidence in support, that "mandated territory" was synonymous with "annexed territory." On the other hand, there have been instances of adherence to the mandate which have encouraged hopes for the success of the international experiment in colonial government.

The allocation of the mandates in Africa has added to the overseas responsibilities of France and Great Britain, especially. In East Africa the greater part of the former German Protectorate, now Tanganyika Territory, is entrusted to Great Britain; the remaining part, comprising the districts of Ruanda and Urundi, which are situated on the high eastern rim of the Congo Basin, have been allotted to the Belgian Congo. The natives of Ruanda-Urundi have not been properly considered in the new political division, for they have been divorced from their natural association with the grassland peoples of the East African Plateau who are of similar culture and traditions to themselves.

Former German South-West Africa was administered

by the Union of South Africa first under Class C Mandate, the terms of which enabled the Union virtually to annex the territory as a fifth province of the federation. The ex-German "colonies" of West-Central Africa, namely the Cameroons and Togoland, were allotted mainly to France, although in each case a strip of territory of considerable significance was added to the British "colonies" of Nigeria and the Gold Coast respectively.

The Second World War destroyed the League of Nations, but after it the United Nations Organization claimed responsibility for all Mandated Territories. Great Britain, France and Belgium have undertaken the international trusteeship, with responsibility to the U.N.O., of the ex-German territories of Africa, of which they formerly held the mandates. The Union of South Africa continues to administer South-West Africa, with all the responsibilities of international mandate, as confirmed by the International Court of Justice at The Hague in 1950 [the Republic of South Africa, however, refuses to recognize U.N. jurisdiction over South-West Africa]. Of the former Italian colonies, Somalia [was] until 1960 under Italian authority; Eritrea, after being administered by Great Britain from the end of the war, was federated with Ethiopia in September, 1952, while Libya became an independent kingdom in the previous year.

British West Africa

In considering British Africa, it is necessary to separate the western dependencies from the eastern ones because of differences in background and problems.

British West Africa consisted originally of six territories: Gambia, Sierra Leone, the Gold Coast, Nigeria, British Togoland, and the British Cameroons. The last two were mandated territories taken from Germany at the end of World War I. Once the slave trade was ended early in the nineteenth century, British interest in West Africa lagged. What energy Britain chose to invest in African ventures during this period was concentrated on the Nile and its approaches. This was a result

of Britain's historic preoccupation with maintaining its
"lifeline" to India through the Mediterranean and Suez.

GOVERNMENT BY INDIRECT RULE: AN INEXPENSIVE METHOD

In West Africa, Britain assumed minimum responsibilities and developed an efficient and inexpensive system
to govern a large area. The following selections describe that system.

From George H. T. Kimble, *Tropical Africa,* 1960.

As was indicated earlier, democratic institutions of a sort
existed in parts of Africa long before the British administrator got there. Many African groups were in the habit
of administering their affairs through councils of elders.
While the members of these councils were seldom chosen
by popular vote, their powers were strictly circumscribed
and frequently subject to abrogation. Even among those
peoples who believed in "chiefly" rule, democratic procedures were quite common. It was customary for the successor to a dead chief to be chosen by the chief's own people through their councils, and these councils had an
uncanny knack of choosing the right man. In the best
democratic tradition, his power could not be bequeathed.

To begin with, the British administrator had difficulty,
understandably enough, in spotting exactly how some of
the African's political institutions worked. More than
once, he found himself backing the wrong man. But at
least he was generally wise enough not to interfere unduly
with the African's institutions. In some cases, it was not
so much a matter of wisdom as of want of men and
money to do otherwise. When Sir Frederick (later Lord)
Lugard introduced, around the turn of the century, the
policy of indirect rule in northern Nigeria by recognizing
the existing administrations of the *emirates,* he did so on
grounds of common sense and economy. As time went
on, though, British administrators everywhere began to
see that tribal institutions could and should be developed
to equip the Africans for the larger life of the Common-

wealth. To this end, customary courts of justice were given official status and considerable powers in the handling of civil and criminal cases. British administrative officers ceased to try cases, except those of a serious nature; they became instead advisers to the native courts. Along with these duties, the chiefs and their councils were given executive responsibilities, as "native authorities," with power to make by-laws and see that they were obeyed. Later they were allowed to levy local taxes and spend them for the benefit of their people. "They became," says Bradley, "embryo 'local authorities' in the modern British sense, and local government was born." (Unfortunately, the chiefs and elders proved less successful in the executive than in the judicial sphere, probably because their functions, except in time of war, had been almost exclusively judicial. They had never had to collect taxes, make roads, control farming methods, or try to improve water supplies and housing conditions.)

THE IMPLICATIONS OF INDIRECT RULE

From Immanuel Wallerstein, *Africa: The Politics of Independence,* 1961.

The men who go overseas for an imperial power often are romantics. In British areas these men got more leeway than in other colonies, often because they were the only ones really interested in colonial policy. The romantics among the soldiers teamed up with the romantics among the anthropologists, and it may be said that out of this union emerged the famous policy of "indirect rule," that policy of allowing the powers of the traditional rulers to remain intact to the maximum degree consonant with imperial rule. Though Lord Lugard, when he initiated this policy in Northern Nigeria, may have had in mind primarily the fact that he had an inadequate number of soldiers and administrators to govern such a large area directly, the extension of the policy elsewhere and its emergence as an ideology can be traced to the responsive note it touched in British hearts.

Though the British may have felt it their duty to accept

the "white man's burden" and bear the responsibility of advancing African interests, they did not assume that Africa . . . one day would be an extension of Britain, or Africans one day British. The bias of the administrator —and more importantly, of the Briton at home—was in favor of the traditional chief in colonial government and not the Oxford-trained lawyer, who was felt to be somehow out of place. In short, British paternalism took the form of pressures to preserve custom, to maintain distance between Britain and Africa, between Briton and African.

The Crown Colony System

The British policy of indirect rule worked under an administrative system which came to be referred to as the Crown Colony system. Typically, it consisted of a Governor appointed by the Crown, an Executive Council made up of the Governor's administrative assistants, and a Legislative Council. This latter body included both "official" members (people with specific government jobs in the colonial administration) and "unofficial" members (private citizens in the area). The unofficial members of the Legislative Council could be appointed by the Governor or elected by the community.

This last feature provided the Crown Colony system with its flexibility. As the people of an area became more ready for self-government and as their demands for it increased, the number of unofficial members could be enlarged, the right to vote could be extended to more people in the area, and the authority of the Legislative Council could be enlarged.

In recent times there was never much question in the British mind that her West African territories would become self-governing. Any disagreements between the British administration and African leaders usually centered around the question, "How soon?" The British never moved quite as fast as the African nationalists wanted them to. Yet, in view of the Belgian tactics in the Congo, the British gradualism may be seen to have some merit.

In spite of tensions about the timetable for independence, the political evolution of West Africa was comparatively painless for one very important reason: there was no white-settler community to complicate the issue. Most of the area was not climatically hospitable to Europeans. Therefore, the European population of these areas consisted of administrative and military personnel, missionaries, and a few merchants. These people were few in number and not likely to develop the deep sense of vested interest that the English farmer in Kenya or the Boer in South Africa developed. Racial tensions have been at a minimum in West Africa, and political evolution to independence was comparatively easy.

British East Africa

British East Africa consisted of the Protectorates of Uganda and Zanzibar, the Trusteeship Territory (ex-Mandate) of Tanganyika, and the Crown Colony of Kenya. Uganda and Zanzibar have no European-settler communities to speak of. In these areas political problems could be dealt with much as in West Africa. Kenya has been a different story.

Nineteenth-century British policy attached more importance to East Africa than to West Africa because of greater interest in the Mediterranean than in Africa proper. Security of the Mediterranean "lifeline" to the East meant a position in Egypt, which meant control of the Nile. Therefore control of the sources of the Nile was a logical extension of the British grand design. Thus they were intensely interested in Uganda and determined to hold their position there. But Uganda was landlocked and could be reached best through the region later called Kenya.

The British wanted to end the Arab slave trade in East Africa, which still flourished after 1890. One way to do this was to make the slave caravan an uneconomical mode of transportation by building competing railroads. It cost two or three hundred times as much to carry a ton of goods by caravan as by rail. Further stimulus was added by the aggressive activities of a

German agent who was clearly planning to add a section of East Africa to the German Empire.

These reasons moved a reluctant British government to authorize the building of a railroad from the east coast to Uganda. The process was difficult because of the terrain and lack of skilled labor. It cost £9500 a mile to build, and proceeded to run at a loss of £150,000 a year. It did end a famine among the Akamba people in 1898–99 by bringing in rice, but continued to operate in the red. From the British point of view it had to be made to pay for itself.

The answer seemed to be to attract European settlers to Kenya. With this in mind the Crown issued an Order in Council in 1901 which took government control over large (and undefined) tracts of land.

After World War I the government encouraged returning soldiers to settle in Kenya by offering them government lands free, or on very favorable terms. This would work toward solving three problems: (1) it would lessen unemployment in England, (2) it would provide customers for the railroads, (3) it would enlarge the white population of Kenya and help to control the African population. Many Africans had served in the British Army during the War and had been encouraged to shoot white men—Germans. The British authorities feared that they might have developed the habit and wanted white reinforcements on hand if necessary.

THE ATTRACTION OF KENYA

Here is a brief description of the Kenya Highlands and its potential for European settlement. Occupation of these valuable lands by whites was a source of racial bitterness in Kenya, for the African was left the poorer land.

From Walter Fitzgerald, *Africa: A Social, Economic and Political Geography of Its Major Regions,* 1957.

This region [the Kenya highlands] has marked physical individuality and, from the standpoint of human relations —especially the contacts of native and immigrant societies—is the most critical land in East Africa. It represents but a small fraction—about one-fifth of the total area of Kenya Colony, and yet, excepting the lofty and vast plateau of Abyssinia, it is the most considerable tract of highland, exceeding 5000 feet, in tropical Africa. . . .

The heart of the Kenya Highlands, which may be conveniently called the Kikuyu Plateau, stretches from the neighborhood of Nairobi to the southern slopes of alternating ridges and river valleys. This is typical of the landscape; yet the Kikuyu Plateau, ranging in altitude from 5000 feet—as around Nairobi—to 8000 feet, at the edge of the Rift Valley, is one of the most densely peopled parts of East Africa and is characterized by extensive and very successful farming, both European and native. Much of the soil, usually deep and rich, is derived from soft volcanic tuffs that supported dense forest down to the time of the incoming of the Kikuyu people. It is very retentive of moisture on account of its fine-grained texture, and remains moist even in time of drought: moreover, it is very light to work and is, therefore, suited to the hoe-labor of the natives. . . .

The foregoing brief description will help to indicate the desirability of the Kenya Highlands from the standpoint of European colonization. In this equatorial region the altitude zone, 6000–7000 feet, is the most satisfactory to the health as well as to the agricultural enterprise of the white immigrants, although the main center of their civilization —Nairobi—is considerably lower (5400 feet). . . . The equable equatorial climate, opposed to prolonged maintenance of vigor, is relieved of its most trying feature—excessive temperature—by high altitude; so that at Nairobi, for example, there is no monthly mean higher than 66°F, whilst most districts of European occupation experience even more temperate conditions.

The rich red volcanic soil, highly suited to mixed farming, and particularly, in some districts, to arabica coffee, covers a large proportion of the plateau highlands and adds a strong inducement to the farmer-settler, so that here—more especially in the districts to the east of the Rift Valley—is the largest colony of Europeans established on the African plateau north of the Zambezi River. From its beginnings in 1903, the European population has grown slowly to the number of about 46,500.

THE MASAI AGREEMENTS

The introduction of a European farming population to a land already inhabited by agricultural or pastoral people was bound to present problems. We will see later just how different the African concept of land ownership is from the European idea. But, even without this mutual misunderstanding, the situation created tension and friction.

The following is an account of how the problem of land was handled in dealing with one of Kenya's proudest groups of people, the Masai.

From Zoe Marsh and G. W. Kingsnorth, *An Introduction to the History of East Africa*, 1957.

The Masai agreement of 1904

Linked with the coming of the early settlers was the problem of the Masai. According to a rough estimate, in 1904 they owned 50,000 head of cattle and 600,000 sheep, they themselves being about 45,000 strong. They roamed over a vast stretch of country which included the land north and south of the new railway line. In view of the danger of clashes between the Masai warriors and the white settlers, it was suggested that the Masai be moved into two reserves linked by a corridor, half a mile wide. The northern reserve was Laikipia and consisted of some 4500 square miles, and the southern, which was of about 4350 square miles, ran down to the border of German East Africa. The area provided was, therefore, generous, but the Masai were given no alternative, and there is some evidence that the tribe were rather unwilling to abandon their claims to the grazing grounds in the Rift Valley.

The Masai agreement of 1911

The agreement covering this move was made in 1904. In a few years it was seen to be working badly: the presence of tick-born disease in the corridor resulted, for example, in the tribe becoming split into two. Lenana, the great Laibon [chief] of the Masai, suggested, therefore, that the tribe should be reunited in one reserve. If the Masai moved from the northern reserve it would mean that Laikipia would be freed for European settlement. Hence the tribe were offered an increase of the reserve in the south to 15,177 square miles, or approximately one and a half square miles of land for each Masai household, which averaged five people. There were complications, however, in carrying out the move, and during this time Lenana sent the following message from his deathbed: "Tell my people to obey the government as they have done during my life. Tell the Laikipia Masai to move with their cattle to the Loieta plains." This message had considerable influence, and the northern Masai expressed their wish to move south. In 1911 a new agreement was drawn up and orders were given a year later for the move to be completed, but when the time came some of the northern Masai changed their minds and asked for the move to be canceled. Eventually, after considerable further agitation, it was completed in 1913. The manner in which the move was carried out has been strongly criticized. Sir Frederick Jackson, for instance, after saying that he was at first against the move wrote in *Early Days in East Africa*, "I then, in the interests of the Masai themselves, changed my view, and was in favor of the move. I am, however, thankful that I had nothing whatsoever to do with the negotiations that led to it, nor with the move itself."

The Carter Land Commission

The Masai were not the only tribe for whom reserves were suggested. There was even a recommendation from the Land Committee that a European reserve should be made. This was not done, but after 1904 native reserves were set aside. In 1915 the government declared that the reserves were Crown Lands and their boundaries were defined by the Crown Lands Ordinance of 1926. Afterwards it was claimed that some of the land which had been included in certain of the native reserves had later been taken for European settlement. Although only relatively small portions of land were involved, it was felt that steps should be taken to remove the grievances felt by the Africans. The boundaries of the reserves were therefore formally proclaimed in 1926, and in 1932 the government appointed a Royal Commission, known as the Carter Land Commission, to investigate the question of native lands. The report of this commission led to adjustments in land which were accepted by the government as the final settlement of claims based on past injustice. A substantial area of land was also added to the native reserves to meet permanent economic needs. The native areas were then transferred from the Crown to the Africans themselves. Their rights to these lands were guaranteed for ever and a Native Lands Trust Board was set up to watch over them. The boundaries of the Highlands area, in which Europeans were to have a privileged position, were also defined and safeguarded by a Highlands Board. These changes created native areas of 52,097 square miles. By comparison the extent of the Highlands in 1950 was 16,173 square miles including 3979 square miles of forest reserve, which is not considered to be available for settlement. The difference between these figures and the total area of Kenya is largely made up of the Turkana and Northern Frontier districts, which are inhabited by nomad tribes observing no fixed boundaries. . . .

Elections to the Legislative Council

In both England and East Africa the end of the war [World War I] brought an extension of the franchise to those on whose support their country had relied, and in 1920 the first election was held to the Legislative Council, which was now to include eleven unofficial members chosen by the European community. Two Europeans were also chosen as unofficial members of the Executive Council, one of whom was Lord Delamere [the acknowledged leader of the settler group]. In this position he was to have a degree of influence which often surprised those who did not realize the value of his experience in a land where officials were not permanent residents.

Devonshire White Paper

The grant of elected representatives to the Europeans alone did not long go unchallenged, and in 1920 the Indians demanded the vote on the same terms. With this they linked the rights to acquire land in the Highlands and to have an unchecked entry into East Africa. Both these claims were strongly opposed by the European settlers, who looked to Lord Delamere to lead them. He accepted this responsibility and led a deputation to England to lay their case before the Secretary of State for the Colonies. A settlement was finally reached in 1923. . . . The White Paper which was issued in 1923 by the Colonial Secretary, the Duke of Devonshire, to cover the terms of the settlement contained also the following important statement:

> Primarily, Kenya is an African territory, and H.M. Government think it necessary definitely to record their considered opinion that the interests of the African native must be paramount, and that if and when those interests and the interests of the immigrant races should conflict, the former should prevail.

This was qualified by the further statement that:

> Obviously the interests of the other communities, European, Indian and Arab, must generally be safeguarded. Whatever the circumstances in which members of these communities have entered Kenya, there will be no drastic action or reversal of measures already introduced.

KENYATTA: EAST AFRICAN TENSIONS PERSONIFIED

The following selection tells something of what it was like to live under British rule and in conflict with the settlers' demands in East Africa. It describes the conditions which were to mold Jomo Kenyatta's intellectual ideals, and suggests a possible course of action which was to become part of Kenyan history in the 1950's: the Mau Mau uprising.

From David Reed, "Jomo Kenyatta, Africa's Man of Mystery," *Reader's Digest*, December 1961.

The old man is Jomo Kenyatta, the mystery man of Africa. Free once more after nine years of prison and enforced exile, he is one of the most controversial personalities in the world today. Kenya's white officials and settlers regard him as a man of diabolic cunning and hold him directly responsible for the savage Mau Mau uprising of a few years ago. Kenya's six million Africans, by contrast, see him as the George Washington of their country, a living symbol of Africa's aspirations for freedom, knowledge and dignity.

In a very real sense, Jomo Kenyatta is Africa itself, with all its conflicts and contradictions. Grandson of a witch doctor, he grew up in a murky, haunted world, where the spirits of dead tribesmen continued to hover above the huts and ridgetops watching over the fortunes of their descendants. As a boy, Jomo learned to throw a spear with deadly accuracy. In those years, too, he drank deep of witchcraft and there are those who say that the delectable taste still lingers on his lips. Yet this same man became a familiar figure in the intellectual salons of England. His charm and razor-sharp mind won him the friendship of many influential Englishmen, and he even hobnobbed with European royalty.

For most of his life Kenyatta has been torn in two directions. As a tribal man, he glories in the tribal past as the golden age of Africa. Yet he also is fond of classical music and impressionist painting. Although Kenyatta has abandoned formal Christianity, he often reads the Bible, as well as works on Oriental religions. A polygamist, he has three wives, one English and two African.

Today [1961], despite his 71 years, Kenyatta is in good health and mentally alert. His eyes are piercing, almost hypnotic. An orator with the skill of a Castro or a Hitler, he can move masses of Africans to tears, rage or laughter. Wherever he goes, Kenyatta carries with him, chained to his wrist, a zebra-tail fly whisk, the symbol of a chief's authority.

Kenyatta's real name was Kamau wa Ngengi—Kamau son of Ngengi. His father, a wealthy man by tribal standards, owned much land and many cattle and goats. His grandfather was a mundo mugo, or good witch doctor: he could foretell the future, make rain and remove evil spells —all, as with any specialist, for a hefty consideration. When the old man made his rounds, he allowed his grandson to carry his bag of magic. And Kamau, trotting up and down the steep ridges of Kikuyuland at his grandfather's heels, saw much that marveled him.

On one occasion, the boy took part in a rain-making ceremony. The method: strangle a lamb, cut it open and drape the intestines on a tree, pour blood on the tree, then feast on the meat and burn the leftovers. Years later, Kenyatta wrote with faintly concealed awe: "Our prayers were quickly answered, for, even before the sacred fires had ceased to burn, torrential rain came upon us. . . ."

One day while guarding his family's cattle, ten-year-old Kamau ran off to a Church of Scotland mission station near Nairobi. There he was taught to read and write English, trained in carpentry, and baptized "Johnstone" Kamau. Eventually he went to seek his fortune in Nairobi, then a bustling little shantytown. He became a clerk in a government office, later a meter reader for the city. He was something of a dandy in those days, fond of dancing, and popular, then as now, with women. He took on a new last name, Kenyatta, referring, in Kikuyu, to a beaded belt he wore; and in time he dropped his Christian name to become Jomo—"Burning Spear."

Racial strife, even in those years, ran high in Kenya.

Although there were fewer than 10,000 white settlers, among the millions of Africans, they firmly believed in their eventual right to rule the country. Heavy taxes were imposed on the Africans to force them to leave their tribal areas and work for the white farmers—usually at subsistence wages. And to make sure that few would remain behind, Africans were not allowed to grow coffee and other cash crops.

For semieducated "mission boys" like Kenyatta, what particularly rankled was the color bar. They were relegated to the lowest jobs, barred from white hotels, restaurants and clubs. Years later, Kenyatta would write: "In the old order of the African society, with all of the evils that are supposed to be connected with it, a man was a man. But today an African is like a horse which moves only in the direction in which the rider pulls the rein."

It is a tribute to Kikuyu intelligence that in the early 1920's, only a few decades after the coming of the whites, the Kikuyu had already formed a Western-style political movement. Kenyatta rose quickly in it, and soon was editing a Kikuyu-language newspaper. Then in 1929 he and a companion journeyed to London to present the grievances of his people directly to the British government.

But the government was not moved by the two "upstart colonials." Disappointed, Kenyatta drifted into the waiting arms of British communists and fellow travelers. For a time, he shared a flat with Paul Robeson, the American Negro singer. On two occasions he visited the Soviet Union, for a total of five months. An official report prepared recently for the British government charges that Kenyatta joined the Communist Party about this time, and adds that it was "reliably reported" he studied revolutionary tactics at the Lenin School in Moscow. Most people believe, however, that Kenyatta dropped his communist connections shortly thereafter. . . .

French Africa

French Black Africa, as distinct from the French-controlled Muslim areas of North Africa, consisted of French Equatorial Africa, French West Africa, the French Cameroons (a trusteeship territory), and Madagascar.

Unlike other colonizing powers, France had the idealism of her Revolution to reconcile with colonialism. A decree from the revolutionary period abolished slavery (1792) and stated that "all men, without distinction of color, domiciled in French colonies, are French citizens, and enjoy all the rights assured by the constitution."

From this stated ideal sprang the political, social, and economic relationships between France and her dependencies. The application of this ideal was uneven. Senegal, in French West Africa, enjoyed the most consistent administration of it, while, ironically, the mandates received short measure.

In the political realm, France soon abandoned the idea of "colonies" and began to consider these areas as "overseas territories," each with elected representatives in the French government in Paris. Many Africans have sat in the French legislature, and more than one has served as a member of the cabinet of various governments. At best, however, the African population was grossly underrepresented. At worst, the principle was ignored and supplanted with authoritarianism; African citizens became subjects. Only since the end of World War II has France, under De Gaulle's leadership, made a strenuous effort to reconcile theory with practice.

The social development of "Overseas France" was keyed to the word "assimilation." Educated and westernized Africans were to be treated as social equals with Frenchmen. This worked as far as it went, but it had two glaring weaknesses: it assumed that every African wanted to abandon his culture for that of France, and the education and other means by which the cultural transition could be made were very scarce. As a result, only a very few Africans became assimilated.

Toward the end of the nineteenth century, the ideal of assimilation was abandoned for the more easily reached goal of "association." This meant that a small elite would be educated and Europeanized. This elite then would be "associated" with the Frenchmen in passing European culture on down to the masses of their countrymen. This group never reached very large proportions.

Economic relationships between France and her "overseas territories" were least affected by liberal idealism. African industries were often discouraged, and tariffs helped create monopolies that enabled France to exploit the areas to her benefit. These periods of economic restriction were mingled with periods of economic neglect when France itself was politically unstable in the late nineteenth and early twentieth centuries.

A COMMENT AGAINST PATERNALISM

Exceptions, and special considerations, of course, mark the general pattern of French West African policy and development. One example is Guinea which of all the French African territory was the most difficult to subdue. The French set up a harsh military administration to which, because it was an unpleasant and uncoveted assignment, all the misfits in the French Army were sent. This did nothing to improve European–African rapport.

With this background, it is perhaps inevitable that when independence came to French Africa, Guinea would choose to cut all ties with France and turn at first to Russia for advice and aid. It is just as logical that Sekou Touré, Guinea's first president, should have come up through the ranks of the labor-union movement rather than from the class of "assimilated" Africans as did most of the other statesmen of French Africa. It may be assumed then, that Touré was more hostile to France than Eboue, Houphouet-Boigny, and Senghor, leaders of former French territories which continued a close relationship with France upon their independence.

In the following reading, President Touré explains why he feels that restrictive French-colonial economic policy outweighed the advantages of "assimilation," and why paternalism is bound to fail.

From Sekou Touré, "Africa's Destiny," in James Duffy and Robert A. Manners, eds., *Africa Speaks,* 1961.

The failure of the colonial concept stems precisely from the fact that the colonial powers, holding the means for the development of wealth, did not use these means to resolve the disequilibrium existing between the standard of living of the colonized peoples and that of sovereign peoples, but on the contrary they accentuated this disequilibrium by the systematic exploitation of goods and raw materials, maintaining the populations in the most degrading poverty and dependence. There is no longer any need to conduct the trial of colonialism insomuch as events and history have clearly pronounced themselves for its complete disappearance. . . .

It is clear that paternalism will be condemned to failure. It has often been noted that, to succeed in their endeavors, certain governments assure themselves of the cooperation of African men or organizations by placing these latter under some obligation to act only in line with these governments' wishes. This is a policy of puppets which will succeed less and less in Africa, because the peoples are more and more organized and determined to fight against all forms of domination, even that by the intermediary of African groups or powers.

For centuries our continent has known paternalism, one might even say various shades of paternalism, depending upon the temperament of the colonizer. But this long practice of paternalism brought no valid progress to Africa. On the contrary, it has taken from certain African leaders their sense of dignity and responsibility, and has rendered them less fit to translate the original virtues of their civilization. For such creatures, corrupted by the colonial powers, is it not shameful to be used in these decisive hours against the most legitimate aspirations of their peoples?

AN AFRICAN SPEAKS AGAINST ASSIMILATION

Our study of the French will be more complete with a look at "assimilation" through the eyes of an African from a non-French area who can study French policy objectively.

Nadbaningi Sithole, an educator and statesman from Rhodesia, wrote a book commenting on colonial systems and their relation to the nationalist mood sweeping Africa in 1959. Sithole's analysis of the French system follows.

From Nadbaningi Sithole, *African Nationalism*, 1959.

But the French system of assimilation has glaring defects since it holds the Frenchman or French culture to be the ultimate goal for the African. It creates the false impression upon many African minds that there is nothing higher than to be a Frenchman, and many an African now resents having to direct all his efforts to becoming a Frenchman some day. The peoples of the world now live in glass houses and their very intimate weaknesses and moral frailties are on public view. The age of subtle pretensions has had its day. The Frenchman can no longer successfully pretend to the African that he is a paragon of excellence. The African is now turning away from his French-aroused desire to become a Frenchman. He wants to remain African and enjoy life to its fullest without being deprived of his rights and privileges on the pretext that he does not look and behave like a Frenchman. It seems to be true all over Africa that the deluded African self that has been on a wild goose chase—becoming Portuguese or French—is returning to its old self. African consciousness, which had been pushed into the background by the advent of European powers since the scramble for Africa in the nineteenth century, is now coming to the fore irresistibly. This new fact of African consciousness as a people renders the French system of assimilation anachronistic.

Belgian Africa

In the section on the scramble for Africa we saw the sordid beginning of the Belgian interest in Africa under Leopold II. After the Belgian government assumed responsibility for the vast Congo territory, sweeping changes in its administration were made.

The Belgians worked from the theory that to minister carefully to the physical needs of the African would mean that he would have no need for or interest in self-government. The validity of this theory has been tested by events which are now history.

The next reading describes the Belgian theory and its application.

BELGIAN COLONIAL THEORY AND PRACTICE

From Alan P. Merriam, *Congo: Background of Conflict*, 1961.

There has probably never been a Belgian policy formally equivalent to the British idea of eventual self-government or the French policy of eventual integration with French metropolitan life. Belgian policy has been sternly paternalistic, with control over the colony the paramount idea. The primary concern has been with economic development, and the colony has been controlled by a coalition of state, church, and business cartels in which the government owned large shares of stock. Control was exercised directly by Belgian administrators, with some evidence of indirect rule. Neither the African nor the Belgian residents of the colony had a voice in the government, and the colonial system was directly responsible to the Belgian Parliament in Brussels. At the same time, the Belgians early recognized the problem of labor provision in the new economy and launched a strong policy of technical training for Africans with the result that many Congolese held highly technical jobs. But there has not been an equal amount of liberal education and the Belgians justified this by a policy of "bringing all the people up to-

gether." Since the war, Belgian general policy has probably changed the least. . . .

Paternalism is defined . . . as "the principle of practice, on the part of a government or of any body or person in authority, of managing or regulating the affairs of a
country or community, or of individuals, in the manner of
a father dealing with his children." No sharper definition
of Belgian policy toward the Congolese exists. In looking
back on the Congo before the movements toward independence began, one sees a "model" colony in which the
Africans were regarded as children virtually incapable of
guiding their own destinies, and in which the Belgians
made provision after provision for the welfare of their
charges. Indeed, the protective coating was applied so
thickly and with such thoroughness that for a long time
the Congo seemed impervious to any sort of outside influence. . . .

This tendency toward the isolation of the Congo in political, economic, and social terms was implemented in
a number of ways, whether consciously or unconsciously.
One of these was the discouragement of white settlement
in the Congo; while the express Belgian insistence here
was, and quite rightly so, that the land should not be al-
ienated by Belgian or other white settlers, the result was
to minimize contacts Africans could make with other nationals, either European or African. Few white settlers
actually owned land in the Congo, with the exception of
the Kivu area, and in general technicians and officials
were not encouraged to settle permanently in the colony,
though some did of course. Those Belgians who wished to
settle in the country could not do so without posting a
sizable financial bond which was forfeited if they were
unsuccessful in establishing themselves. The results of this
policy were at least twofold. In the first place, isolation
was strengthened, and contacts between Africans and Europeans were kept relatively small. In the second place,
the policy tended to make the Belgian inhabitants of the
Congo feel temporary. . . .

This attitude was to some extent created and certainly
reinforced by the fact that Belgians as well as Congolese

had no voting rights in the Congo. The aim of this policy was partly democratic and partly protective. In the first instance, the administration felt that if the Congolese were not allowed to vote, neither should the Belgians, and this was simply a matter of honest democracy, although democracy in the reverse. As a protective measure, it was felt that legislative power should be reserved to the administration, not only because the Congo was not ready to vote, but because if Belgians were allowed the franchise they might exert a preponderant influence and thus put into jeopardy the welfare of the Africans in the colony. The nonvoting policy in respect to Belgians certainly did much to stifle initiative, to intensify the feeling of the Belgians in the Congo that their stay was at best temporary, and thus to turn their thinking toward Belgium rather than toward the Congo.

The tremendous degree to which the Congo has been controlled essentially by outside forces, is emphasized in the three-pronged unofficial organization among the State, Church, and business. We have already had occasion to note that the Congo was administered directly from Brussels. The Governor General was the representative of the Crown, all edicts and directives came from Brussels, and the Congolese were not consulted in the administration of their own affairs. Further, the Governor General was relatively little troubled by political affairs in Belgium, had no local legislative assemblies to guide or check his policies, and was responsible directly to the Belgian Parliament. The extent, then, of direction of the Congo on a governmental level from outside its own borders was immense, and local movements when they did exist were in a sense ignored because they represented local rather than Belgian views.

The Roman Catholic Church formed the second dominating power in the Congo, and this to some extent grew logically out of the fact that Belgium itself is more than 90 per cent Catholic. In general Catholics have been dominant in governmental positions, but their greatest influence came through the educational system which was administered in the Congo through missions. In 1925 the Belgian government gave the Catholic church an absolute monopoly on government subsidies to education, and this continued until 1945 when Protestant schools were included: the decree became effective about 1948. In general, then, Catholic influence has been strong in the government, not necessarily a bad thing in itself except as it has created something of an interlocking directorate between Church and State.

The third member of this directorate was business. In 1952 it was reported that five holding companies controlled approximately 70 per cent of all Congo business, a tremendous concentration of economic power. But further, in all five the State held a strong interest, ranging up to 50 per cent, and in other corporations a substantial, sometimes controlling interest. The result was that the State not only collected taxes from the companies, but dividends as well.

The five big companies were Brufina which controlled the Banque de Bruxelles as well as certain industrial organizations; Unilever, through its Belgian subsidiary Huilever, which controlled various vegetable products; Cominière, a mining and agricultural concern; the Banque Empain with strong interests in transportation; and the Société Générale which held mining rights and many other interests. John Gunther has commented on the Société Générale:

> This last immense and proliferating holding company was founded in 1822, has capital reserves of more than two billion Belgian francs ($40,000,000), and is the kind of colossus that might be envisaged if, let us say, the House of Morgan, Anaconda Copper, the Mutual Life Insurance Company of New York, the Pennsylvania Railroad, and various companies producing agricultural products were lumped together, with the United States government as a heavy partner. This is monopoly with a vengeance. The Société Générale is bigger than the other four companies put together. Its interests are extraordinarily multiform. It is much more than a mere bank or holding company. For instance it controls the

CCCI (Compagnie Congolèse et Industrie) which in turn controls subsidiaries in cotton, sugar, pharmaceutical products, automobiles, and beer. It has interests in railroads, insurance, Sabena (the Belgian aviation company), diamonds, cattle, shipping, and cold storage.

But none of this is what makes the Société Générale really count. What counts is the mines. . . .

The financial structure is complicated. Under the Société Générale and the CCCI is an organization known as the Comité Spécial du Katanga. . . . Also an organization known as the Compagnie du Katanga is important. Underneath these is the celebrated Union Minière du Haut Katanga, one of the foremost and most successful mining companies in the world. The Belgian government owns a two-third interest in the CSK, which in turn owns 25 per cent of the Union Minière. . . . About 20 per cent of Union Minière stock is owned by the Société Générale. The Union Minière . . . pays for instance, between 45 and 50 per cent of all Congo taxes.

It should be pointed out that Gunther's last statement has been refuted by Jan Albert Goris who says that "the percentage is not higher than twenty per cent," and a distinction should be clearly made that it was the Congo and not the Belgian government which was the owner of interests in Congo companies; according to Goris "this revenue is used only in the Congo."

In any case, the closed nature of the triumvirate is clear; the government of the Congo is directly responsible to Belgium; the Catholic Church is strongly supported by the government which, quite naturally contains a high percentage of Catholic members; and the large companies are not only dependent upon the government for continued good favor but are also partially, at least, controlled by that government. Such an arrangement represents a strong power system; the Congo was definitely controlled, and almost the entire organization contributed, consciously or unconsciously, to the stifling of independence and independent thought on the part of both Congolese and Belgians.

BELGIAN PATERNALISM

The widely traveled American journalist John Gunther gives us a glimpse of the application of paternalism in the daily life of the Congo. His description applies to the period before independence.

From John Gunther, *Meet the Congo and Its Neighbors,* 1959.

The Belgians, who are a humane and advanced people, like to say that color bar does not exist in the Congo, but of course this is not strictly true. Africans may be given opportunity, but they are not given equality. I have already noted that towns like Leopoldville and Elizabethville have an almost complete system of geographic segregation—they are double cities with one compartment for whites, one for blacks. And the white city is, of course, overwhelmingly favored in all respects.

There are still all manner of minor discriminations. Africans in the Congo cannot travel without a permit, they cannot possess firearms, and in theory they are not allowed to drink anything stronger than beer. They are permitted vocational education, but only up to a point. The ceiling is a curious one. A Congolese Negro can become a carpenter or a mechanic, but not an engineer. He can be a bishop, a journalist, an accountant, a medical assistant, a teacher, a civil servant, or a druggist—but not an architect or attorney. There are Negro lawyers in British and French Africa, but not one in the Congo. To the Belgians, lawyers mean politics, and politics is one thing that the Belgians do not want their Africans to have.

One vital point of difference between the Belgian system and that of the British and French is that the Belgians do their utmost to keep their Africans out of Europe and particularly out of Belgium itself. They do not want them to see how Europeans live in Europe. Hundreds of African boys from British or French colonies have gone to British or French universities in Europe, such as Oxford or the Sorbonne. But practically no Congolese boys are allowed to go to a Belgian university.

This is because the Belgians do not want their Africans to become tempted and dissatisfied. They feel that if Africans see what life in Europe is like they will become discontented and harder to handle politically when they return home. The Belgians do not want the Congolese to hear about things like habeas corpus, a free press, and trial by jury.

Africans in the Congo are given good social services and hospitals and so on, and are for the most part allowed to live pretty well with chances of economic advancement, but this does not mean that they are babied. We entered the Congo from Uganda and our chauffeur was a Uganda boy—a British subject. He was terrified of every Belgian we met. He had a bad cold, and we were up in the mountains in freezing rain. But he said that if we asked the hotel manager to give him a room (normally chauffeurs in Africa sleep in their cars) he would be arrested. I said that this could not possibly happen since he was a British subject, not Congolese. "Makes no matter," he replied.

I asked him if he thought that Africans in the Congo had any advantages that they did not have in British Africa. He answered, "People here have no anything."

This was an exaggeration, but certain abuses do still exist in the Belgian Congo. For instance, British officials out in the field rely largely on persuasion when they want to get something done, for example, in improving agricultural techniques or controlling erosion. But the Belgian official simply commands a peasant with some such words as, "Plant thirty trees here next month—or else!"

One complaint I heard was that if any European housewife reported that a Congolese servant had committed some misdeed, he was automatically subject to a sentence of six months in jail without a trial. Another was that boys out in the country are made to marry very young, whether they want to marry or not. The Belgians want a big, quickly expanding population. Also young men are made to work in forced labor gangs.

A PASSIONATE REBUKE

The role of the late Patrice Lumumba, the Congo's first Prime Minister, has yet to be defined by history. He has been viewed as either the principal villain or a martyred hero of the Congo's struggle for independence and unity. He may turn out to be a bit of both. Whatever role history ascribes to him, however, his evaluation of Belgian paternalism is quite clear.

From Patrice Lumumba, "The Independence of the Congo," in James Duffy and Robert A. Manners, eds., *Africa Speaks,* 1961.

We have known the back-breaking work exacted from us in exchange for salaries which permitted us neither to eat enough to satisfy our hunger, nor to dress and lodge ourselves decently, nor to raise our children as the beloved creatures that they are.

We have known the mockery, the insults, the blows submitted to morning, noon and night because we were "nègres." Who will forget that to a Negro one used the familiar term of address, not, certainly, as to a friend, but because the more dignified forms were reserved for whites alone?

We have known that our lands were despoiled in the name of supposedly legal texts which in reality recognized only the right of the stronger.

We have known the law was never the same, whether dealing with a white or a Negro; that it was accommodating for the one, cruel and inhuman to the other.

We have known the atrocious suffering of those who were imprisoned for political opinion or religious beliefs: exiles in their own country, their fate was truly worse than death itself.

We have known that in the cities there were magnificent houses for the whites and crumbling hovels for the Negroes, that a Negro was not admitted to movie theaters or restaurants, that he was not allowed to enter so-called "European" stores, that when the Negro traveled, it was on the lowest level of a boat, at the feet of the white man in his deluxe cabin.

And, finally, who will forget the hangings or the firing squads where so many of our brothers perished, or the cells into which were brutally thrown those who escaped the soldiers' bullets—the soldiers whom the colonialists made the instruments of their domination?

From all this, my brothers, have we deeply suffered.

Portuguese Africa

The Portuguese, who first opened the way to Africa, still cling to large holdings on the continent. The poverty and lack of progressiveness which characterizes Portugal herself cannot help but be mirrored in her colonies.

PORTUGUESE POLICY

From George H. T. Kimble, *Tropical Africa,* 1960.

. . . Portuguese policy has tended to be tradition-directed; and for an understandable reason. With only a handful of people—a million at the most in the early sixteenth century—the Portuguese managed to colonize Brazil, maintain establishments in India, off the coast of China and around the coasts of Africa from Tangier to Malindi, to send missionaries to practically every pagan country, to maintain research enterprises second to none in the fields of navigation, cartography and astronomy, and to trade with practically every country in the known world.

It was a stupendous and heroic achievement, one that Lusitanian poets and historians have never tired of telling, and one that has often been memorialized in shrine, monument and institution. Perhaps the very brevity of her Great Age has served to focus attention on it and to strengthen the affection of the Portuguese for the past and for those institutions, such as the Catholic Church, that have resisted the erosive agencies of time and fortune.

There have been shifts and twists of emphasis, but the objective of Portuguese policy down the years has seldom been in doubt. In Commander Sarmento Rodrigues' words, it has been "to Christianize, colonize and civilize.

. . . In diffusing our blood, our language and our religion, our only purpose was that high aim of making others equal to us and uniting them in the bonds of brotherly love."

Though the moral aspects of Portuguese colonial policy are not always the most apparent, they are continually exercising the minds of its exponents. And it must be said to their credit that, even in the early days, the Portuguese seldom made a man's race or color or status the subject of discriminatory legislation. . . .

If they did despise the majority of the Moors, it was because they were unbelievers. But they knew a powerful alchemy for turning unbelievers into brothers. Just as the Romans employed the device of citizenship whenever they needed or wanted to swell their ranks with barbarians, so the Portuguese employed the device of conversion. To qualify for membership in their club, it was not necessary that a man be white, only that he be a Christian—a man with human dignity, with aspirations worth fostering, and with all the makings of a brother. . . .

In other words, when the African has learned to speak and write Portuguese, has thrown over tribal traditions and accepted the moral sanctions of Portuguese culture, is willing to live with one wife and generally to work and behave like a Portuguese, he may become a Portuguese citizen and so enjoy full juridical equality with the citizens of Lisbon. Class distinctions may remain, as they do among the citizens of Lisbon, but not racial distinctions. . . .

. . . the Portuguese have no use for self-determination, and equally no use for the commonwealth concept.

Central to all their political thinking is, in Dr. Armindo Monteiro's words, "the overriding idea of national oneness." There is only one state, one territory, one population, one citizenship, one government. Portuguese Guinea, Angola, Mozambique are provinces of Portugal. . . .

The economic unity is not as evident as the political unity, but it is a favorite theme of Portuguese ministers, students of government and businessmen. Like France,

Portugal is poorly off in many of the necessities of a modern, diversified economy. She has little coal and no iron ore to speak of, and, of course, none of the tropical and subtropical ingredients of manufacturing industry such as rubber, cotton, sisal and palm oil. In the circumstances, it is natural that the Portuguese should be drawn to the idea of developing the overseas and metropolitan provinces on complementary lines, using "colonial" raw materials wherever possible in metropolitan factories and shipping back the products of those factories to the overseas provinces. And they have been no slower than any other colonial power to exploit the idea—to the extent, in some instances, of requiring raw material producers to sell their goods at prices below, and to purchase their manufactured necessities at prices above, those to be obtained on the open world market. . . .

A CRITICAL VIEW OF PORTUGUESE POLICY

From James Duffy, *Portuguese Africa,* 1959.

No questions have aroused greater controversy in the history of Portuguese Africa than those of slavery and contract labor, and on no question have the Portuguese been more sensitive. The last century and a half has been frequently marked by domestic and international polemics. With England in particular Portugal has had a lingering dispute over these problems. Nor is it by any means certain that the arguments have run their course, for the Portuguese colonial administration is obviously not yet disposed to abjure its repressive exploitation of African labor on which the present expansion of the economies of Angola and Mozambique is largely based.

To meet the blunt accusations of slaving and improper labor practices Portugal has been forced in the past one hundred and twenty-five years to respond with the creation of an elaborate legislation, some of it genuine, as, for example, Sa da Bandeira's antislavery decrees, and other parts of it synthetic. If this legislation has sometimes failed to convince most foreign critics, it has probably convinced a majority of the Portuguese, even some of those who have been as critical as foreigners of the African labor situation in the overseas provinces, for many Portuguese seem to have an almost mystical faith in the solution of problems by reports and complicated legislation. Nor have Portugal's traditional policies on the use of African labor always been lacking for support from outside Portuguese territory, and it is not unusual to hear the cliché in many parts of Africa, "Only the Portuguese know how to treat the native."

In recent years the Portuguese government has tried to soften the unpleasant implications of contract labor by emphasizing such terms as "the dignity of labor," "spiritual assimilation," "cultural evolution," and "black Portuguese citizens" when speaking of its native policy, but the reality is pretty much the same today as it has been for four hundred years: the indiscriminate use of the African for Portuguese profit. Had this vision of the African shown any marked change in these centuries, beyond the final abolition of slavery and the creation of an ambiguous legal language to define the African's status vis-à-vis the colonial administration, a discussion of slavery and contract labor would be only a historical exercise, but there has been no such change, and a study of this aspect of Angola and Mozambique should contribute to an understanding of present tendencies. Whether the African has been an export commodity, a domestic slave, a *liberto, contratado,* or *voluntario,* his fundamental relationship with the Portuguese has remained the same— that of a servant. When the African is supposed to emerge from his centuries-old apprenticeship and tutelage into a role of responsible citizen of Greater Portugal cannot be known (historically, a few Portuguese Africans have always been able to achieve a position of economic and social responsibility in the clergy, commerce, and lesser administration, thus giving some validity to Portuguese assertions of racial equality; and in recent years the emergence of the *assimilado,* especially in the cities and larger towns, has shown a slightly encouraging progress), but the idea of an Angola or Mozambique for the African seems to have about as much significance in Portugal's colonial plans as the notion of a United States for the Indian has in American deliberations. . . .

Until recent years native policy was only incidental to the administration and exploitation of Angola and Mozambique. The African population in its majority was ignored, enslaved, or conquered depending upon the necessities of the age, and based on little more than expediency. The slave trade was, of course, given its extent in the two possessions, a sort of native policy, but in a larger sense it was another aspect of Portugal's economic exploitation. Economic considerations still dominate colonial schemes, but not so nakedly, and a major effort of the New State's overseas policy has theoretically been based on the social, as well as the financial, integration of Angola and Mozambique. From the traditions deriving from Portuguese conduct in Africa in centuries past and from the authoritarian purpose and mystique of the present the Salazar government has evolved a philosophy for the African provinces: cultural assimilation. Still more precept than practice, this policy is advertised as the answer to Africanism and the ultimate hope for European colonialism in Africa.

IN DEFENSE OF PORTUGUESE POLICY

From A. J. Alfaro Cardoso, *Angola Your Neighbor*, 1950.

It is a fact commented upon by everybody that in the Portuguese colonies, whether localized in Africa, Asia or Australasia, a peaceful atmosphere has prevailed now for centuries, in startling contrast to the state of affairs at present observed in the same continents, in territories governed by other nations.

This fact is the outcome of our policy of assimilation of native peoples, markedly realistic and based upon an experience of long centuries of civilizing action, by means of which we are gradually raising them to our level so that in time we will make them all as Portuguese as the

Portuguese of the Mother-Country, distinct from these only in their color.

To attain this end, we do not close our eyes to the objective reality which the native problem presents, and therefore do not confuse the civilized and semi-civilized natives living in towns and their outskirts, which constitute a minority, with the vast mass of raw, uneducated natives peopling the remainder of the territory.

In our opinion, to mix up a native of the bush with one that has lived close to us, absorbed our ways, habits and ideals—in a word, our civilization—and to seek to apply to the former the methods of approach that we adopt with the latter, is to run away from the reality of fact, leaving the problem without adequate solution.

The raw native is unacquainted with the most elementary principles of hygiene, whether with regard to his dwelling or his feeding or still the care of his body; he works his land by using the most primitive implements and processes; he raises his cattle by following the teachings of nature learnt in the observation of the life of wild animals around him; he practices fetish-worship, endowing trees, streams and all inanimate objects with life and believing that they can influence him for good or evil.

This raw native has to be looked at as an adult with a children's mentality—and as such he must be considered. He needs to be tutored as if he were a minor, taught to feed and clothe himself properly and to withstand the dangers that face him on all sides, shown how to get the most out of his own land by the best methods, guided in the choice of work suited to his abilities—in short, educated, physically, morally and professionally.

What he consequently requires is protection and teaching, until he grows up and as a civilized man, can take his place beside us.

Bearing this in mind, the enlightening action of the Portuguese in Africa has been characteristically "paternal," slowly but surely improving the native's standards of living and bringing him towards our sphere of life and into closer touch with ourselves, so that gradually he will come to adopt our culture, language and faith. . . .

The result of the foregoing is that we do not practice racial discrimination. What we want to see is that the individual, be he white, yellow or black, should possess moral and civic education and culture—should be, in a word, a civilized man.

All those who reach our standards enjoy among us the same rights, and stand in a position of perfect equality with us, irrespective of the color of their skins.

Germany, Italy, and Spain in Africa

In a historical sense, Germany's role in Africa has been largely a catalytic one. Germany's emergence as a major power after 1870 and her entry into the field of colonial competition seemed to accelerate the partition of Africa.

When the Great Powers decided to settle their territorial claims at the Berlin Conference, Germany emerged in control of German East Africa (Tanganyika/Tanzania), German South-West Africa, the Cameroons, and Togoland. Her brief administration of these territories was marked more by efficiency than by humanitarianism, and was terminated by her defeat in World War I.

In this way, too, she served as an involuntary catalytic agent in history, because the problem of dividing her colonies among the victors was solved with the development of the Mandate System under League of Nations supervision—a new concept in the administration of dependent territories.

The transfer of mandated territories to the jurisdiction of the UN's Trusteeship Council, and the still unresolved dispute over the Republic of South Africa's right to administer South-West Africa under it, had their origins in German Africa.

Like Germany, Italy entered the European power arena late, but unlike Germany, she lacked military strength. Her ambitions in North Africa were, therefore, largely thwarted by France. She did, however, take Libya in 1911.

Farther south, meanwhile, she had acquired Somalia and Eritrea, which flank Ethiopia on the southeast and northeast respectively. In 1896 she was badly defeated by an Ethiopian army when she attempted to add Ethiopia to her empire. It was not until the Mussolini era of the 1930's that she made good her ambition and conquered the ancient African kingdom.

The League of Nations' inability to cope with this act of aggression, despite a historic plea from Emperor Haile Selassie, contributed greatly to the decline of that organization in the decade before World War II.

With the defeat of Italy and the Axis Powers in 1945, Ethiopia found herself liberated, with little to remind her of the brief Italian occupation apart from a few well-built roads, bridges, public buildings—and the opportunity to annex Eritrea, which gave her access to the Red Sea.

Italy remained in Africa after the end of the war, however, to administer her former colony of Somalia as a UN Trust Territory. This responsibility ended with the eventual independence of that country.

Spain's interest in Africa has, quite naturally, focused on North Africa, although in modern times, like Italy, she could make little headway in that area in the face of France's ambitions.

The few enclaves she holds on the West African coast trace their origins to the first era of European contact with Africa—a period dominated by the slave trade and during which Spain was preoccupied with her holdings in the New World.

They still survive largely because they have never been important enough to disturb anyone very much. But they are anachronisms in the twentieth century and are significant only in that their now independent neighbors are not likely to tolerate this vestige of colonialism indefinitely.

Some Conclusions

In this presentation of the features of the colonial systems of the European powers, some generalizations emerge. The common denominator in all cases was paternalism, which took different forms, depending on the culture of the colonial power.

In British Africa there was the emphasis on law, native political development (when it did not conflict with British settlers' interests) and a degree of social distance which amounted to a color bar.

The Belgian system was marked by a stark materialistic paternalism calculated to perpetuate a very profitable investment in the Congo. They focused so completely on the concept of the well-fed, happy African that they were unable even to conceive of the idea of independence until it was too late.

The French and the Portuguese systems shared two features. Both insisted on considering their dependencies as integral parts of the mother country, and both had a more relaxed attitude in the matter of social distance. They dropped the color bar for those willing and able to Europeanize themselves. But here the likeness ends.

France has been strongly conditioned by the heritage of her Revolution: liberty, equality, fraternity. This she has at least attempted to apply to her colonial administration.

Portuguese history, on the other hand, never included a Declaration of the Rights of Man or a successful experiment with republicanism. The Portuguese can therefore be thoroughly consistent as they rationalize their oppressive, exploitive system.

When Alien Cultures Meet

We are all vaguely aware that something tragic happened to the American Indian after 1492. We tend to see it in terms of wagon trains stuck full of arrows and the cavalry arriving in the nick of time. But even if white men had met red men without violence, the impact of totally different cultures would have created serious problems. This is what happened in Africa—sometimes with, and sometimes without, violence. However, in America the white man far outnumbers the Indian; in Africa the European is a small minority. But until very recently, the white man in Africa wrote the laws and imposed his point of view on the indigenous majority. Such a situation produces clashes of values and misunderstandings which can lead to violence.

COOPERATION IN A PRE-INDUSTRIAL SOCIETY

In the following reading, the anthropologist Margaret Mead examines attitudes of a pre-industrial society. The concept of communal ownership should be compared with Western ideas. Analyze the problems which might be faced by a Peace Corpsman who comes to work in such an area.

From Margaret Mead, *Cultural Patterns and Technical Change,* 1957.

Western social scientists find cooperating units in many parts of the world. But the concept of cooperation in most areas is different from that known to the West. Western cooperation refers usually to a group which has been created in terms of future ends for the benefit of the individual members; it is individual collective effort converging toward a unifying end. The cooperating units we find in Africa, Latin America, the Middle East, and China, however, are units with an organic basis deriving from the past and originating in birth, repeating past patterns, not reaching toward the future. Here an individual is born into a family, a village, a church group, and when he acts for the welfare of the unit, he is often merely filling his prescribed role; the "cooperation" is incidental. To the outsider, they may appear to be cooperative, but within themselves they often are not, since they are not collective. . . .

The communal ownership of land and communal responsibility in agriculture offer its members security and make possible certain valued social patterns. Among the Tanala of Madagascar individual ownership was introduced indirectly as a by-product of the introduction of wet-rice culture, which made the continuous farming of one tract possible and so led to individual ownership. One of the clans, which valued its joint-family ownership and cooperative labor above material wealth, outlawed the disruptive change and returned to dry-rice culture. The chiefs of Basutoland, who also prize community solidarity, discourage measures essential to the preservation of land, such as tree-planting or the fencing of pasture lands, because these imply individual rights over the communal land and may lead to individual ownership.

Against the advantages, moreover, may be set the paramount disadvantage of communal ownership and the cooperative work group: its resistance to change. From Bechuanaland and East Africa comes the objection that improvements such as drainage, terracing, planting permanent crops, reduction of stock as an anti-erosion measure, meet with little incentive under this system because the results of the individual would be lost to him without the cooperation of his neighbors, and whereas these do cooperate along traditional lines, there is no pattern for doing so in introducing the new practices. And the individual, unable to get financial support from his group for improvements, cannot even borrow for them when he cannot give land as security. . . .

Obstacles to the establishment of an industry are often encountered, arising from the values of the culture involved. The Masai, for example, will not work for wages, since tending cattle is the only valued occupation, and cattle themselves are the highest good. In many parts of Africa the relationship of obedience to someone without traditional authority is lacking. The Zulus, considering themselves a dominant warrior race, think it degrading to accept the discipline of industrial labor; they are ready, however, to accept domestic service, since this falls within a differently structured relationship. The Tiv say that only boys who are asocial and who do not fit into the group are ready to live away from home earning wages; that is, boys who are essentially maladjusted. On the other hand when the railroad went through Tiv country, groups of people from the district concerned worked happily for wages, and revealed qualities much liked by their employers.

A MISSIONARY'S DESCRIPTION

Anthropologists and missionaries frequently feud with each other. The anthropologist appreciates and studies a culture as he finds it, while the missionary is dedicated to changing it. Therefore, the anthropologist would say missionaries do not make the most objective observers of cultural processes. Making allowance for a possible missionary bias, however, the following selection gives us glimpses of the changes being wrought in the everyday life of Africans. The authors of the following reading are missionaries who have followed their calling in various parts of Africa for many years.

From Emory and Myrta Ross, *Africa Disturbed*, 1959.

The educational process from the West has been a major creative disturbance in Africa, brought and, for a hundred years, carried principally by Christian missions. Education is generally rated a slow process. But "slow" is a relative term. Traditional evolution from the stage of animistic communal societies has taken mankind generations, and even centuries, in the past. In contrast, education in the last fifty years in Africa has been almost explosive in its effect on society. There is no parallel in history for the impact that education has had on so large a mass of people in an animistic communal society. . . .

As Africans seek to build unity out of the interplay between their own diverse cultures and the varieties of ideas and techniques brought to them from the West, they involve themselves in entirely new relationships. One of these relationships is indicated by the words "cash economy."

We were sitting with two friends in a comfortable home in Leopoldville, talking about the many changes in the Congo.

"Among the hardest things is this," said one of our friends. "In the old days we had land and forest and water, and we ourselves could get everything. Now we have to depend on someone else with money, or we starve. That is hard."

"But you could go back to your village," we said in jest. "The land, forest, and water are still there; you can still get everything."

They laughed. "No, we don't want to go back. There

are new things here that we want. But the money matter is strange and hard."

It is easy to discern a number of practical reasons why a cash economy suddenly introduced into a barter society would seem "strange and hard." But one other reason is not so clearly visible to the West. In animistic communal societies, the things that are bartered and how they are bartered are usually closely bound by the spiritual beliefs and practices of the tribe.

The late John T. Tucker, in *Drums in the Darkness,* told of a primitive Angola tribe in which "to ensure future success a trader's child when a few days old is made to eat special food obtained by the father at great cost. The special dish consists of the eye of a fish, a piece of elephant's ear and the diaphragm of a lion; the eye is believed to confer clearness of perception for future business dealings; the elephant's ear prevents deafness, earache and noises in the head, the future trader thus being guaranteed keen hearing; the lion's diaphragm imparts invincible strength whether on the path or in overcoming other traders."

An African removed a generation or two from such a background is likely to feel that Western cash economy is quite divorced from spiritual sanctions. If he becomes a Christian, he may expect that Christianity will exert a strong influence over its followers' attitudes toward wealth. It will disturb him to discover how little relationship there seems to be between Christianity and a cash economy.

We were invited to a home one Sunday afternoon in Nairobi, Kenya, with a number of others—storekeepers, a foreman, a bank clerk, government clerical employees. Our conversation turned to the problems of land and a cash economy.

"I get what could be considered a fairly good salary," our host said. "But we have no land here in the city, so my wife can't grow food. You see these two girls visiting us? They're my nieces. They've come from the country for a visit and they've been here two weeks. It's a custom we have always observed. When we lived in the country ur relatives came to visit very often. We liked to have hem. Our land produced our food—we never sold the xtra. When visitors came there was plenty to eat."

"But now you have to buy food," one of his friends put n. "Family visitors come as is our custom. Food costs nore money than we've got. How can we feed guests?"

"Also it is our custom when relatives visit to give them presents to take home," our host continued. "In the counry it could be food or pots or mats, something we had grown or made. Now it must come from the shops. We don't want these girls or our relatives or ourselves to feel shame when they bring no gifts home with them or when he gifts are poor. The girls must take welcome gifts home. That's our custom. But where to get the money? The new life has many hard things."

AN ECONOMIC VIEW

> We have heard from the anthropologist and the missionary on the subject of European-induced change in Africa. The following reading will deal with the subject from the standpoint of economics.
>
> *From* Frank R. LaMacchia, "African Economies: Basic Characteristics and Prospects," *Annals of The American Academy of Political and Social Science,* March 1955.

Before European penetration, the traditional indigenous economy was one of agricultural production for subsistence and barter, with money playing a relatively insignificant role. Under the impact of European cultural settlers, plantation owners, and government officials along with their Western values, morality, patterns of behavior, and institutions, profound and lasting changes have occurred in the native economic and social systems. Tribal wars have been halted, famines have been averted, infant mortality has been lowered, the general death rate from disease has been reduced, and the use of money both as a medium of exchange and a standard of economic values has been steadily enlarged. All these contributed to increased physical well-being and a rapid increase in the

human and livestock populations of many areas. In man
areas serious population pressures occurred. In regions c
European settlement they were aggravated by the reserva
tion of the better lands for European use. On the othe
hand, the introduction of the plow and other improve
hand implements made it possible to cultivate large
areas, although sometimes with harmful effect to the soil
Under the influence of traders, Africans became increas
ingly aware of the cash value of cereals and other crop
as a means of obtaining cloth, pots and pans, and othe
simple consumers goods, and later, tools, sewing ma
chines, and bicycles. The requirements of governmen
also made them conscious of the need for cash to pa
taxes. Missionaries not only brought Christianity but gav
basic and practical education, instilled habits of cleanli
ness, and provided medical care.

Transition to exchange economy

The Western-type money economy reached into every
corner of Africa. The rapid expansion of transport and
communications and the development of mining, industry
and European plantation agriculture brought a persisten
and heavy demand for African labor. As a result today
there is virtually no African community which does no
depend in some measure on money earnings. The transi
tion from subsistence native economies to full-scale ex
change economies is, however, by no means com
plete. . . .

Effect on native economies

The steady movement of labor into money-earning activi
ties outside of the native economies has had serious
effects. The demand in European areas has been largely
for male labor without their families. The result has been
to reduce the number of employable males in the native
economies, completely denuding some villages of eco
nomically productive males, leaving only the women and
children and a few aged and feeble men to perform the

necessary work. Food production has been adversely affected and countries formerly self-sufficient—although at minimal nutritional levels—are now importing considerable quantities of foodstuffs to supplement local production. However, the diversion of resources from subsistence agriculture to export and ancillary industries has enabled Africa to produce more for export; with increased foreign-exchange earnings it can pay not only for the additional food it requires but for capital equipment for development as well.

The disruptive effects of separating families have also been felt in the urban, mining, and European agricultural areas. It has contributed to high turn-over rates in industry, which in turn have retarded the growth of a skilled African labor force. . . .

The transition from subsistence economies to exchange economies is accompanied by many noneconomic stresses, particularly in areas of relatively large European settlement. As Africans become more integrated into the exchange economy they become more responsive to monetary incentives, but they quickly learn that ability, initiative, and skill are not necessarily rewarded by advancement in status and income. The relegation of Africans to an inferior political, economic, and social status stimulates resentment, bitterness, and frustration. Under these circumstances, the growth of a middle-class of Africans having a vested interest in a harmonious, evolutionary process of development in cooperation with the new enlightened members of the European community is exceedingly difficult, if not impossible.

AFRICAN REACTIONS TO EUROPEAN CULTURE

To continue our study of interacting cultures we turn once more to anthropologists, who see the problem more in terms of the indigenous cultural backgrounds.

From William R. Bascom and Melville J. Herskovits, *Continuity and Change in African Cultures,* 1959.

The diversity of African cultures and of African reactions to European culture presents a major obstacle to understanding contemporary Africa, even for experienced observers. . . .

The degree of variation in African cultures is equaled by contrasts in the acceptance and rejection of Euroamerican innovations. Thus, in Kenya the Kikuyu were so eager to adopt European ways that, when frustrated in their desires, many resorted to the violence of Mau Mau. The Masai, Pakot, and other Nilotic peoples in the same country have followed the opposite course, remaining aloof and proudly indifferent to European influence; except for minor details, they have withstood the efforts to change their ways. Between these extremes, the Ganda of neighboring Uganda, with a cultural background which included a highly organized political system, have adapted to European culture with less resistance than the Nilotics but with less enthusiasm than the Kikuyu.

These differences in reaction to European contact cannot be explained solely, as is so often implied, in terms of variations in colonial policy or of duration and intensity of contact. Equally, if not more important are the pre-established patterns of African culture. The tendency to neglect the factor of traditional modes of behavior and systems of belief has had far-reaching practical consequences where the framing of programs for economic or political development has been involved.

Nigeria affords a classic example of the effect of cultural backgrounds on the course of recent events. The policy of indirect rule was first applied among the Hausa in the north, where political authority was centered in the Emir and where taxation, courts, and other governmental institutions comparable to those of Europe were already in existence. It was extended with little difficulty to the Yoruba in the southwest, since their traditional political structure was sufficiently similar. But the attempt to apply it to the Ibo in the southeast failed because comparable political units on which to superimpose the new system were lacking. The development of Nigeria's federal form of government and of the different systems of representation which operate in its three regions cannot be explained without taking these cultural differences into account. Despite these differences and contrasts, of which any serious student of African culture soon becomes aware, there are underlying similarities between the cultures of neighboring African peoples and in the processes of culture change for sub-Saharan Africa as a whole. . . .

Another complication that faces one who seeks to understand contemporary Africa arises from the fact that, even where it is least apparent on the surface, all groups take over innovations selectively. Some things are accepted, while others, not considered desirable, are rejected because they are incompatible with preexisting custom or unsuitable to the natural environment, to name only two of the possible reasons. The Tutsi of Ruanda, for whom cattle are so important, have accepted modifications of earlier custom in political procedures, diet, and, to a degree, in agriculture, but they have stubbornly resisted and bitterly resented administrative efforts to destock their herds, although the population problem in their territory arises out of pressures not only of human beings on the land but of cattle as well. . . .

Even where selectivity in the acceptance of cultural elements from outside is recognized, analyses of the contemporary African scene too often fail to grasp the fact that selection is additive and not necessarily substitutive. European cloth adds to the range of fabrics and patterns; kerosene lamps are used together with traditional ones; and European-manufactured china and ironware expand the range of goods produced by African potters and blacksmiths. In time they may come to displace the African-made products, but despite the severe competition of European machine-made goods, African weavers, smiths, and potters are still active. . . .

In religion, where substitution has clearly been the end of proselytizing, this principle clarifies an otherwise puzzling situation. For, whatever their verbalizations, Africans have by no means given over their allegiances to traditional supernatural forces when they have accepted the deity of another people. Rather, the new deity is added to the totality of supernatural resources on which they can call for aid. . . .

AN EXAMPLE OF CULTURAL BLENDING

A good example of the blending of beliefs is cited in the following short selection.

From Rhona Churchill, *White Man's God*, 1962.

Just how close to the witch doctor's spirit world is that of the native Christian became still clearer in a talk I had with one of the church wardens, Diniwe Madala. His Kraal is a short walk from St. Cuthberts. His two dogs barked ferociously as I approached unexpectedly, but his plump wife called them off. Her husband, a dignified, elderly, gray-haired man, ushered me into his guest hut and sat me down on a well-sprung sofa. His two grandsons were playing ball in the yard outside. He is regarded as one of the most sincere Christian Africans for miles around.

"I've just been talking to Father Rumsay about witch doctors," I told him. "He says you know more about them than he does."

"Perhaps I do. Perhaps I do," he chuckled. "I had a friend who was a witch doctor until he felt the good spirits calling him to become a Christian. He consulted them on his decision. But they must have been annoyed, for soon after he was baptized into the Church he became very ill.

"Because he had been a witch doctor he knew at once the cause of his sickness. He knew the evil spirits were angry and determined to kill him, so he asked Father Lee to give him sick communion. After he had had it he called up the evil spirits and told them straight, 'Jesus is stronger than you are. Do your worst. Kill me. But you can't touch me beyond the grave, because from there I go to Heaven,' then he died, peaceful and content."

"And do you believe he really talked to the evil spirits and was killed by them?" I asked this church warden who had been a Christian for fifty years and had had a mission school education.

"Of course," he said, "We all know it was so." And there was not a hint of doubt in his voice.

> For some, blending of old and new religious belief is not easy. The difference between the white man's preaching and practice is all too obvious to the rising generation of Africans.
>
> Here are the words of a worried missionary in the Republic of South Africa, reported by Miss Churchill.

"There was complete trust of the European thirty years ago," [the missionary] said. "The African felt he was moving forward. Now he has lost hope and become demoralized. We see it here in the Reserve all too vividly. A lad who has accepted Christianity and respects our missionaries, goes off to the mines, sees how the white man behaves in the towns, sees how the laws are stacked against him, and comes back anti-Christian. Because he still wants a religion he reverts to heathenism.

"It's happening every day, before our eyes. Those of our first generation Christians who are alive are still very enthusiastic, but the second generation Christians are less so, and most of the third generation ones are Christians only in the sense that they wear western clothes, have had some schooling and were baptized as infants. The pull back to heathenism is strong and the root cause is the disillusionment caused by the Apartheid laws. When we came to this land we met friendly Africans eager to learn our ways, and follow our example, eager to move forward to a fuller life, eager to rise above menial work. The tragedy of South Africa is that she has missed a unique opportunity of building a really fine, prosperous and civilized multiracial society. She could have set an example to the whole continent."

Two Case Studies of Social Change

To catch the real meaning of social change we turn to two case studies of representative African groups.

A case study is to the anthropologist what the laboratory report is to the physical scientist; it is the record of his study and observations. In the following case studies we will see two groups: one in the natural environment of the rain forest, and the other in the newly created city environment. The impact of Western culture is described and to some extent evaluated.

THE RAIN FOREST PEOPLE

From George H. T. Kimble, *Tropical Africa*, 1960.

[The Cameroonian rain forest groups] traditionally followed the same livelihoods—hunting (for small game as a rule) and the cultivating by the usual bush-fallowing methods of such subsistence crops as yam, manioc and banana. They formerly did little trading, as their surpluses were few and unreliable; and they seldom went far from home, partly because of fear and partly because of linguistic difficulties. Among the more important of these groups are the Fang and the Bulu.

During the past fifty to seventy-five years these forest dwellers, like all other colonized peoples, have come to accept the fact of interference. They have become accustomed to the exactions (mostly small) of the commandant, the ministrations (mostly welcome) of the mission teacher, pastor and doctor, and the pushing and shoving of the entrepreneur (mostly unavoidable). Many of them, too, have become accustomed to living in towns, without which the white man—or so it seems to them—can do nothing well. . . . Those—still by far the great majority —who continue to live in the forests have become accustomed to the idea of growing cash crops. Cocoa, coffee, tobacco, peanuts, bananas and palm kernels enable them to pay their taxes and to be in the market for a limited range of goods.

To what extent has the social order of these rain forest

peoples been changed by these changes in their economy? In externals, at least, it has been greatly changed. To start with some of the most obvious and agreeable changes: Slavery has disappeared and along with it the practice of burying slaves alive (sometimes wives, too) in the graves of their masters. Cannibalism has also disappeared, assuming one can discount the stories that still, from time to time, come out of the deep forests of killings made for the sheer pleasure of eating human flesh. Most of the secret societies that used to terrorize everyone have been snuffed out. There has also been a satisfactory decline in the status and activity of the sorcerer.

Coming to more prosaic matters, there have been changes in the stratification of society, in its family institutions and relationships and the day-by-day doings of its members.

Leadership

In pre-European times there were no chiefs, either hereditary or elected. Each village was run by a group of older men belonging to the clan family. Though no one man had greater power than any other, because of the prestige attaching to wealth the word of the richest man usually commanded greater attention than that of the not so rich; the rich man was, in fact, an uncrowned king—the headman of the group.

Today this old one-level society (the head man of it was never more than the first among equals) is slowly being replaced by a three-level society, founded on Western criteria of schooling and civilization, instead of on the African criteria of wealth and prestige. Horner [George R. Horner, author of a paper from which Kimble drew the information for this study] characterizes the three levels as follows:

1. The elite class, composed of government officials, rich and educated planters and store owners, directors of schools, pastors, priests, etc.

2. The evolue class, consisting of lesser school and government functionaries, clerks in commercial employ,

small planters, carpenters, and ebony handicrafters, tailors, and educated women.

3. The great mass of uneducated, illiterate or preliterate villagers—all those living where there are no schools, or where schools have been started too recently to have produced a literate class.

This is not a classification that means anything to more than a few Africans. As Horner says, "Only a small percentage of the elite class, those who have given up their culture for Western culture, would recognize these social divisions." The rest have not yet begun to think of themselves as belonging to a society in which there are superiors and inferiors, privileged and unprivileged, in which favor is to the evolue and riches to the elite.

Most people, nevertheless, have begun to see that they belong to a society that does not stop where the village stops. The ties that bind them to their ethnic kin in other clans and villages may be loose, and articulated poorly if at all, but the awareness of the ties is there. Nowadays language is no longer the barrier to understanding it was, since almost every man, if not yet every woman, has a smattering of French. Insecurity is no longer the barrier to travel it was, for a man may go the length of the land without fear of being attacked or maltreated. Many, indeed, have gone beyond the length of the land—and to North Africa and Europe as part of the Free French army that played so large a role in the liberation of Occupied France—and in doing so have discovered how little of the world they know who only know the rain forest. The postwar awards of citizenship, voting rights, representation in the French National Assembly, and scholarships for bright students served to enlarge the intellectual borders still further. Some of the rain foresters are today more conscious of country than of tribe or group; and a few are world-conscious—to the extent of seeing, and winning, U.N. recognition of their political hopes.

Effects of schooling

A number of changes have come about as a result of

sending children to the white man's school. If they go to a day school, they are away from home from early morning to late afternoon. If they go to a central, or boarding school, they may be away from home for months on end. In either case they are no longer free to work in their parents' fields or go hunting or fishing except during vacations; and they are no longer able to spend large amounts of time, if any, in the "bush schools"—the initiation societies of their age groups. Whether they go to day or boarding school, the disciplinary role of the parent is diminished. Most teachers assume the role of father. In doing so they oblige children to work for them, in both house and garden, and to submit to their jurisdiction in all social matters. Frequently this spells punishment far more harsh than any the child will have known at home.

The schools, particularly the central schools, are responsible for other, more disturbing changes. Away from their home communities, boys and girls find it easy to break the traditional rules governing sexual conduct. They find it equally hard to obey white man's rules, with the result that neither the old nor a new code of behavior has real meaning for them. This has not been without effect on the system of marriage and divorce.

Marriage and divorce

As in most other parts of tropical Africa, marriage was traditionally thought of in the rain forest as a community matter. Its primary function was to ensure the survival of the two families concerned, and so of the community of which they formed part. Accordingly, a marriage had to be arranged, and the terms of the contract agreed upon, not only by the two contracting parties but by all the elders of the village, or villages, from which the parties came. Bride wealth formed an important part of the contract. Characteristically the securities transferred took the form of two or more bundles of iron bars (each bundle containing twenty pieces), ivory, sheep cloth and a dog.

Today marriage means different things to different people. To many young men and women it means little more than elopement and a clandestine home in the bush. To many others it means a quick civil ceremony performed, with or without the families' and elders' consent, by the nearest available government official. To baptized Christians it means vows performed in a church or chapel, often followed at a discreet interval by a traditional pagan ceremony in the woman's village.

In the first case, no payments or securities are required; and it is probable that none are available, since the commonest reason given for the "bush marriage" is the inability of the man to find the cash or goods demanded of him by the woman's people. In the second case, it is unusual for payments or securities to be required for it is an un-African form of marriage to begin with, and one that is not generally approved of by the families of the contracting parties. In the third case, the practice regarding payments or securities varies widely. Some parents, Christian and pagan, require that certain specified gifts be made by the man; but others do not. On the whole the churches, Protestant and Catholic, discourage the practice, both because it is un-Christian and because the amount of cash or goods demanded in these days makes "legitimate" marriage increasingly difficult for most young men. And the demands are high. Writing in the mid-1950s, Horner reported that even in the bush they would commonly include a phonograph, a suit for the bride's father, a sheep (worth the equivalent of about $12), a saw (worth about $50) and $300 in cash—more (up to $500) for a well-educated girl. To come by such wealth takes most young men more years of hard work than they are willing to wait.

Along with the consequent increase of unrecognized marriages has gone an increase in divorce. In the old days divorce was rare. A man could divorce a woman for one of three reasons only: sterility, adultery and refusal to cook. A woman could not divorce her husband legally for any reason, though she could leave him if he were too cruel or would not eat the food she prepared for him. Nowadays a man can demand a divorce on any of four grounds: adultery, crime, prolonged absence from the home, and plain bad conduct. A woman now can demand a divorce, on any of four grounds: beatings, venereal disease, "continual infamous condemnation," and, in the case of a polygynous household, failure to treat her on an equality with the other wives. For this easing of divorce, both church and state must, it seems, be held responsible; the church by insisting that a polygynist could not become a member in good standing until all but one of his wives were divorced, and the state by increasing the number of grounds on which divorce could be obtained and by insisting that marriage needed neither the blessing of the church nor the approval of village families—that it was a matter which could be ended as it was begun, by consent of the parties concerned.

Dress, food, and housing

There have also been changes in the way the rain forest dwellers dress, feed and house themselves. Today it would be hard to find a young Bulu man or woman who does not aspire to be able to dress—though not necessarily to be dressed all the time—in the style of the European. So strong is this aspiration in many minds that the question of the suitability of a given fashion for local use scarcely arises. If close-fitting slacks for women are the mode in Paris, then they become the mode in Douala, notwithstanding the notable difference in the figure of the average Parisian and the average Doualan. If white buckskin shoes are in style on the paved promenades of the Riviera, they are likely to be fashionable in the unpaved, muddy tracks of the bush—on the heads, if not the feet, of their owners.

It is difficult, of course, for the man or woman who wants to be able to look like a European not to want to be able to live like one. More and more are seeking to do it—to the extent, at any rate, of having chairs to sit on, beds to lie on, bicycles to ride, and metal on the roof, linoleum on the floor, windows in the walls, canned goods in the cupboards and "canned" noise everywhere. Some

Bulu town houses are far better appointed than some town houses in metropolitan France.

The pull of the forest

There is, then, no minimizing the changes that have taken place, and still are taking place, in the culture of the rain forest peoples. At the same time, the cultural climate and the "soil" of the rain forest—the sources of strength and inspiration of the forest dwellers—appear to have changed very little; the lopping, pruning, trimming, clearing, and planting up with exotic growths that have been going on have altered little more than its looks.

At heart, Horner contends, the man of the rain forest is still unrepentantly African. As supporting evidence he cites, among other things, the increasing incidence in recent years of polygyny. In a society as poor in things as the old rain forest society, wealth must be measured by other criteria. One of the most widely accepted of such criteria, both in and out of the rain forest, has long been the number of wives and children a man has. A man with one wife was considered poor, for two reasons. First, women, as wives, were the only ones he could normally get to work for him in his gardens; men and boys shun manual work, while girls marry and leave home almost as soon as they are capable of doing a day's work. Second, death rates being what they were, a man would not expect one woman to raise enough children to assure him of a succession. Consequently almost every rain forest man desired to have more than one wife. Frequently he would be abetted in his desire by his wife, who looked forward to having less work and more prestige in a polygynous household. For a while it looked as though the strictures of the Christian church would strangle sentiment for the old pagan creed, but this has not proved to be the case. As the incomes of the rain forest peoples have increased, thanks to the demand for their cash crops and their services in commerce, industry and government, so has the number of those willing to give up membership in the

Christian church for the privilege of living in the manner of their forefathers.

Other lines of evidence pointing in the same direction are the fact that most rain forest people, Christian and pagan, still strongly approve of the traditional ways of arranging a marriage and of stabilizing it with the help of payments or securities, and the fact that most of them show no desire whatever to cut themselves loose from their homes. As Horner puts it, "Though many young men and women leave home these days, hardly any of them leave home psychologically." Away from home they may dress and talk and eat like Europeans, but at home they are not like anybody; they are themselves. There they will frequently discard not only the speech, dress and living style of the European, but also his way of thinking and his skills.

Horner tells of a trained medical assistant who, on returning to the bush after working in a modern hospital, gave up using Western medicines in favor of native ones. When asked why, he replied that the white man's medicine did not always work for Africans. "He would never have said this while working at the hospital, that is, while he was a 'European'; but now, at home, he was once more an African and solved his conflict of identification by becoming a member of the group and once more—at least for six months—following the established customs and mores of his culture."

As further line of evidence—in Horner's view, the most important line of all—we may cite the fact that the highest good and chief end of the ordinary rain forest man remains what it has ever been: wealth and status. Only the methods used to reach this end have changed and these not always greatly. Thus, whereas a man interested in winning status or keeping it was expected to divide up the bag of a hunting expedition according to a long-established "division of wealth" procedure among a group that included his wife, his close friend, his village brothers, his parents and parents-in-law, nowadays he is expected to follow much the same procedure with the earnings of his crops. Upon receipt of cash for his crop, he is expected to give his wife any sum she asks; to give his close friend usually the equivalent of twenty kilograms of cocoa; to give something to any village brother who asks for it; to help a village son raise his marriage money; to send gifts to his parents and parents-in-law; and to give aid to any stranger who asks it.

Again, whereas in the old days a man sent gifts to a village brother in the hope of receiving richer gifts and of raising his prestige with his neighbors and relatives in the process, now he is quite likely to send gifts to the nearest white man since, by the sender's standards, he is almost always rich in goods, influence and power. Or, again, whereas in the past a boy would spend time in the bush school being initiated into the secrets of his people's greatness and learning how to become as great as they, today he is likely to spend much more time in the white man's school being initiated into the secrets of the white man's greatness; for, increasingly, "white" and "wealth" are thought of as two sides of the same coin. Horner tells how a man insisted on bringing him, over a period of months, regular supplies of chickens, eggs, bananas and other foodstuffs for which he would take no money. Then one day he asked Horner to adopt his elder son and send him to America for an education; thus equipped, the boy could not fail, on returning to his people, to make both himself and them rich.

The fact that much of the white man's education is unrelated to the needs of bush life does not seem to matter greatly. Indeed, where an "Africanized" curriculum, complete with instruction in local geography and folklore and the care of the locally grown cash crops, is offered as an alternative to the standard curriculum, the student is commonly encouraged by his people to choose the latter, on the grounds either that it is a stronger kind of magic or that to study like a white man is, in time, to have his wealth and status.

It is perhaps not too much of an exaggeration to say that almost the only things the ordinary rain forest man wants as yet of the white man are his "power tools" and symbols: the ability to read, write and calculate (many men argue that this is the basic tool, and that now they have it, they are "as good as the white man"), the ability to make and maintain machinery, travel fast, and grow fine crops, print money ("you are rich because you print all the money," is a complaint that is often heard) and, when it serves his social purpose, to eat, live and dress like a white man. Insofar as the white man is willing to put him in the way of these tools and symbols, the ordinary rain forest man is happy enough to court his company; but once the willingness ceases to be apparent, the courtship flags.

As for the other things the white man has been offering him—politics, citizenship, nationhood, the Code Napoleon, sectarianism, class distinctions—the rain forester remains for the most part unconvinced of their relevance to his social good, let alone of their intrinsic goodness.

When asked by Horner if he thought the white man had brought "good" to the African, a Bulu replied: "We Bulu will not know if you have brought good until fifty years after you have gone." Not that every Bulu, any more than every Briton or Brahmin, is above finding uses for things that his descendants half a century from now will decide were really very bad for him!

CITY DWELLERS

To savor fully the taste of social change, from its sickening worst to its astringent best, one must go to the town. . . .

With the exception of the "native" towns of West Africa, such as Timbuktu, Kano and Benin, a few "Arab" towns along the eastern coast, such as Zanzibar and Bagamoyo, and one or two Portuguese ports like Luanda and Mozambique, there were no towns in tropical Africa before the present century. Now there are hundreds. The town therefore represents a new milieu for almost all of those who live in it, one to which the traditional sociological criteria of "normalcy" do not apply. It is neither clan nor country, neither hallowed ground nor fruitful earth. It neither feeds a man's children nor lodges his ancestors. It is an uncharted wilderness, for which tribal man lacks both guiding star and measuring rod. European man made the town, and made it for European ends—which, as has been shown, were not African ends.

While every one of these towns could provide grist for a case study of social change, not many of them have as yet been through the sociologist's griddle. Of those that have, few if any have been sieved and sifted as carefully as Stanleyville, capital of the Orientale Province of the Belgian Congo. From 1952 to 1954 Stanleyville was under almost continuous scrutiny by a three-member team of the International African Institute, working in collaboration and under contract with UNESCO. . . .

Stanleyville is situated at the upper limit of navigation of the middle Congo, roughly a thousand miles above Leopoldville, at the foot of the rapids known as Stanley Falls. When H. M. Stanley saw the locality in 1877 it was nothing but a fishing village backed by seemingly endless, uninhabited and untamable bush. Today Stanleyville is a center of trade, transport (rail, road and river), administration and industry. Of its approximately 75,000 inhabitants, more than 70,000 are Africans. More than 80 per cent of the Africans live in the three separate quarters, known as Belge I, Belge II and Brussels, which very roughly form the apexes of a triangle in the middle of which lies the European town. Almost all of the rest live in a large *arabisé,* or Moslemized, village a half mile or so from the European town, and in the railway workers' camp beside the station.

What sort of people are these Africans? What did they do for a living before they went to Stanleyville? And where did they come from? Approximately two-thirds of them were born in the bush. At the time of the UNESCO study nearly half of them had been in Stanleyville less than five years; only slightly more than one-sixth had been there more than twenty years. Although there is bush and bush, for all practical purposes this means that most of the inhabitants of Stanleyville were raised in the world of village, clan and tribe, a world strong in local loyalties, weak in central authority. It also means that they were raised in a world of self-sufficiency (or semi-self-sufficiency since the coming of the Belgian administration), of simple living, and of scant opportunity for acquiring wealth and power.

Of the 66 different tribal groups making up the population, not one was represented by more than 6,000 people at the time of the survey, and only five by more than 2,000. Fifty were represented by groups of less than 500. While the great majority of these tribes had their homes within 200 to 300 miles of Stanleyville, not less than 15 per cent of the persons surveyed by the team came from outside the Orientale Province, some from as far as Katanga, Kasai and Ruanda-Urundi, upward of 750 miles away.

What sort of people are they becoming? What are they doing, and how are they living in Stanleyville?

Education

Most of them are getting some education. At the time of the survey more than half of the adult males had had at least one year of general schooling, and nearly four-fifths of the boys between the ages of 6 and 15 were attending school. Even one-third of the girls between those ages were attending school. But not many of them were as yet getting much education. "Only a minute proportion leave school equipped for the new life awaiting them. The majority have not been trained for any particular trade and have no idea how to fit into a changing economy" (Nelly Xydias, *Social Implications of Industrialization and Urbanization in Africa South of the Sahara,* UNESCO, Tensions and Technology Series, Paris, 1956). Only 15 to 20 boys were being graduated each year from the Stanleyville technical school, out of a total working population of approximately 20,000. Not many Stanleyville Africans as yet see the need for much education. After putting a boy through five or six years of primary schooling the parents like to think that he has a claim to a white-collar job, if only that of a junior clerk. A girl after two or three years of primary schooling—if she gets as much as that—is generally thought to be wasting her time—and she probably is, in the context of the life her parents led when they were young.

Occupational status

Largely because of this limited schooling, most of those who are gainfully employed do work for which very little previous education or experience is required. They are laborers, night watchmen, messengers, and helpers to truck drivers, mechanics, masons and the like. Exact figures are unavailable, but the ratio of unskilled to total workers is perhaps 4 to 5. The remaining 20 per cent of the labor force is made up of skilled and semiskilled wage earners (chauffeurs, mechanics, cobblers, masons, carpenters, painters, cooks, houseboys), white-collar employees (clerks, schoolteachers, medical orderlies, managers of European-owned shops serving Africans), and self-employed persons (shopkeepers, dealers in palm wine and beer, cultivators and so on).

What education can do—and does—for the worker is clearly shown in the table. As more schooling becomes available—or as some schooling becomes available to more people—the occupational status of the African may be expected to improve. Indeed, it is already doing so. Thus, whereas 46.1 per cent of the "first-generation" workers—those who began life in the bush—were engaged in unskilled work at the time of the survey, only 27.7 per cent of the "second-generation" workers were so engaged. The corresponding figures for those engaged in skilled and semiskilled work were 46.3 and 53.5 per cent; and for those in white-collar work, 7.6 and 18.8 per cent. Where there has been an improvement in occupational status, it is reflected in the worker's way of life: in the growing amount of luxury spending being done (on such things as radios, phonographs, tobacco and beer); in the unwillingness of increasing numbers of white collar workers to let their wives live like bush women; and in the for-

mation of workers' councils and occupational unions—
though it must be added that it is European more often
than African interest that so far has kept most of these
alive.

PERCENTAGE DISTRIBUTION OF ADULT AFRICAN MALES (16 PLUS) BY OCCUPATIONAL CATEGORY AND LEVEL OF EDUCATION STANLEYVILLE, BELGIAN CONGO, MID-1950s

Occupational Category	Years of General Schooling				Number
	0	1–3	4–6	6+	
Total	49.5	20.9	23.0	6.5	1,894
Unskilled wage earners	64.7	21.2	12.3	1.8	694
White-collar employees	7.9	7.8	42.6	41.7	176
Skilled & semiskilled wage earners	43.4	25.2	28.8	2.6	812
Self-employed	73.3	12.4	10.7	3.6	88
Not gainfully employed	48.2	17.0	25.9	8.9	124

Source: Jacques J. Maquet, quoting the preliminary report of
the UNESCO–International African Institute research team.

Earnings

Most of the Africans living in Stanleyville are still poorly
off; their earnings are "insufficient to enable [them] to
feed well and live decently in an urban center" [Maquet,
op. cit.]. At the time of the survey most of the unskilled
workers were getting less than 850 francs (approximately
$17) a month, and most of the white-collar workers less
than 1,750 francs ($35). [By way of comparison, the av-
erage monthly pay and allowances of the European civil
servant was 37,500 francs, or approximately $750.]
Many workers supplement their wages by income from
family "side lines," covering everything from hawking fish
caught in the Congo to hairdressing and laundering. On
the other hand, it is only fair to say that many salaried
workers were making more than 7,000 francs (approximately $140); that every worker was entitled to free dis-
pensary and hospital treatment and to receive from his

employer the amount of the food ration and one-quarter of his wage whenever he was certified sick. Further, every worker was insured by his employer against industrial accidents and occupational disease.

The city as home

With the increasing attractiveness of urban employment, many Africans are coming to think of the city as a place where a man may make a permanent home, raise a family, form new associations, and fashion a new kind of community. Evidences of this line of thinking abound. The occupational ambitions of African school children show it clearly. Whereas 21 per cent of the primary school boys questioned on the subject expressed a desire to become mechanics of various sorts, 24 per cent a desire to become clerks, and 30 per cent carpenters, only 6 per cent wanted to become farmers. Whereas 9 per cent of the secondary school boys questioned expressed a desire to become either doctors or medical assistants, 24 per cent teachers, and 59 per cent clerks, only 2 per cent wanted to do manual work. Only 15 per cent of the primary school boys stated that they wanted to follow the work of their fathers (or brothers); as for the secondary school boys, not even one per cent of them wanted to do as their fathers did. The preferences expressed by girls attending primary school were even more "uncustomary." Thirty-three per cent of those questioned wanted to become seamstresses, 21 per cent embroiderers, 21 per cent teachers, 10 per cent either nurses or midwives, 2 per cent nuns, while 13 per cent wanted nothing more than to go on with their studies.

Equally far removed from tribal life were the preferences expressed by educated grown-ups when questioned about their choice of friends and about the kind of community they would like to live in if they could choose freely. Already it is clear that common interest is for many educated people at least as strong a tie as "brotherhood" or kinship. Thus, 69 per cent of the clerks questioned had a teacher, mechanic, or clerk for one or more of their

hree best friends. Only 35 per cent of the drivers ques-
ioned had friends, one or more, in these occupational
categories, and only 27 per cent of the unskilled laborers
questioned had such friends. Though the answers given to
he "kind of community" question were harder to analyze
statistically, they were on the whole "untribal" answers.
"People can be of the same tribe, but have very different
situations in life. Tribe is not enough." "You feel freer
when the tribes are mixed." "One must take into account
education, occupation, the home, the private life, de-
cency, wealth." Sentiments like these were expressed by
evolue Africans often enough to constitute something of a
trend.

The phenomenon of the voluntary association is also
indicative. The African, ever a lover of tribal group activities, ritualistic and recreational, secret or otherwise, is
busying himself increasingly in the work of groups designed to fill the empty hours—and the emptiness—of his
new town life. He has organized voluntary associations
for almost everything from "helping the dead" and getting
more pay for the living to promoting true religion and
comradeship. In some of these causes the women are as
active as the men. A few associations are open to both
men and women—tribal apostasy if there ever was! Some
are single autonomous groups; others, like the Brotherhood of Congolese Veterans, form an integral part of
large organizations. Almost all make a feature of mutual
aid, and increasing numbers of them are interested in
broadening the basis of membership and in fostering the
moral and intellectual progress of the members along the
still rough paths of their new social domain. And as the
basis of membership of a given association broadens, the
range of its interests ceases to be parochial, bound by
tribal and regional attitudes of mind. Instead it becomes
concerned with "the gradual integration of the various
subgroups (ethnic, religious, professional . . .) of the
urban centers' advanced community into a society as a
whole" [Maquet, op. cit.].

The tribal bond

At the same time, most of the Africans of Stanleyville still have more than half a foot in the bush. They may be urbanized, civilized, and Christianized (or Moslemized, as many are), but very few of them are completely detribalized. There may have been some weakening of hereditary bonds and authority, but most of the traditional institutions of bush society, such as the kinship system . . . bride wealth, age sets and brotherhoods, retain their vigor. Few if any town families have renounced the customary bush practice of accommodating those of their kin, brotherhood, and acquaintance to whom they are beholden. As in the bush, when "brothers" settle down on a man's compound, while waiting to find work or on the occasion of a visit, they are put up free. And as in the bush, the visit may last for the remainder of a lifetime. Even in *evolue* households, tribal values die hard. Thus, while many educated men try to get their wives to play the part of an equal—by sharing in the conversation of the table or by developing some outside interests—few have succeeded, and many say they have given up trying.

Most town dwellers, first and second generation alike, periodically go back to the bush, either for the pleasure of it or to honor tribal obligations. A large proportion of them belong to associations open only to persons of their own tribal or ethnic group. In such associations what counts is not so much a man's education, economic status, or ability to speak French, as his knowledge of tribal custom and language, and the qualities of leadership prized by the tribe.

The durability of the old tribal bond is nowhere seen to better advantage than in marriage forms and procedure. A random sample study covering 77 case histories of marriage disclosed the following facts:

1.   More than two-thirds had married within the tribe.
2.   Nearly nine-tenths of the marriages were of the customary sort, binding not only the individuals but also

e families or groups of relations; only about 11 per cent
f them involved a religious (Christian or Moslem) cere-
ony.

3. Payments in cash or kind were made in all but one
ase, and in the case of more than one-third (35.1 per
ent), payment was made either partly or wholly in kind.

4. More than one-fourth of the marriages had been
rranged by members of the family.

5. More than half of the married persons questioned
dmitted to having been divorced one or more times—a
atio not substantially smaller, it would seem, than that
revailing in the bush. The grounds for divorce were, for
he most part, the customary ones: loss of desire, deser-
ion, refusal to live as man and wife, barrenness, neglect
f household duties, quarreling, "in-law" troubles, habit-
al adultery, and so on.

Even in regard to marriage, nevertheless, the old order
has been coming in for its share of battery and assault.
ncreasing numbers of marriages break up because the
parties concerned are drawn from different tribal backgrounds and fail to make the necessary adjustments. Increasing numbers of men resort to concubinage because
of the exorbitant marriage money demanded of them. Increasingly, also, urban marriage is coming to be a matter
for decision by the principals only, not by parents and
clans.

But this is not to say that the old order, whether in
marriage, home, village, or community, whether in
Stanleyville, the Teita Hills, or the Cameroonian rain forest, is done for. If its days are numbered, nobody is telling—not even the sociologists.

Conclusion: The Exclusiveness of European Culture

Everywhere in Africa Europeans introduced new ho-
rizons, new needs, new desires, new economic possibilities—in short a new culture was either directly or indi-

rectly paraded in front of and sold to the Africans
This does not mean that every African wants to "g(
European." It does mean, however, that many African.
would like to choose freely those facets of Europea)
culture which appeal to them. He has found, however
that this is not always possible. Once the European ha(
created this vision of what could be, he proceeded t(
exclude the African from participating in it with him
If we understand this, we can understand much of th(
bitterness which characterizes the African attitude toward the European today.

PART V

Africa Since World War II

Nationalism: A Dynamic Force

Nationalism as a historic force is primarily of European origin. It was born of the French Revolution and the Age of Enlightenment, and dominated the political development of Europe during most of the nineteenth century.

By the early twentieth century, Asian nationalism was pitted against European national interests. After World War II, sparks of nationalism burst into flame all over Africa, although not without modifications as it grew in this new environment.

Nationalism is difficult to define because it is an emotionally loaded term which has different meanings for different people. Whatever force makes people *feel* that they belong together *is* the basis of their nationalism. In Africa there are geographic, linguistic, religious, racial, and traditional tribal nationalisms, as well as nationalisms based on the largely artificial colonial boundaries drawn by the European powers.

Perhaps the element most common to these manifestations of African nationalism, however, is resentment —resentment of the centuries of discrimination and rejection which the African has suffered at the hand of the European. It is bad enough to be treated as an inferior under any circumstances, but it has become increasingly unbearable for Africans to find themselves treated as exploited inferiors in their native land.

AN AFRICAN JUSTIFICATION OF NATIONALISM

Tom Mboya, a leader of the nationalist movement in Kenya and a cabinet minister in the government since the country's independence, rose to prominence through the trade union movement. In the following selection he comments on the need for and goals of African nationalism.

From Tom Mboya, "Vision of Africa," in James Duffy and Robert A. Manners, eds., *Africa Speaks*, 1961.

Despite its force as a stimulus to Africa's economic development, colonialism has been the biggest hindrance to the development of the indigenous people. Under colonial rule, little attention has been paid to the need to invest in education, health, technical training, and general community development for Africans. Partition of Africa and the use of territories as sources of raw materials for metropolitan economies have not allowed the planning of continental or regional development. Instead, colonial divisions have treated each territory in isolation from others.

Africans are convinced that economic and social conditions cannot be considered apart from their political setting. Self-government and independence open great possibilities for economic and social development. Self-government permits people not only to embark on development programs serving purposefully the needs of their own country which they know best, but also enables them to establish relations with other countries on the basis of equality and to coordinate progressively the economy of their country with those of others. Full economic and social emancipation is not possible without political emancipation. Above all, it is through becoming masters of their own fate that the energies of the people are fully released for the arduous task of economic and social development

The subjection of a people, in any form, including forced labor, apartheid, or colonialism under the guise of assimilation, is wholly inimical to economic and social development. This is the answer to those who argue that African territories must wait until they have a viable economy and have acquired enough experience before they demand freedom.

This argument for delay, which smells of a passive betrayal of democracy, ignores the fact that experience has shown that it is only after independence that most countries have embarked on large-scale economic and educational projects, and that in all cases it is only after independence that the world has begun to be conscious of a country's economic and social problems. In fact, the foundations for stable government have been laid only after independence, which makes nonsense of the plea of colonial governments that they are training Africa for self-government. In every case, colonial powers have left their African territories only when the organized pressure of the people has made it impossible for them to govern without serious consequences. . . .

Like most of the underdeveloped areas of the world, Africa needs rapid economic development. She has to do this in the shortest possible time and often with very limited personnel and capital. While engaging in her new development plans, she has also to face up to the task of reconstructing her economy from the colonial structure to one suited to the needs of an independent state. This task is not made any easier by the East-West power competition, but Africa must avoid being involved in this competition and be free to further her effects through multilateral or bilateral economic arrangements with whatever country will supply her with her immediate needs on the easiest terms and without political or other strings.

In the process of economic reconstruction African states may have to think of broader ties with neighboring states and possibly of a pooling of resources and coordination of efforts. Development of power, communication, and research are fields in which such action is immediately advisable. The establishment of the United Nations

Commission for Africa is an important contribution in this respect.

Every African leader hopes that independence will remove colonial barriers and facilitate the growth of African unity and possibly one day a United States of Africa. All leaders would in fact like to work for such a development. But it would be naive not to recognize that a number of problems, including those of language, tribalism in some areas, poor communications and great distances, conflicting personalities and political opinions, etc. will have to be recognized and resolved. This calls for statesmanship and mutual respect and understanding of each other's genuine interest.

"THE GENTLEMEN OF THE JUNGLE"

> The following fable is an allegorical presentation of African nationalism as seen by the great Kenyan nationalist Jomo Kenyatta.

> *From* Jomo Kenyatta, "The Gentlemen of the Jungle," in Peggy Rutherford, ed., *African Voices,* n.d.

Once upon a time an elephant made a friendship with a man. One day a heavy thunderstorm broke out, the elephant went to his friend, who had a little hut at the edge of the forest, and said to him: "My dear good man, will you please let me put my trunk inside your hut to keep it out of this torrential rain?" The man, seeing what situation his friend was in, replied: "My dear good elephant, my hut is very small, but there is room for your trunk and myself. Please put your trunk in gently." The elephant thanked his friend saying: "You have done me a good deed and one day I shall return your kindness." But what followed? As soon as the elephant put his trunk inside the hut, slowly he pushed his head inside, and finally flung the man out in the rain, and then lay comfortably inside his friend's hut, saying: "My dear good friend, your skin is harder than mine, and as there is not enough room for both of us, you can afford to remain in the rain while I am protecting my delicate skin from the hail-storm."

The man, seeing what his friend had done to him, started to grumble; the animals in the nearby forest heard the noise and came to see what was the matter. All stood around listening to the heated argument between the man and his friend the elephant. In this turmoil the lion came along roaring, and said in a loud voice: "Don't you all know that I am the King of the Jungle! How dare anyone disturb the peace of my kingdom?" On hearing this the elephant, who was one of the high ministers in the jungle kingdom, replied in a soothing voice, and said: "My lord, there is no disturbance of the peace in your kingdom. I have only been having a little discussion with my friend here as to the possession of this little hunt which your lordship sees me occupying." The lion, who wanted to have "peace and tranquillity" in his kingdom, replied in a noble voice, saying: "I command my ministers to appoint a Commission of Enquiry to go thoroughly into this matter and report accordingly." He then turned to the man and said: "You have done well by establishing friendship with my people, especially with the elephant, who is one of my honorable ministers of state. Do not grumble any more, your hut is not lost to you. Wait until the sitting of my Imperial Commission, and there you will be given plenty of opportunity to state your case. I am sure that you will be pleased with the findings of the Commission." The man was very pleased by these sweet words from the King of the Jungle, and innocently waited for his opportunity, in the belief that naturally the hut would be returned to him.

The elephant, obeying the command of his master, got busy with other ministers to appoint the Commission of Enquiry. The following elders of the jungle were appointed to sit in the Commission: (1) Mr. Rhinoceros; (2) Mr. Buffalo; (3) Mr. Alligator; (4) The Rt. Hon. Mr. Fox to act as chairman; and (5) Mr. Leopard to act as Secretary to the commission. On seeing the personnel, the man protested and asked if it was not necessary to include in this Commission a member from his side. But he was told that it was impossible, since no one from his side was well enough educated to understand the intricacy of jungle law. Further, that there was nothing to fear, for the members of the Commission were all men of repute for their impartiality in justice, and as they were gentlemen chosen by God to look after the interests of races less adequately endowed with teeth and claws, he might rest assured that they would investigate the matter with the greatest care and report impartially.

The Commission sat to take the evidence. The Rt. Hon. Mr. Elephant was first called. He came along with a superior air, brushing his tusks with a sapling which Mrs. Elephant had provided, and in an authoritative voice said: "Gentlemen of the Jungle, there is no need for me to waste your valuable time in relating a story which I am sure you all know. I have always regarded it as my duty to protect the interests of my friends, and this appears to have caused the misunderstanding between myself and my friend here. He invited me to save his hut from being blown away by a hurricane. As the hurricane had gained access owing to the unoccupied space in the hut, I considered it necessary, in my friend's own interests, to turn the undeveloped space to a more economic use by sitting in it myself; a duty which any of you would undoubtedly have performed with equal readiness in similar circumstances."

After hearing the Rt. Hon. Mr. Elephant's conclusive evidence, the Commission called Mr. Hyena and other elders of the jungle, who all supported what Mr. Elephant had said. They then called the man, who began to give his own account of the dispute. But the Commission cut him short, saying: "My good man, please confine yourself to relevant issues. We have already heard the circumstances from various unbiased sources; all we wish you to tell us is whether the undeveloped space in your hut was occupied by anyone else before Mr. Elephant assumed his position?" The man began to say: "No, but——" But at this point the Commission declared that they had heard sufficient evidence from both sides and retired to consider their decision. After enjoying a delicious meal at the expense of the Rt. Hon. Mr. Elephant, they reached their verdict, called the man, and declared as follows: "In our opinion this dispute has arisen through a regrettable misunderstanding due to the backwardness of your ideas. We consider that Mr. Elephant has fulfilled his sacred duty of protecting your interests. As it is clearly for your good that the space should be put to its most economic use, and as you yourself have not yet reached the stage of expansion which would enable you to fill it, we consider it necessary to arrange a compromise to suit both parties. Mr. Elephant shall continue his occupation of your hut, but we give you permission to look for a site where you can build another hut more suited to your needs, and we will see that you are well protected."

The man, having no alternative, and fearing that his refusal might expose him to the teeth and claws of members of the Commission, did as they suggested. But no sooner had he built another hut than Mr. Rhinoceros charged in with his horn lowered and ordered the man to quit. A Royal Commission was again appointed to look into the matter, and the same finding was given. This procedure was repeated until Mr. Buffalo, Mr. Leopard, Mr. Hyena and the rest were all accommodated with new huts. Then the man decided that he must adopt an effective method of protection, since Commissions of Enquiry did not seem to be of any use to him. He sat down and said: "Ng'enda thi ndagaga motegi," which literally means "there is nothing that treads on the earth that cannot be trapped," or in other words, you can fool people for a time, but not forever.

Early one morning, when the huts already occupied by the jungle lords were all beginning to decay and fall to pieces, he went out and built a bigger and better hut a little distance away. No sooner had Mr. Rhinoceros seen it than he came rushing in, only to find that Mr. Elephant was already inside, sound asleep. Mr. Leopard next came in at the window, Mr. Lion, Mr. Fox, and Mr. Buffalo entered the doors, while Mr. Hyena howled for a place in the shade and Mr. Alligator basked on the roof. Presently they all began disputing about their rights of penetration, and from disputing they came to fighting, and while they were all embroiled together the man set the hut on fire and burnt it to the ground, jungle lords and all. Then he went home, saying: "Peace is costly, but it's worth the expense," and lived happily ever after.

Much silence has a mighty noise.

AFRICAN SELF-CONSCIOUSNESS

Since 1919 there have been Africans of stature who were concerned about the fate of the African people as a group. The following reading presents African ideas of what it means to be African. Whether the idea was called Pan-Africanism, Pan-Melanism, or Negritude, it became part of the African self-awareness that preceded and accompanied movements for self-determination and self-government.

From Thomas Hodgkin, *Nationalism in Colonial Africa*, 1957.

The idea of general African liberation has been expressed also in terms of "Pan-Africa"—i.e., the concept of the eventual union of all African peoples in a single State. . . . Periodic Pan-African Congresses have been held—the first in Paris in 1919, at the time of the Peace Conference, under the Presidency of the Senegalese deputy, M. Blaise Diagne; Pan-African literature published; and Pan-African policies advocated by such African politicians as Dr. Azikiwe in Nigeria, Dr. Nkrumah in the Gold Coast, Mr. Kenyatta in Kenya, and Mr. Nkumbulah in Northern Rhodesia. In French Africa the theory, as essentially separatist, is rejected by most of the older generation of political leaders. But many of the younger generation seem inclined to accept the view that "nowadays the policies of the most intelligent African leaders are explicitly Pan-African." M. Cheikh Anta Diop, for example, argues that "only the existence of independent African States, federated around a democratic central government—from the Libyan coast of the Mediterranean to the Cape, from the Atlantic to the Indian Ocean—will enable Africans to develop fully and make themselves respected." Independence on anything less than a Pan-African scale, M. Diop suggests, would mean the creation of relatively weak African States, still in practice dependent upon external Powers.

It is not always easy to distinguish between Pan-African and Pan-Negro (or "Pan-Melanist") ideas. Pan-Africanism is, however, a fairly precise geopolitical concept, according to which the future United States of Africa is usually conceived as including the admittedly non-Negro peoples of Egypt and North Africa. Pan-Negrism is more in the nature of a mystique, which directs its appeal to Negroes (and colored people) wherever they may be— including the Negro communities of America and the West Indies. Like Pan-Slavism . . . Pan-Negrism depends for its effectiveness not so much upon a political program as on a metaphysic—the belief that the Negro peoples of the world are the carriers of certain values, and that the assertion of these values is bound up with the cause of Negro emancipation, not simply from colonial rule, but from all forms of racial discrimination and opposition. The term coined expressing this sense of a common Negro inheritance and destiny, among French Africans . . . is *Negritude*. . . . For M. [Jean-Paul] Sartre *Negritude* is essentially a revolutionary concept, reflecting the status of the Black people as the proletariat of the world. It includes such elements as the idea of liberty as earned through suffering:

> To the absurd utilitarian agitation of the White the Black opposes the long authenticity of his sufferings. . . . The Black represents himself in his own eyes as the man who has taken upon himself all human misery and who suffers for all, even for the White.

Belief in the enjoyment of nature as more valuable than sheer technical efficiency:

> Of technique the White knows all. But this merely scratches the surface of things; it is unaware of the substance, of the life within. Negritude, on the contrary, is a comprehension through sympathy.

Belief in the abolition of racial privilege as the universal mission of the Negro peoples:

The Negro creates an antiracist racism. He does not at all wish to dominate the world . . . he affirms his solidarity with the oppressed of all colors.

M. [Léopold] Senghor has on various occasions emphasized a rather different aspect of *Negritude.* In his view the great achievement of the African and Negro peoples has been *la sagesse*—the art of living; expressed through their democratic social structures; their religion; their attitude to birth, marriage, and death; their work; their arts; their rhythms. . . .

THE EFFECT OF SUCCESSFUL ASIAN NATIONALISM

From George H. T. Kimble, *Tropical Africa,* 1960.

The political "coming out" of Asia during the past generation has been followed with the keenest interest by African nationalists. As early as 1927 Ladipo Solanke affirmed that "It took the white race a thousand years to arrive at their present level of advance; it took the Japanese, a Mongol race, fifty years to catch up. . . . there is no reason why we west Africans should not catch up with the Aryans and the Mongols in one quarter of a century."

Solanke's time scale, like his ethnology, may have been on the rough-and-ready side, but few of his African contemporaries would have quarreled with it; and none would have quarreled with the conviction that what the people of Asia could do, the people of Africa could also do. Nor could any say that the people of Asia were not "doers," when almost every year of the past score and more has seen a new independence movement gather speed or a new Asian name added to the scroll of sovereign states.

Of all the Asian independence movements, the Indian movement has undoubtedly stirred the imagination of African nationalists the most. And it is not difficult to see why. First, there was the personality of Mahatma Gandhi. The message cabled by the National Council of Nigeria and the Cameroons (NCNC) on his death expressed the sentiments of all African nationalists, for whom Gandhi was "the bearer of the torch of liberty and oppressed peoples," whose life had been "an inspiration to colonials everywhere." Second, there was the passive nature of it. Most of the African nationalists have been raised in the conviction—part religious and part political—that the really durable victories are the bloodless ones, and that a good cause is advanced much faster by going to prison for it (as many Indian and African leaders have done) than by dying for it on a battlefield. Third, there was, and still is, the kinship between Indian and African students living in London and elsewhere—a kinship fostered in the early days by the interest of Indian nationalists in the West African Students Union and in the short-lived but influential journal *Pan-Africa* (to which many of them contributed articles), and, more recently, by the presence of Indian groups along with African ones in the Movement for Colonial Freedom. Fourth, there has been the consistent condemnation by Indian government spokesmen of African colonialism and race discrimination. This condemnation has been widely voiced in the press, on short-wave radio programs beamed to African countries, and at international conferences. At the Colombo Conference of Asian Prime Ministers in early 1954, Prime Minister Nehru, the most consistent and respected critic of them all, himself a "prison graduate," affirmed that "colonialism is a violation of fundamental rights, and a threat to peace," and in the following year at the Afro-Asian Conference in Bandung he pleased his African admirers even better by affirming that it is an "intolerable humiliation for any nation of Asia or Africa to degrade itself by becoming a camp follower of one or the other of the power blocs . . ." Fifth, there had been the generosity of the Indian government in providing scholarships and travel grants to African nationalist leaders, actual and potential, and in encouraging its own elite to learn about Africa. (Since 1954 there has been an African Studies Program in the University of Delhi, in which work up to the doctoral level is offered.)

In [James S.] Coleman's view, "the continued assertion by India of the role of leader of the newly independent and colonial areas of the world will mean a continuing Indian influence upon emergent African nationalism and in favor of neutralism." He also believes that "the real significance of the Indian factor is that it has given and continues to give African nationalists a sense of power derived from external allies, as well as conviction that their cause will triumph."

THE INFLUENCE OF THE COLD WAR

The speed with which African nationalists achieved their goal of independence is partially due to Cold War pressures on the colonial powers and the United States. The division of the industrial countries into the Western and Communist blocs led to competition between the blocs for the favor and allegiance of the underdeveloped countries. In most situations, the West had the advantage of physical presence, experience, and control, but Russia, and later China, sought to displace Western influence.

The Communist bloc welcomed African students and nationalists, and offered assistance to new nations. Pamphlets and radio broadcasts in African languages proclaimed the evils of colonialism and imperialism.

European nations found it awkward to be occupying a position which could be called "oppression" while their Marxist competitors spoke of "freedom" and "social justice." Accordingly they sought means of gracefully relieving themselves of colonies. In West Africa this was accomplished rapidly, but where large numbers of white settlers were involved, the process was slower and more painful. Portugal alone has doggedly refused to follow suit.

The United States wished to preserve Western influence in Africa. America saw African independence as inevitable, and thus concentrated on creating conditions that would foster the development of the Western concept of freedom. Therefore America frequently pressed her European allies to fulfill African demands for independence. These nations were sometimes resentful of American support for African aspirations in Angola, the Congo, South Africa, and Rhodesia. Resulting strains in the NATO alliance led to compromises between American and European views.

This is not to say that the growing Western approval of African aspirations was hypocritical. In fact, self-determination is consistent with the philosophy of the Western democracies. But it took the competitive pressure of the Cold War to translate vague sympathy into positive action. While African leaders tend to decry the Cold War, African nationalism has generally profited from it.

The Communist attempts to influence Africans are illustrated in the following selection. Even though the events referred to occurred before the Cold War was a recognized fact, the foundation of influence was being laid. One must not jump to the conclusion, however, that just because a man received some training in Moscow, he was destined to be a 100-percent Russian-oriented Communist for all time. The political philosophies and leanings of many of the men mentioned below have shifted a good deal since their introduction to Marxism in the 1930s and 1940s.

From George H. T. Kimble, *Tropical Africa*, 1960.

If communism is not the most powerful of forces within the African nationalist movement, it is not from want of effort. This effort has been sustained and intelligent, and devoted to the twin purpose of seduction and disaffection. While most of the effort appears to have been directed by national communist parties and front organizations, notably those of the United Kingdom and France, some of it has undoubtedly been directed by international agencies. The primary target of the metropolitan communists has been the African students in their midst. Their tactics, as Coleman describes them, have followed the customary lines: "solicitation regarding lodgings, social relations and entertainment; unconditional support of all nationalist objectives; arranging of summer tours behind the Iron Curtain; and the stimulating vision of a return to Africa armed with funds and the potential might of the Soviet Union to become leaders in African Soviet Republics."

Although few were won by this wooing, many were moved by it to the point of a benevolent interest. Prominent among those Africans whose nationalism was fed, in part at least, on a diet of communist comfort and dialectic, are Jomo Kenyatta (who spent some months in Moscow in 1931), I. T. A. Wallace-Johnson, co-editor with Nnamdi Azikiwe of the *African Morning Post* (Accra) in 1934–1935, founder of the West African Youth League, and leading radical nationalist of Sierra Leone for over twenty years; Ladipo Solanke, founder and long-time leader of the West African Students Union; Dr. Felix Houphouet-Boigny, founder and first president of the Rassemblement Démocratique Africain, which in its early days (about 1945) had close connections with the French Communist Party; and Kwame Nkrumah, who still speaks of himself as a "Marxist socialist."

THE NATURE OF THE COLONIAL ADMINISTRATION

The kind of colonial environment within which the various African nationalisms developed naturally shaped the courses which they took. The political philosophy of the mother country, its assumptions about the colony's future, and the presence of a settler population were all factors in conditioning the nature of nationalism within a given territory.

From Immanuel Wallerstein, *Africa: The Politics of Independence,* 1961.

As a result of their special framework of thinking concerning the colonies, the British were the first to begin the process of decolonization. Their attitude could be traced in part to their unhappy experiences in British North America. Having suffered the American Revolution, the British sought to avoid a repetition in Canada and thus began to consider how to devolve powers on the colonists, and how to do it before an explosion occurred. The British tradition of local government plus the fact that the people to whom these powers were at first transferred were largely Englishmen (Canada, Australia, New Zealand) made decolonization a relatively painless procedure.

In the middle of the nineteenth century, legislative bodies on which local people served were created in British colonies in Africa. Thus, the political experience of British West Africans, experience in modern parliamentary government, had a long history and would come to serve this area well. By the same token, in the settler areas of southern Africa, the British also created local legislative bodies, but here the power went in part to white settlers. As these white settlers got more and more autonomy, they eliminated African participation in government, at least until a much later stage of African nationalism. This was the history notably of the Union of South Africa. After the Boer War, the British were generous in their willingness to turn back power to the population of South Africa: the Boers were given coequal rights with the English colonists, but there were suffrage rights and parliamentary representation for Coloureds and Africans as well. When Britain went all the way and granted independence to the Union of South Africa, the dominant white population began to eliminate first the Africans, then the Coloureds, from any political role. Similarly, in Southern Rhodesia the white settlers received substantial autonomy, and in Kenya they received some, for a long time to the detriment of African participation in government.

The British acceptance of the devolution of powers, of the legitimacy of the objective of national independence, led to a situation in which African nationalism could flourish in West Africa and white settler nationalism could flourish in East, Central, and South Africa, until African nationalism caught up with the latter and began to force a rethinking of the political situation, both by the settlers and by the British government. What should be underlined here is that autonomous development, the ultimate acquisition of independence, were always considered reasonable, indeed inevitable, objectives of British colonies in Africa. Once Britain had expanded her previously white Commonwealth after the Second World War to include the Asian dominions of India, Pakistan and Ceylon, there seemed no reason why African countries, first of all the Gold Coast and Nigeria, should not proceed along in this path. Thus, the pace of constitutional development in British nonsettler Africa was rapid and marked by a minimum of violence and antagonism. The rapid transfer of power was to serve as the model and impetus for it elsewhere in Africa.

The French had experienced no early colonial revolt such as the American Revolution leading to the development of a white Commonwealth whose structure could be extended later to nonwhite nations. The French concept of constitutional advance was to draw colonies closer to France, not push them farther away. The Second World War forced France as well as Britain to reconsider its colonial policy. For one thing, the Free French movement had received early support in black Africa, and after the war, therefore, the government thought that such loyalty deserved to be rewarded. . . .

The French concept of illegitimacy of independence meant not only that the constitutional patterns were different from the British but also that the organizational patterns were different. African political parties were sometimes mere extensions of metropolitan parties (such as the SFIO in Senegal). But even if they were not, the fact that they had elected members in France's parliamentary bodies meant that, for reasons of parliamentary survival and influence, they had to attach themselves (*apparenter*) to a party in France. . . . More important even than this political attachment was the fact that various kinds of nonpolitical associations were also organized as branches of French organizations. This was true of everything from boy scouts to war veterans, but it was most significant in the case of trade unions; for a long time all African trade unions were part of the three French federations, the CGT, the CFTC, and the Force Ouvrière, particularly the first. . . .

These were not the only differences. One thing the British were very eager to export was their particular version of parliamentary government. In the process of turning over power, the British used their influence as a pressure toward the development of a multiparty system. The

French did not seem to care. When the French were fighting the nationalist party, they created opposition parties; when they decided to come to terms with the nationalists, they seemed just as happy to have only a single group with which to deal. But as we shall see, after independence the pressures of the social structure toward a one-party state were more important than Britain's effort to encourage multiparty systems.

The fact that the British officialy proclaimed the object of independence and the French officially rejected it caused a different attitude during the crucial period of the dyarchy on the question of creating larger political federations. The British worked hard and actively toward achieving the constitutional formulae which permitted Nigerian federalism and Ghanaian regionalism. The British also worked for East African unity. The French officially abstained from, unofficially worked against, the achievement of federations in French West and French Equatorial Africa, partly because at critical moments those forces which pushed toward federalism seemed to be pushing toward more rapid independence, which was still anathema to the French. Nevertheless, as we shall see again, the forces pushing toward unitary structures within states (for example, the breakdown of regionalism in Ghana) and toward new ties between independent African states were such as to eclipse the importance of the different attitudes of the British and French during the transition period.

Another difference in heritage was the concept of the role of the civil service. Great Britain has long placed great emphasis on the nonpolitical role of the civil service. Senior civil servants are forbidden to engage in partisan political activity, even as private citizens, in order to reinforce the norm that they impartially serve alternating political masters. The French exclude only the most senior group. Not only are a larger number of positions in a ministry overtly political (*le cabinet privé du ministre*) but most permanent civil servants have the rights of all other citizens in terms of active politics. Indeed, the result is that there are clans of French civil servants "linked" with French political tendencies—a rarer occurrence in Britain. This difference, carried over into Africa, was very important during the colonial period. Since the government was the chief employer of the elite, an African civil servant often had to choose between keeping his job and active association with the nationalist movement. The choice of "apoliticism" did not make the civil servants popular with the future leaders of their country. In French areas there was no such conflict. The French could retaliate against a civil servant who was a nationalist by transferring him, but they could not fire him. The dichotomy between African civil servant and African political leader was therefore never as sharp. But once again, after independence, the conflicts between civil servant and politician deriving from their different interests would far outweigh the importance of the different norms that ex-British and ex-French Africans derived from their colonial heritage. In short, although the British differed from the French in terms of their attitudes toward a multi-party system, the construction of political federations, the nature and role of the civil service, these differences became less important as African nations faced the new imperatives of the postindependence era.

• • •

THE POLITICAL INSTITUTIONS OF NATIONALISM

From Thomas Hodgkin, *Nationalism in Colonial Africa*, 1957.

Congresses: Their origin, structure, and function

The political associations which dominated the scene in British and French West and Equatorial Africa and the Sudan during the early postwar years conformed roughly to a common pattern—though, naturally, differences in local conditions gave rise to important divergences of aim, strategy, and organization; as well as to differences in their cycles of birth, maturity, and decay. They belonged to the type referred to here as "congresses" or "fronts" rather than parties. The main points of contrast between congresses and parties can perhaps be summarized as follows. First, the congress claims to represent "all the people"; to embody the national will, made articulate. Its dominant concept is "popular sovereignty," and its spiritual ancestor Jean-Jacques Rousseau. Second, structurally, the congress normally takes the form of a loosely knit, even amorphous, amalgam of local and functional organizations, grouped around a nuclear executive or working committee. Third, the strategy of the congress is, in general, aggressive—expressed in such terms as "the struggle against imperialism," *la lutte contre la colonialisme*—and may involve any or all of the recognized techniques of popular pressure: national boycotts, general strikes, civil disobedience, mass demonstrations, press campaigns, as well as petitions, deputations, and agitation through traditional channels. The party, on the other hand, though it may still claim to represent "the mass," or "the best elements," of the nation, recognize that there are other parties and groupings, as well as the colonial administration, with which it has to compete for power. It attempts to achieve a more tightly knit, pyramidal structure, with its basis in local branches and individual party members (though there are important differences, discussed later, in the point to which this articulation is carried). And its strategy is, in most cases, more flexible and gradualist—directed toward the use of electoral machinery and representative institutions as the main means of securing or retaining political power.

These contrasts between congresses and parties have been presented schematically. In practice, of course, the distinctions are much less clear-cut. But in both cases there is an evident connection between theory, organization and strategy. . . .

The terms which these bodies used to describe themselves—"Congress," "National Council," "Convention," "Rassemblement"—have a certain significance. They imply a notion of universality—the idea that the organization does really express the "general will," and has a moral right to challenge the legal authority of the Administration on that account. . . .

Structure is related to function. Congresses, because they claim to represent "all the people," try to build up connections of some kind with "all the people." This is essential, if only to avoid the traditional reproach of all colonial administrations—that the nationalist leadership speaks only for itself and a small group of urban, educated "malcontents"; with the corollary that the true interpreters of the popular will are District Officers and loyal chiefs. . . .

Congress strategy is frequently aggressive, for the simple reason that it seeks to bring about a fundamental, and fairly rapid, change in the power relationships between Africans and Europeans; and the congress emerges at a time when the colonial power shows little inclination to permit such a transformation to occur. Hence congress leaders, although they may . . . be far from revolutionary in their personal outlook, have accepted the necessity for the use of extraparliamentary techniques, as a means of wearing down the resistance of the Administration. And though they may attach importance also to the pressures which can be brought to bear through parliamentary channels, they are usually unwilling to draw nice distinctions between "constitutional" and "unconstitutional" methods.

Parties as agencies of nationalism

Is it possible to point to any common characteristics of these new African parties? It is necessary first to draw a broad distinction between parties with a relatively primitive, and those with a more modern, type of structure. This contrast can also be presented schematically, somewhat as follows. Parties of the former type are dominated by "personalities," who enjoy a superior social status, either as traditional rulers or members of ruling families, or as belonging to the higher ranks of the urban, professional elite (lawyers, doctors, etc.), or on both grounds. Their political machinery, central and local, is of a rudimentary kind, consisting of those individuals, *chefs de canton,* notables, men of property, who naturally gravitate toward the party, and function, intermittently and principally at election times, as a party committee. Their annual, or occasional, congresses are largely concerned with giving an ovation to the party leaders and confirming them in office. They have little, if anything, in the way of a secretariat or full-time officials: the work of running the party is regarded as a leisure-time occupation of the party leaders. For party funds they look in the main to wealthy backers, as need arises. They depend for popular support less upon organization and propaganda than on habits of respect for traditional authority, or wealth and reputation, among the mass (above all in the rural areas). . . .

Parties of the second type aim at, even if they do not always achieve, a much more elaborate structure. Since their chief claim and function is to represent the mass, they are committed to a form of organization that is (certainly on paper, and to some extent in practice) highly democratic. The party leaders are "of the people" in the sense that they have achieved the positions through dint of personal talent rather than birth or privilege. The basic unit of the party is the local branch (or in towns the ward). . . . The party annual conference is a serious affair, which may last several days; it receives reports on organization and membership, finance, press and propaganda, youth and women's work, economic and social affairs, local government, etc.; passes numerous resolutions; defines party policy, and (if an election is approaching) approves the party's electoral program; as well as electing the national executive committee. The local leadership of a party of this type consists, as a rule, of members of the local intelligentsia—school-teachers, clerks in government departments or commercial firms, traders, women as well as men—most of whom are active also in other organizations, tribal unions, trade unions, farmers' associations, etc., and on this account a source of strength to the party. Parties of this type are able to achieve a much higher level of efficiency than the "parties of personalities"; not only because they can depend upon an organized, politically conscious body of supporters, but also because they possess a continuously functioning central office (and, often also, regional and branch offices), and employ a staff of full-time party officials with administrative and organizing responsibilities. . . .

It . . . requires a party newspaper, or newspapers; party colors, emblems and badges; a party flag; party slogans; party rallies and tom-toms; party songs, ballads or hymns; and, above all in Africa, party vans. It depends for its strength not on the backing of traditional authority but upon propaganda, designed to appeal particularly to the imagination of the young, to women, to the semi-urbanized and discontented; to those who are outside the local hierarchies, and interested in reform and change.

ORGANIZED RESISTANCE TO WHITE SUPREMACY: THE MAU MAU

> In Kenya, some Kikuyu tribesmen, faced with unyielding settlers and chafing under long-standing grievances over the loss of their land, formed a secret organization devoted to achieving reforms even if it meant violence. The outburst of 1952 known as the Mau Mau rebellion was alleged by the British to be under the direction of Jomo Kenyatta. Many of the wounds of Mau Mau have healed, but the rebellion remains a classic example of violence bred by the frustration of the colonial experience.

> From David Reed, "Jomo Kenyatta, Africa's Man of Mystery," Reader's Digest, December 1961.

After World War II, Kenyatta and exiles from other British colonies in Africa, including Kwame Nkrumah now president of Ghana, began to make plans for the liberation of Africa. Peter Abrahams, a Cape Coloured from South Africa, recalls that on one occasion Nkrumah proposed that the three of them form a secret society, and that each spill a few drops of his blood into a bowl and so take a blood oath of secrecy and dedication.

"Kenyatta laughed at the idea," writes Abrahams in Holiday. "He conceived of our struggle in modern twentieth-century terms with no ritualistic blood nonsense. I the end, Nkrumah drifted away from us. We were too tame and slow for him."

In September 1946 Kenyatta returned home, leaving wife and son in England, where they have remained ever since. Kenya had changed little in 15 years. The color bar remained rigid. Because of a sharp rise in the Kikuyu population, the land question was more explosive than ever. As the colonial government kept turning down the Africans' demands for reforms, Kikuyu politics were growing increasingly subversive.

Soon afterward, reports started to drift in of a new organization, the Mau Mau, which administered blood oaths. Sheep and goats were sacrificed; then, facing sacred Mt. Kenya, the Kikuyu tribesmen pledged to drive the whites into the sea. The oathing ceremonies became more and more depraved. Cannibalism and sexual perversions made their appearance in midnight rites.

Through it all, Kenyatta sat impassively in his home near Nairobi, reading Nietzsche and Schopenhauer. Over his house flew the flag of his rebel political movement, the Kenya African Union—black for Africa, red to show that an African's blood is the same color as anyone else's, and green for the fertility of the Kenya highlands. Frequently British officials demanded that he denounce the burgeoning Mau Mau movement. But Kenyatta would counter with his own demands for political reforms, and when these were not met he would stand before thousands of cheering Kikuyu and say, "Mau Mau, what is that? I've never heard of it." On another occasion he told a mass rally: "The land is ours. Don't be afraid to spill your blood to get the land."

The storm broke in the autumn of 1952. White settlers and their families were murdered, often chopped to bits with machetes. Cattle belonging to white settlers were hamstrung and otherwise maimed. At night the sky over Kikuyuland was lighted by the burning huts of those Kikuyu, most of them Christians, who refused to go along with the savage movement.

The settlers armed themselves; British troops were

flown in. The Mau Mau was an anti-white uprising. Yet the terrorists murdered fewer than 100 Europeans and more than 2000 of their own people who refused to join with them. Officially, white troops and police, with their anti-Mau Mau African allies, killed 11,500 terrorists. But trigger-happiness and blood lust were not unknown; the actual toll was several times the official figure.

Kenyatta was arrested at the start of the emergency. Later brought to trial, he was given seven years at hard labor for managing an illegal society. Then he was flown to prison in the remote northern-frontier desert of Kenya. The evidence against Kenyatta at the trial was not impressive. But it was undisputable that he was the sole leader of extremist Kikuyu nationalism, and that only a fine line separated it from the Mau Mau.

Even while Mau Mau still raged, great changes rolled over Kenya. Convinced that the Mau Mau disease could be cured only by far-reaching reforms, the Kenya government took an African into its council of ministers in 1954. Three years later African representation in the colony's legislative council, or future parliament was increased. Finally, by 1961, Africans were in the clear majority. And independence was coming.

For Kenyatta, in the desert heat of his prison, surrounded by a lunar landscape of lava rubble, rock, and bitter lakes, these were years of hardship. In 1959 he completed his sentence, with 28 months off for good behavior. Instead of being given his freedom, however, he was taken to another desert village, there to live out his remaining days in enforced exile. But his memory continued to burn like a bush fire in the hearts of his countrymen.

As late as 1960, Governor Sir Patrick Renison declared that Kenyatta was a leader "to darkness and death." The Africans hooted in derision. Unrest boiled up and many ex-Mau Maus, just released from detention, retook their beastly oaths.

Sir Patrick bowed to the inevitable. Last August [1961] a police plane brought Kenyatta, his third wife, and their two daughters back from exile to his home near

Nairobi. Thousands of tribesmen were on hand. Drums sounded, barefooted women danced and shrilled, "Kenyatta is home! Thank you, Jomo!" Kenyatta acknowledged the welcome with a lordly wave of his zebra-tail fly whisk. Then, embracing his 90-year-old stepfather, he came close to tears. "It has been raining," Kenyatta said, "but now the rain has stopped and all is well with the world."

Nairobi today is a city of baby skyscrapers and traffic jams. A great economic revolution has transformed Kikuyuland into a showplace of African agriculture. Africans are allowed to grow cash crops these days. Hundreds of young Kenyans are studying at universities in the United States and England. The color bar is gone, the farmland of the white highlands is open for purchase by anyone, and Africans are rapidly being promoted to top positions in government and in private business.

Ironically, Kenyatta and other African leaders are now urging the white settlers to remain, realizing that they are a great economic asset to the country. But among the settlers there is uneasiness, and many of them are leaving the colony. Some fear a "Night of the Long Knives," or Congo-type vengeance, on the coming independence day. . . .

> It is one of the ironies of history that today the European population regards Kenyatta as their best defense against the zealous who would "Africanize" everything at once. Kenyatta staunchly supports the idea of Kenya as a multiracial state.

THE ANGOLAN REBELLION

The tide of African nationalism reached isolated Angola after the Congo became independent in 1961. A bloody rebellion dragged on into a prolonged guerrilla war. Supplies and trained Angolan revolutionaries were flown into the jungle bases from friendly countries. The Angolan rebellion represents the type of warfare which is likely to be an expression of nationalism in places where the European minority still refuses to grant Africans self-determination.

A journalist, Albert Meyers, observed the war from territory securely held by Portuguese troops.

From Albert J. Meyers, "A Firsthand Story of Today's Hottest War," *U.S. News & World Report,* August 28, 1961.

Undetermined numbers of black Africans—some of the estimates run as high as 25,000—have lost their lives in this war between the Portuguese colonial regime and those who are fighting to overthrow it.

Compare the war in Angola with events in the Congo and you find that the toll here in six months far surpasses that in the Congo in twice the time. Whereas in the Congo Belgian colonial administrators quickly capitulated to the independence demands of African nationalists, here in Angola the Portuguese are determined to hang on. Whereas in the Congo relatively few have been killed, here in Angola violent death has become almost commonplace. . . .

It is a strange hit-and-run war.

I drove from Luanda northeast beyond the small town of Caxito on the road to encircled Carmona. In this area you see hundreds of Portuguese troops, both white and black, engaged in military operations. You see no rebels, except for a few prisoners. Yet this is one of the "hot zones" of the war.

What's it like to fight this type of jungle warfare? This is the way a young Portuguese paratroop captain puts it:

"These terrorists are experts in camouflage. And their tactics in ambush show they've been trained by someone, somewhere—well trained."

The Portuguese strategy is to encircle the rebels and seal off the border with the Congo—thus closing the hatch through which the rebels receive supplies and reinforcements. But so far, they haven't been able to do it. And when the rainy season starts in a few weeks, it will make operations more difficult for the Portuguese and easier for the rebels.

Caught up in the war are many American missionaries, some 250 of whom live and work in this area. The Portuguese charge that some of these missionaries have aided and abetted the rebel cause. Missionaries, in turn, charge that thousands of innocent blacks have been slaughtered by Portuguese troops and civilians. . . .

Portugal's "jewel," Angola is a vast country lying along the southern border of Africa's Atlantic Coast, just south of the Congo. . . . The territory is as big as France, Germany, and Italy combined.

It is a country of great open spaces, 13 times the size of Portugal, with a population density of less than five persons per square mile. It is home for some 5 million black Africans and about 250,000 white Portuguese.

One reason Portugal is determined not to give way to the wave of African nationalism now sweeping across the continent is the simple fact that the Portuguese have been here for 500 years—two centuries longer than white men have inhabited the Union of South Africa. . . .

Yet you quickly notice a difference between Angola and neighboring South Africa. In South Africa, separation of the races is the law of the land. But in Angola integration is permitted in some cases—at least in theory. . . .

In Luanda you see whites and blacks working side by side on construction projects and mixing in shops and cafés. In the slum areas on the outskirts of the city you can see white families living in tumbledown shacks next door to African families, whose housing is no worse and no better.

Actually, there is a lot of unofficial segregation not recognized by law. You seldom see an African guest in Angola's best hotel. Hotel jobs, except for the most menial, are reserved for whites. Your taxi driver in Luanda is white.

With all of this, however, there is no doubt that color-consciousness in Angola is much less prevalent than in many other areas of Africa. . . .

What part, if any, the Communists are taking in the rebellion is widely discussed here. Portuguese officials say they have captured no weapons that can be traced directly to Communist sources. They also say they do not believe the Holden Roberto group is Communist, though it may be receiving some Red support.

The Conakry-based group is believed by the Portuguese to be Communist-dominated, but has had little to do with the guerrilla operations so far.

You don't have to be here long to reach this conclusion: There's no question that, if Portugal is forced to quit Angola, a situation far worse than that in the Congo can develop. Here in Angola, there are very few Africans in the educated and professional classes, and none who are really trained, politically. It is doubtful if the territory's blacks are even as ready for self-government as the natives were in the Congo.

Ready or not, they're not going to get the chance if the Portuguese have anything to say about it. The Portuguese simply will not grant independence. Said one Luanda resident:

"This is our home. We may die here, but we will never leave."

The Portuguese are very bitter over the criticism from abroad of their treatment of the natives on two scores: contract labor and punishment for crimes.

Portugal maintains a system here under which every able-bodied African must work at least six months of the year. Contract-labor brokers pay tribal chiefs for the services of African laborers. The brokers then sell the services of these Africans to planters, construction workers, and stevedoring companies.

The contract laborer is paid at a higher rate than a voluntary worker, and in addition is furnished food, housing, and medical services.

Another practice widely criticized abroad is a system of physical punishment for African wrongdoers. A native caught robbing is not sent to jail. He is beaten on the hands.

Both practices—contract labor and physical punishment—have brought condemnations of the Portuguese for allegedly using repressive methods in dealing with the native population.

Yet, when you add everything up, the Angola native probably is no worse off than the native anywhere else in

Africa where colonial powers still are in control. Neither
is he better off. . . .

Richard Mathews entered Angola through the Congo,
and his guides were Angolan nationalist rebels. Contrast the overtones of this article with the previous one.

From Richard Mathews, "A Visit to the Rebels of Angola," *The
Reporter,* September 28, 1961.

We rolled south through the darkened towns, past Congolese Army check points where sleepy soldiers blinked
at us and looked at our papers. Unanswered questions
raced through my mind: What had caused the exodus of
130,000 refugees from Angola into the Congo? What lay
behind the five-month-old rebellion? Was Holden Roberto,
a Baptist and former Leopoldville clerk, the real leader of
the rebellion, with his União das Populacões de Angola
(UPA)? . . .

We were still in the Congo, and there was still a Congolese village between us and the frontier, some two miles
away. Half an hour later, we found ourselves on the top
of a low, bush-covered ridge. Along it, from east to west,
ran a cleared swath, perhaps thirty feet wide. Fidel said:
"*Voilà l'Angola, monsieur.*"

Garcia and Fidel, UPA members both, were treated
with warmth and admiration, I noticed. It was the same
story in all the villages we passed through and the same
with all the other UPA members I talked with. It seems
undeniable that the UPA and the revolution have real popular support, at least in large parts of northern Angola.
Indeed, it would be difficult to explain its success
otherwise.

It impressed me that I, a white, was warmly welcomed.
This was true in the villages as well as later among the
rebel troops. Holden Roberto and his colleagues had told
me in numerous interviews that they were not leading an
anti-European movement. The revolution is not anti-
white; it is simply—and brutally—anti-Portuguese. There
is a great fund of good will, for example, for the Protestant

missionaries, nearly all of whom are either British or American. . . .

A little before four we reached a village called Kambamiole. By 4:10 we were approaching the fringes of Fuessa; we could already see the roofs of the first few huts. Suddenly Fidel told me to run with him into the forest bordering the trail and to lie low. The reason became evident immediately: a drone could be heard off to the southwest. It was a Portuguese reconnaissance plane, an ancient one-engine craft, probably unarmed. I wondered why all the fuss for a little spotter so far off. I learned soon enough: at 4:15 a much more resonant drone filled the sky. The spotter must have been searching for designated targets, and on finding them, radioed the other planes. Two minutes later the Portuguese dropped their first bombs and made their first strafing runs about half a mile to the north of us, at Kambamiole.

At 4:30 it became apparent that Fuessa was also on the day's list of targets. First there were several low reconnaissance passes. Then a few grenades were dropped on the north side of the village (luckily we were on the west). Next the strafing began; there were six passes in all. I could not tell which of the three planes we had seen made them because at the time I was trying to bury myself in the roots of a clump of thorn palms. Thirty-caliber machine-gun bullets were crackling off into the trees all around. Some of the forty-five UPA guerrillas who were the presumed target of the Portuguese sniped at the planes as they swooped low on the strafing runs. I found later that their arms consisted of twenty locally made muzzle-loaders, eight Enfields, six Mausers, and one automatic machine pistol. If the rebels wasted ammunition, they certainly demonstrated considerable courage—and they told me they had downed more than twenty Portuguese planes in the last four months with similar weapons.

By five the Portuguese either thought they had sufficiently crippled the rebel band or had run out of ammunition. It only remained for them to burn the villages they had already strafed and bombed. This they duly did with three gasoline bombs. Their mission ended, they flew off.

When we entered Fuessa, we had to skirt a burning hut where ammunition had been stored and from which bullets were now flying in all directions. The village's few women were pouring water on the thatched roofs of four huts that had not caught fire. As the fire subsided into smoldering heaps of ashes, the women began raking out what they could save—the ten-gallon pans they carry on their heads, smoking bits of colored cloth, roasted peanuts and manioc, hoes and jungle knives with charred handles. By now the Fuessa fire had spread up the grassy hillside on the eastern side of the village.

The UPA soldiers, ragged men and boys from fourteen years old on up, hardly seemed perturbed. Fidel explained that there had not been a single rebel casualty in all three villages. As far as I could determine he was right about at least the first point, if one was to exclude the marginal case of a Mauser-carrying seventeen-year-old whose cheek was slightly scratched. The Portuguese had sent out four planes and bombed for forty-five minutes, without weakening their enemy's potential.

All evidence I could gather indicated that the operation against Fuessa was typical of the Portuguese military effort in large parts of northern Angola. To the south, around Bembe and Carmona, where there is some semblance of battle lines, the situation is probably different, but in northern Angola, the UPA guerrillas move almost at will and there is apparently nothing Portuguese aviation can do about it. If the Portuguese send in troops, they will be fighting at a disadvantage despite their superior equipment, for the nationalists know the virtually roadless terrain, have the support of the local population, and, as guerrillas, can choose the time and place of combat. Though poorly equipped and untrained, the rebel groups I saw were determined and well organized. Holden Roberto recently stated that shortly after the September rains come, "The UPA will be the absolute master of all the territory north of Luanda."

On the night of the burning of Fuessa, I was given a reed bed in one of the four remaining huts. At dawn

Fidel woke me. "We had better go off into the forest," he announced. "The Portuguese usually come back the next day to see what fine things they've done. It's best not to be around." I readily agreed, but we decided to go first and see Kimbuaku—or what had been Kimbuaku the day before. There was nothing left but the charred pole skeletons of huts surrounding a pit dug by an exploding grenade. About thirty feet away we found a yard-long, drum-shaped aluminum case. On one side of it was a red label that read: "110 gallon Gasoline Bomb. Property of United States Air Force."

That evening we camped in the forest with about forty UPA guerrillas and those of the civilian villages who had not already left for the Congolese refugee camps. Early next morning thirty-four UPA soldiers and porters arrived from the north with a cargo of nineteen boxes of nine-millimeter cartridges, a few light automatic weapons, some bags of salt (something desperately needed in the south), and medicine. Directing the rebel convoy was Louis Ingles, a thirty-four-year-old former tailor and now UPA military commander in the Santo Antonio do Zaire region in the extreme northwest of Angola. The five hundred guerrillas of the area, he said, were fighting desperately, and were in dire need of heavier equipment.

"You know," he said, "of course we suffer terribly, but the war is teaching us a lot—how to work together and accept discipline and sacrifices. When we get independence we won't be like the Congo."

Ingles passed out sheets of general instructions written in Kikongo and signed by Holden Roberto in Leopoldville. Among the ten points was an order demanding that each village select an individual to transmit information and receive UPA commands. The man chosen was to express opinions "not according to his own views, but the views of the whole population." Another point warned against stealing by UPA soldiers; a third stated that no item seized from the Portuguese should be kept. A fourth point urged cooperation and mutual respect between youth and elders; a fifth demanded that money the rebels could lay their hands on be sent to the UPA's directors in

Leopoldville because "if we do not have money our work for independence cannot continue." . . .

Over watery, home-grown coffee, I asked Nones how the Portuguese administration had behaved in Uga. What he—and most other Angolans I talked to—resented most was the forced-labor system. I knew that Africans who could not prove they were supporting themselves and their families were obligated to become *contratados,* that is, to accept six-month "contracts" as workers on roads and plantations. They were supposed to be paid modest sums, fed, housed, and doctored. This was written into the "province's" laws and was public information. But according to Miguel, the laws had little bearing on reality. When the *chefe de posto,* the official most directly concerned with native policy, came down to Uga from his headquarters in Buela, he knew exactly how many workers were needed. Whether or not these workers were supporting themselves and their families did not concern him. Since many of the men at Uga had migrated to the Congo (while continuing to pay taxes to the Portuguese), where prospects were infinitely brighter, the *chefe de posto* would often take women and children from eight years old up. Miguel said the *chefe* of the Buela district was inspired by a kickback from the plantation owners.

In the Carmona coffee region, the *contratados* work from dawn to dusk every day except Sunday. If a worker fails to pick a pre-established quota of coffee, his (or her) hands are beaten until bloody with a wooden paddle called a *palmatoria. Contratados'* wages, though below twenty-five cents a day, are often withheld. Worse still, their six-month "contracts" are often renewed against their will for periods running into years.

Captain Henrique Galvão of Santa Maria fame, formerly a colonial inspector, sent in a report on Angola in 1947 which was so damning to the Portuguese administration that he was jailed. He noted that "only the dead are exempt from compulsory labor." And James Duffy, whose *Portuguese Africa* is the only scholarly study of the subject in English, found in 1959 that "the reality is pretty much the same as it was four hundred years ago:

the indiscriminate use of Africans for Portuguese benefit."

. . . If Angola was peaceful until last spring, it was enjoying the peace of a slave state. Now it is experiencing the violence of a slave rebellion. If the nationalists hack Portuguese noncombatants to death with their sinister, two-foot katana knives, the Portuguese, better equipped, do the same sort of thing on a larger scale. They are reliably reported to have lined up the entire population of suspect villages, marched them to the banks of a river, machine-gunned them all down, and watched their corpses float off to the crocodiles.

We left Buela in the dark; before midnight we passed the undemarcated Congolese frontier. We were to meet a UPA gun-running truck at 2:00 A.M. It never came, so we set off on foot for the railroad station at Moerbeke. During the course of the morning, I was arrested by two drunken Congolese policemen and detained for two days. I feared the worst (newspapers exaggerate incidents so much), but they did me no harm.

My arrest was not surprising. Anybody—black or white—having anything to do with the UPA is likely to be apprehended. At the present time the guide who showed us from Songa to the frontier is incarcerated in the district jail at Songololo. If the local Congolese authorities along the frontier are not in the pay of the Portuguese (and many share my opinion that they are), they behave as if they were.

After I had been transferred from the hands of the policemen to the subgovernor of the territory, my detention was agreeable enough. The subgovernor finally agreed to allow me to take the morning train back to Leopoldville. I had never thought that I would look on that troubled city as a center of civilization.

The Political Evolution of Representative African States

FRENCH EQUATORIAL AFRICA

What was French Equatorial Africa now comprises the sovereign states of the Central African Republic, the Congo (Brazzaville), Chad, and Gabon. Other French African dependencies were organized into the administrative units of French West Africa and Madagascar. These are referred to here, but not considered in detail.

From Smith Hempstone, *Africa–Angry Young Giant,* 1961.

. . . Felix Eboue was midwife to [French Equatorial Africa]. This thickset Negro from a South American pepper port (Cayenne, French Guiana) was born in 1884, a descendant of slaves. He did well in school and was sent to France to study in the school of colonial administration. Eboue served in the French Sudan and Guadaloupe, worked himself patiently up through the colonial hierarchy to become governor of Chad, the northernmost of French Equatorial Africa's four territories.

As Nazi Germany forced France to her knees, Eboue, who risked not only his career but his head in so doing, led Chad and two other Equatorial African territories into the Allied camp, blocked Rommel out of central Africa, provided Britain with the only feasible overland supply route to Suez when Hitler's bombers closed the Mediterranean to Allied shipping, and gave homeless Charles de Gaulle real estate upon which to mount his Cross of Lorraine [symbol of the Free French]. Overnight, Eboue became a symbol both of Free France and of a renascent Africa, worthy of honor and capable of action. The words "This is Radio Brazzaville calling . . ." for five long years spelled self-respect and hope to millions in Occupied France. Although Eboue's fame has been overshadowed by that of his military colleague, in history he will share with de Gaulle the role of savior of France's honor in her darkest hour. The people of Little Rock, Algiers, and Notting Hill would do well to remember that they owe much to this black man.

But Eboue was very much more than a brave Frenchman. He was an accomplished musician who could play with equal facility the most intricate sonata or pound out a message on the piano understandable to the players of Africa's talking drums. He was a perceptive anthropologist and a wise administrator who urged France to treat the African "as a human being capable of progress in his own environment and, in all likelihood, lost if he is taken from it." Few wiser words have been written about Africa and Eboue well deserves his resting-place in the Pantheon in Paris.

The Brazzaville Conference

His last act was just as important as his defiance of Vichy: in reward for and recognition of Africa's contribution to the cause of freedom, a conference was held in Brazzaville with Eboue as host in January 1944. Filled with the spirit of the Resistance and warmed by the knowledge of the coming Liberation, de Gaulle met with Eboue and other African leaders to blueprint the economic and political structure of a greater Franco–African community.

Although the men of Brazzaville specifically ruled out any definition of French Africa without France, they guaranteed to Africans the right to participate in the drawing up of the new constitution and to be represented in all assemblies of the French Union. In Africa itself there was to be a decentralization of administrative control, the election of territorial assemblies by universal suffrage wherever possible, land reform, extension of the French labor code to Africa, a vast program of economic development in which the needs of the African territories would receive equal recognition with those of France and the abolition both of forced labor and of the *indigénat* (the legal differentiation between French citizens and French subjects). Taking a leaf from the book of Caracalla, emperor of third-century Rome, full French citizenship was to be conferred upon all those living within the boundaries of France's empire.

Eboue died a few months later and de Gaulle retired from public life. As a consequence, the spirit of the Liberation and of Brazzaville was diluted and smaller-minded men of the it-can't-be-done stamp came to power. But if not all of the hopes of Brazzaville were immediately realized, substantial gains were won: France's feet were set upon the path from which there is no turning. Even the watered-down caricature of the spirit of Revolutionary France acknowledged that, henceforward, Africans were to have a major say in shaping their own destiny.

Brazzaville was followed by a decade of jockeying and indecision as a France fearful of communist agitation in her closed colonial preserve, angered at the outbreak of warfare in Algeria and Indo-China, fearful of aggressive American capitalism, and mistrustful of Black nationalism, hesitated between liberalism and reaction. . . .

The loi cadre

In 1956, the new Socialist premier, Guy Mollet, took two Africans into his cabinet and tabled before the French Assembly the so-called *loi cadre* (enabling law) which was to revive the spirit of Brazzaville and even extend the promises of that conference. Black Africa was not yet actively restive but events in Indo-China indicated to the jittery statemen that the pressure of events might soon leave France with no alternative south of the Sahara.

If carried to its logical conclusion, Overseas France would have 248 deputies in a 520-member French Assembly. This, of course, was and is politically impossible and unrealistic for many sound reasons. But the *loi cadre* did increase African representation in the Metropolitan assemblies, establish universal suffrage throughout the Union, create a single electoral college for blacks and whites, reorganize the civil service, enhance the powers of the local assemblies, and elevate the top Africans in each territorial assembly to local cabinet rank.

This did much to satisfy Equatorial Africa's political aspirations but little to solve her pressing economic problems: then as now, she imports £3 worth of goods for every £2 she sells and two-thirds of her exports by value consist of two products prone to price-shimmering, wood and cotton. Neither French liberalism nor the often fuzzier brand peddled by the United Nations can do much about the fact that three out of every four inhabitants of [French Equatorial Africa] live more than six hundred miles from the sea in areas without easily navigable rivers or the possibility of railway construction. Nor can merely wishing it so make the Muslim population any less suspicious of Western education. Belgian administrators were able to say with some truth that, if their blacks lacked the political freedom afforded by the *loi cadre,* they at least had full bellies and shoes on their feet. But even more startling political developments were in store for the Gallic giant.

De Gaulle's return and plan for a French Community

Wearied of the political merry-go-round which had given each French government for thirteen years an average life-span of six months, fearful of the neofascist threat posed by Algeria's *colons* and rightist factions within the army, France turned in the summer of 1958 to her wartime savior, Charles de Gaulle, to restore her stability and her honor.

It was characteristic of de Gaulle, as a man of Brazzaville, that he dared to present French Africans with the choice between independence and closer identification with France and, having dared, won. De Gaulle made only one whirlwind trip through Africa a month before the September 28 referendum in an attempt to rally Africa to his proposed French Community. The General offered the African territories political independence (with an end to French financial aid) or autonomy within the French Community and continued economic assistance. Where, the African politicians wondered, would the money come from to fulfill their promises of more schools, roads, and dams, a better standard of living for their people? Perhaps more important, who would pay the politicians' fat salaries, provide them with free mansions, cars, servants, and four round-trip air tickets to Paris each year? The African, ever a materialist, got the message.

De Gaulle promised that an affirmative vote would not bind a territory to France indefinitely. Implicit but unsaid was the future formation of a French Community resembling the British Commonwealth of Nations. For the moment, however, the Community, dominated by France, was to retain control of foreign affairs, defense, currency matters, overall economic planning, and higher education.

"In effect," said a Frenchman in Gabon, "de Gaulle said 'Take our money as long as you need it; if you ever want complete independence, just drop me a postcard.'"

Despite the scope and generosity of this offer, it appeared at election time that de Gaulle might well go down in history as the man who lost France her African empire in one throw of the dice. Thirty-five days before the election, Reuters stated that "French-African leaders are presuming that Madagascar and at least nine of twelve territories of French West and Equatorial Africa will vote for independence." In the event, de Gaulle rolled up an affirmative vote in these territories. Only Guinea exercised the right to opt for independence.

Reasons for de Gaulle's victory

The British pundits erred by underestimating the force of four things: the economic factor, racial goodwill created over the years by the policy of identification, the appeal of de Gaulle's personality to the average African, and the confidence of the African leaders that, at a later date, they would be able to obtain a more liberal revision of the Community's ground-rules. This revisionist movement was led by the politicians of Mali and Madagascar, who persuaded the General to grant their countries full independence in 1960 while still retaining loose links with France. Their success inspired the remainder of the

French African states to follow their example and all did so before the year was out. . . .

Gaullism, particularly within the four territories of French Equatorial Africa, is literally a cult. Fetishist tribes sacrifice chickens to images of the General encased in bottles. Neo-Christian sects include de Gaulle in their Trinity with the Father and the Son. Even those less spiritually inclined who have never heard of Louis XIV, Napoleon, Rousseau, or Foch smile with pleasure at the mention of the General's name.

In part this adulation is based on de Gaulle's war record. But de Gaulle's magic speaks even to those Africans—and there are more than a few—who are unaware that there was a world war. The General is everything that the African seems to like and respect in a leader: tall, hefty, imperious, calm and at the same time flamboyant, a speaker in parables, and a wearer of braid and feathers. It is highly unlikely that the able Pierre Mendès-France could have sold the same program with an equal degree of success: physically and emotionally, he just doesn't coincide with the African image of a leader.

Just to reinforce the General's magnetism, in the days when the outcome of the referendum seemed in doubt, the French army and officialdom launched a well-organized propaganda drive in his behalf. Colorful posters slapped indiscriminately on city skyscrapers and bush huts informed such of the electorate as were literate that a vote for de Gaulle was, among other things, a vote for equality, liberty, fraternity, prosperity, community, Africa, and France. All of this turned out to be as necessary as a Democratic doorbell-ringing campaign in Georgia during an election year. There was no anti-Gaullist propaganda in Equatorial Africa and one government publicist, worried about how this would look to the outside world, pleaded (unsuccessfully) for a little government money to "print and scatter around a few *Non!* posters."

As far as the political leaders of Equatorial Africa were concerned, the structure of de Gaulle's Community offered much, denied little. As Boganda put it, "the choice was between being allowed to drive your own batered Chevrolet with a nearly empty tank or being chauffeured by a white driver in a new Cadillac as far as you like. And, in the end, one has always a chance of acquiring title to the Cadillac."

On the day of the referendum bare-breasted Bakongo women and Ubangi damsels with plates in their lips jostled with pale Arab bedouins, Frenchmen with existentialist beards, and sallow mulattos from Libreville to cast their votes. When the tally was finished, the dimensions of the Gaullist vote were totally surprising to most and reached proportions almost embarrassing to some. Metropolitan France had voted four to one for de Gaulle; Eboueland (Middle Congo, Ubangi-Shari, and Chad) gave him a 99 per cent *oui* vote; even in Gabon, the fourth territory of Equatorial Africa and the one that stuck longest with Vichy, the General received a majority of 92 per cent. In the event, the black political leaders of Equatorial Africa had opted for the Cadillac rather than the Chevrolet.

Unity or disunion

Having assented to belong to the French Community, Equatorial Africa had then to decide whether it would become a large unitary state, a federation of states, a department of France, or four autonomous republics each with an individual relationship to France and none to each other. Afrer considerable jockeying, the same centrifugal forces which nearly wrecked the United States within months of Yorktown smashed Equatorial African unity. [French Equatorial Africa], which had never been more than an administrative reality, dissolved into four political entities. But events outside Equatoria were at least partially to re-create this unity: the independence of Mali (the republics of Senegal and Soudan) coupled with the sudden Belgian granting of freedom to the Congo drastically altered the concept of the Community and strengthened the hand of the four territories of Equatoria —Congo, Central African Republic, and Chad joined to-

gether to form a customs union within which many con-
sumer services are shared.

Gabon, which has both a history of separatism and a
strong economy, remained outside the union.

. . . Premier M'Ba knew that Gabon would have to
bear most of the cost of the unification of Equatorial Africa while having virtually no say in the political fortunes
of the state. In the proportional allocation of seats in an
eighteen-member assembly, for instance, dirt-poor Chad
would have ten seats and the Central African Republic
(Ubangi-Shari) would have four, while Gabon and the
Congo Republic, which is also relatively rich, would have
only two each. Despite all the talk about Pan-Africanism,
M'Ba was unwilling to share Gabon's wealth with her
poorer sister republics and he was instrumental in seeing
to it that his country, at least for the moment, remains
outside the union of the other three equatorial African republics. With a relatively stable government and a burgeoning economy, Gabon gives promise of becoming one
of the most prosperous black republics of the French
Community.

TANGANYIKA: THE EVOLUTION OF A TRUST TERRITORY

Tanganyika was a German colony until after World
War I, when it was given to Great Britain as a mandate
under the League of Nations. When the United Nations replaced the League of Nations after World War
II, the title was changed to trust territory, but the idea
remained the same. The trustee power had the obligation to administer the territory with the best interests of
the inhabitants in mind and with an aim toward eventual self-government or independence. The Trusteeship
Council of the United Nations sees that the obligation
is being fulfilled.

Until its large-scale involvement in the Congo after
1960, the United Nations' major responsibility in Africa
had been exercised through its Trusteeship Council.
Since newly independent ex-colonies are members of
this body, it is natural that it should tend to exert maximum pressure toward independence for areas remaining under its jurisdiction.

Tanganyika, now Tanzania, illustrates how effective this pressure can be. When, in 1954, the Trusteeship Council recommended independence in twenty years for what was then Tanganyika, the British flatly rejected the proposal. Yet, working in the spirit of the recommendation, they were able to grant Tanganyika complete independence within the Commonwealth by 1961.

From Martin Lowenkopf, in *Africa Report,* December 1961.

Although Tanganyika lacks the material wealth of Kenya and Uganda and has a far thinner layer of educated Africans than either of these neighbors, it has moved peacefully ahead of them toward full independence on December 9 [1961].

The most obvious reason for Tanganyika's unexpected emergence as a pace-setter is Prime Minister Julius Nyerere, who has molded the disparate races and political forces of his country into a cohesive national political movement that contrasts sharply with the politico-tribal struggles for power elsewhere in East Africa. Nyerere's accomplishment is the greater because he has been able to gain this objective without sacrificing the confidence of Britain, his own credibility as an African nationalist, or the course of nonalignment he has set for Tanganyika in world affairs.

In building up the Tanganyika African National Union [TANU] into the powerful monolithic force it has become, Nyerere has enjoyed certain advantages not shared by nationalist leaders in Uganda or Kenya. Perhaps most important, Tanganyika has no white settler "problem" comparable to that of Kenya. Of its 9,000,000 people, more than 98 per cent are Africans. Of some 125,000 non-Africans, the great majority are Indians, Pakistanis, and Arabs; only about 20,000 are Europeans, and, of these, perhaps only 3,000 are permanent residents.

Homogeneity an asset

In addition, Tanganyika enjoys a degree of linguistic and

ethnic homogeneity rare in Africa. Because Swahili is the lingua franca throughout the country, it has been far easier for TANU organizers to communicate on a meaningful level with all elements of the population. And while there are 127 different tribes within Tanganyika's borders, there is no single grouping comparable, in political or economic strength, to the separatist-minded Baganda in Uganda.

While a man of Nyerere's stature would have been likely to rise to the top in any environment, his predominance is at least in part due to the fact that he was able to build TANU in his own image before there were many other educated Africans capable of competing in the political arena. In 1954, when TANU was founded, Nyerere was one of two overseas university graduates in Tanganyika. By the time there were others who might have been inclined to start competitive political movements, TANU was clearly established as the only vehicle to power and Nyerere's position in it virtually unassailable.

Nyerere has constructed TANU out of both traditional and modernist elements, using his own charisma to blend the two into a working organization. The middle-class leaders of the cooperative societies which handle much of the marketing of Tanganyika's cotton and coffee have long been a mainstay of the party's leadership, and George Kahama and Paul Bomani, both Ministers, are their leading representatives in the government. Many returning war veterans, semieducated townsmen, and others were drawn to TANU because it seemed to offer a way of reducing the power of the nonrepresentative "chiefly" administration and securing democratization of native councils. At the same time, Nyerere successfully won the support of a number of traditional chiefs for TANU's goals of self-determination, once it became clear to them that the mass of the people supported the party. Chief Abdullah Fundikira, Minister of Lands and Surveys in the present government, was an early supporter of TANU. The trade union movement, which is in a sense an offspring of TANU, built new bonds between the party and an important element of the population.

In assessing the sources of TANU's strength, special attention must be given also to the party bureaucracy itself. TANU has become the employer and sacred cause of some 2,000 persons—mostly former teachers, clerks, and small businessmen. Although these officers enjoy little discretion under the TANU constitution and organizational machinery, they are a distinct force in the country, because they are part of the power structure of the state and close to the people as well; more important, they are a force independent of the different elements which go to make up the party . . .

Economic problems loom largest

The overriding problem facing an independent Tanganyika is economic—or, as Prime Minister Nyerere has phrased it, to conquer "poverty, ignorance, and disease." Most of the country's inhabitants are engaged in subsistence agriculture. Production is hampered by uneconomic land usage, lack of water and variable rainfall, widespread infestation of tsetse fly, and, in consequence, an ill-distributed population. Two-thirds of the people of Tanganyika live on one-tenth of the land, and only seven percent of the total land area is devoted to production of export crops. Largely because of the postwar sisal boom and increased production of coffee and cotton, Tanganyika's exports and its gross national product have increased sustantially in the last few years and it presently enjoys a favorable balance of trade amounting to $53,-200,000. However, its three export crops are acutely sensitive to fluctuating world prices and the upward trend of recent years has not continued in 1961. . . .

Political tensions exist

Although TANU remains one of the most cohesive political movements in Africa, its bureaucracy is not a collection of "yes" men and open opposition to Nyerere's policies exists among some elements of the population. These differences of viewpoint are likely to grow rather than diminish once the all-encompassing goal of independence is achieved, and as the educated elite develops in size and the range of its aspirations. There is already a "ginger group" in the National Assembly which takes issue with many of Nyerere's policy decisions, and there is obvious dissatisfaction among some TANU back-benchers who have been moved from the "inner circle" to less significant positions to make way for younger but better-educated appointees to executive office. Some TANU regional officials, discontented by the size of their representation in the Assembly, tend to identify with this group. . . .

The question of citizenship

This was demonstrated recently when Prime Minister Nyerere found it necessary to stake the government's life on a Citizenship Bill which will allow persons born outside Tanganyika but who have lived in the country for five or more years to become citizens two years from date of application. Although the legislation eventually passed, the debate in the National Assembly revealed that there is considerable opposition within the governing party to Nyerere's commitment to a nonracial Tanganyika. It may be increasingly difficult to contain the sensitivity which exists in many quarters toward the relative wealth of the immigrant community—particularly the 100,000 Asians.

It is as impossible to analyze Tanganyika's political and economic prospects apart from Nyerere's position in the country as it is to discuss India without reference to Nehru. The very real tensions which exist in Tanganyika can be kept in check as long as Nyerere remains the adored leader of the masses, the patron and constitutional leader of the most important elements in the country, and the kind of responsible and imaginative leader who attracts concrete assistance from abroad to help him meet his people's rising expectations. His significance goes far beyond the borders of Tanganyika, moreover, because he is the close confidant of African nationalist leaders throughout English-speaking East and Central Africa, and a chief architect of the projected East African Federation.

Tanganyika clearly represents a new and powerful voice among the . . . independent nations of Africa.

TANZANIA: A PROGRESS REPORT

The unpredictable nature of African politics was demonstrated in April 1964 when Tanganyika and the island state of Zanzibar announced their union as the new state of Tanzania.

This surprise move was preceeded by disturbances in both countries. In December 1963, Zanzibar had undergone a revolution in which the Arab-dominated government was replaced by an African-dominated one. The leadership of the rebels was such that the move was generally regarded as a long step forward for communist influence in East Africa.

The following year a mutiny in the Tanganyikan army was regarded by some to be an extension of the same sort of influence to the mainland. This fear appeared to be unfounded, however. The mutiny was quickly put down by British troops flown in at the request of President Nyerere and the grievances of the mutineers were found to be of a nonpolitical nature.

Then in the spring of 1964 came the union of the two troubled countries. Again there were observers who saw this as an extension of communist influence from Zanzibar to the mainland. Events to date have not borne out this supposition. If anything, the converse is true.

The following selection comments on some of the problems the newly united republic faced.

From "Honeymoon Trials," *The Economist,* August 29, 1964.

Arguing against impatience the other day, President Nyerere told thc Tanganyikans that they should not blame a brick for not being a wall. He may be tempted to repeat these words this weekend when he makes his first ceremonial visit to Zanzibar since the two countries joined in a united republic on April 22 [1964]. For the first three months after union there was little if any evidence of the two countries merging.

During the last month, however, progress toward real union has begun. There are plenty of bricks about for President Nyerere to see—and not just the 5,000 tons of them that the East Germans brought all the way from Europe to rebuild part of the Ngambo slums. Since they all went to conferences in London and Cairo, there seems much closer rapport between the Tanganyikan and Zanzibari leaders. The United Republic flag flew on the island for the first time when the Vice President, Mr. Karume, returned from Cairo and it now flies even over the houses of remote area commissioners. Mr. Karume, who a month ago hardly mentioned Tanganyika, was last week daily telling the people of the northern island of Pemba how the union had made both countries strong.

Integration has gone fastest in the police forces, helped by the sending of 300 Tanganyikan police to Zanzibar within a week of the January revolution. The merging of the armies was clearly more difficult. Tanganyika had to raise new battalions after the mutiny, while the People's Liberation Army, containing Zanzibar's most radical revolutionaries, was soon being trained by Russian instructors in deadlier weapons than their original antique armory. But a Tanganyikan officer, Brigadier Serikikya, has paid several visits to Zanzibar this month, and the barrack room word is that many Zanzibari soldiers will soon be posted to the mainland.

The question for President Nyerere is what to do next. There are obvious areas of discouragement. His own junior minister, Mr. Rowland Mwanjisi, now has a hand in administering Zanzibar's home affairs, but there is an unyielding attitude among Zanzibari leaders about the surrender of immigration control. They must, they say, keep the power to exclude undesirables, and the resulting visa difficulties have meant a slump in tourist bookings for months ahead. The timing of the union made it impossible to coordinate Tanganyika's [£]246-million development plan with schemes for Zanzibar, which two months later announced its own [£]24-million plan. Some of

Zanzibar's leaders appear intent on choosing their own sources of aid and deciding what conditions of investment are unacceptable. . . .

By the summer of 1967 the union had not progressed much beyond the point described in this 1964 article. Zanzibar was still controlling most of its own affairs under relatively little influence from the mainland. Economic necessity however, did produce a liberalization of the visa policy and a revival of tourism.

Meanwhile, on the mainland, in March 1967, President Nyerere took a long step toward the implementation of "African socialism." He pronounced the Arusha Declaration which underscored his theme of "self-reliance" and resulted in the nationalization of banks and major businesses.

NIGERIA: A CRISIS SURVIVED

West Africa received only secondary consideration from the British imperial planners during the latter half of the nineteenth century. By 1890, in the area later to become Nigeria, the warlike Moslem emirs of the northern area had been pacified in order to protect the more commercially valuable southern sector and to balance French colonial expansion from the north. This became the Protectorate of Northern Nigeria. About the same time a coastal area called the Oil River Protectorate and the Lagos area were merged in what was called the Colony and Protectorate of Southern Nigeria. The economic and administrative advantage of a union of these areas became obvious, and Lord Lugard brought it about in 1914.

Centralized administration was not, however, without its problems. The practice of "indirect rule" with the preservation of traditional forms of government was developed by Lugard and applied with success in the north and southwestern parts of Nigeria. It did not work equally well in the east, however, because of the diverse organization of the indigenous societies. Because "indirect rule" was not adapted to the social patterns of the eastern district, it was replaced early with local governments based on the English pattern. Modern political development has been rapid in this area.

Other cultural and ethnic differences divide the people of Nigeria. As a result, independent Nigeria emerged as a federation of three states: the North, the East, and the West. Within each of these regions there are numerous minority groups which fear for their existence at the hands of the majority. The greatest danger to the progress of Nigeria is the centrifugal force created by ethnic diversity and reinforced by the federal constitution.

The framing of this constitution in stages between 1946 and 1958 was no slight achievement. Each of the three regions has its own parliament and the federal legislative authority is in the hands of a national House of Representatives. The seat of the federal government is Lagos, located in the Western Region but given status similar to the District of Columbia.

The first nationwide elections held after independence in December 1964 precipitated a crisis which threatened to end in the breakup of the federal state. An adjustment of the unequal sizes of the three original regions, a heritage from the colonial period, was attempted through a census in 1964 and by the creation of a fourth region, the Mid-West. This adjustment increased the ill will between the two major political organizations, the Northern Peoples Congress (NPC), and the National Council of Nigerian Citizens (NCNC). A regrouping of political factions resulted in the polarization of forces on a north–south basis. The NCNC organized the United Progressive Grand Alliance (UPGA) with southern emphasis, and the NPC reacted by creating the National Nigerian Alliance (NNA) which showed a northern orientation.

The biggest campaign issue was which area should control the federal government. The UPGA charged that the incumbent NPC government was "feudalistic," and proposed the creation of smaller states within the federation to create greater national unity. It promised to "reorganize the national economy of Nigeria on a sound socialistic basis," and characterized the NPC government's generally pro-Western foreign policy as being "muddled."

This sort of conflict is, of course, a healthy part of the function of a two-party system. What precipitated the crisis, however, were charges by the UPGA that NNA governments in the West and North were preventing the nomination of opposition candidates, and generally interfering with normal pre-election campaigning. Receiving no satisfactory response to these charges, the UPGA boycotted the election and the Eastern region threatened to secede.

When the balloting was over only 4 million out of a possible 22 million votes had been cast. President Azikiwe threatened to resign rather than invite the NNA to form a new government on such a basis. For a period of four days, dissolution of the Federation seemed imminent. At the insistence of both the Chief Justice of the Federation and the Chief Justice of Eastern Nigeria, and after long deliberations between chief Nigerian political leaders, a compromise program was agreed upon. The compromise allowed the NNA to form a broadly based government, pledged the investigation of the election's legality, a review of constitutional and electoral machinery, by-elections in areas where the number of votes cast was small, and dissolution of the Western Region's government to ensure popular support for a new government there.

From Richard Harris, "Nigeria: Crisis & Compromise," *Africa Report,* March 1965.

The compromise appears to have preserved constitutional government for the time being and averted the secession of Eastern Nigeria and the breakup of the federation. It revealed, too, that Nigeria's political leaders continue to be motivated by a desire to maintain the unity of the nation in spite of their serious differences. Faced with the frightening possibility of imminent disintegration of the federation, both the UPGA and NNA leaders appear to have been shocked into hurriedly concluding an agreement to preserve the unity of the nation.

This compromise reached at the brink of disaster has

solved none of the underlying causes of the crisis. Nothing has been settled politically . . .

In summary, the enormous size of the Northern Region remains the most serious deterrent to political stability in Nigeria. Any political party which controls the conservative, Moslem North and wins most of the 167 seats allocated to that region in the federal house, can dominate the whole federation even if it does not win a seat in the South. It was for this reason that the controversy over the 1964 census, as well as the recent election, assumed such serious proportions. The census confirmed the fact that Nigeria has one region bigger than all the rest combined. The NCNC alliance with the Action Group was the only real alternative to accepting the domination of the federation by the NPC. Some argue that the only logical solution to Nigeria's political problems lies in the creation of more states, particularly out of the Northern Region. Since it is unlikely that the Northern politicians will agree to such a move so long as they hold the majority position at the center, the most logical solution is not within the realm of possibility.

THE BREAKDOWN OF DEMOCRATIC PROCESSES IN NIGERIA

The pessimism of the foregoing article was not unfounded. All of the problems referred to—accentuated by a massive and growing corruption at all government levels—frustrated Nigerian democracy. As has so often happened in developing nations, impatient young nationalists in the military took matters into their own hands. In January 1966 the army seized control of the country and conducted a bloody purge. The results and implications are assessed in the following article.

From *The Christian Science Monitor*, January 26, 1966.

In a moment of anger, the Nigerian people have performed an act of national purging unparalleled in the story of the emergent African countries.

A country firmly set on a course of political, social, and economic integrity, respected by its African neighbors, envied perhaps by the less fortunate of them but above all occupying high place in world opinion, may have thrown all this away.

Nigeria's international image has been tarnished for some time to come by a military coup which may have neither a lasting effect nor achieve the aims which its organizers desired.

The origins are still obscure and almost certainly complex. They must, however, stem—like everything in Nigerian politics—from the tribal imbalance which essentially revolves around the inevitable electoral domination of the Yorubas of the west and the Ibos of the east by the massively populated Hausa-speaking Moslem north.

Reaction to corruption

After the 1965 federal election, a northern government predictably emerged with, as its ally, a sort of puppet government in the west, reinstalled three months ago by regional elections blatantly rigged and without semblance of finesse.

Since then, the fury of the electorate in the three regions of the south has been unabated. Widespread violence in the west was mostly due to the attendant frustration.

At the same time, there was growing steadily a deepseated reaction to the massive corruption which undeniably existed in high places and which the government appeared to condone.

Against this background the young army officers plotted. Over the last few years the Nigerian Army, British trained, efficient, had bred a small elite class of officers still in their twenties who had received rapid promotion to the rank of major—many of them Ibos from the East.

They clearly felt dissatisfied with their superiors who represented the establishment, the old Nigeria and were "beyond redemption"—even though their commander in chief, Maj. Gen. Johnson Aguiyi-Ironsi is only in his early forties and rose through the ranks.

It may never be known exactly what happened. It is claimed by Maj. Chukwamwa Nzegwe, who assassinated the northern Premier, that about half a dozen were in the plot. It must have been extremely well organized for it involved the simultaneous slaying of regional premiers in widely separated capitals as well as the Prime Minister and Cabinet members in Lagos.

(It is perhaps significant that in the coup no major political leaders were killed in the two Ibo-populated regions.)

New questions arise

After that loyalties seemed a little confused. Certainly the northern coup seemed to be taking an independent course, and there was, it was believed, an attempt on the life of the commander in chief, now head of the military government. That attempt resulted in summary executions, though not in the large numbers which were reported. Was someone trying to finish off the plot in a last throw?

It seems certain that General Aguiyi-Ironsi was not privy to the conspiracy and may have been a marked man himself. But he appears to have gained control of the situation with the cooperation of the Navy and the police. He has appointed military governors in the regions and set up a supreme military council to include the governors, the heads of the three services, and the police.

Impression explained

And the young majors? Presumably like Major Nzegwe they are accepting the new order—for the moment.

What about the popular reaction to all the bloodshed? There has been remarkably little. Chief Akintola, the assassinated western Premier, was highly unpopular. The northern Premier, Sir Ahmadu Bello, the Sardauna of Sokoto, who was aristocratic, autocratic, contemptuous of southerners, had many enemies and was not, as popularly supposed, an influential religious leader.

Sir Abubakar Tafawa Balewa, the federal Prime Minister, essentially a scholar, a man of the people (the northern people of course), and one of Africa's first statesmen, was incredibly regarded by the Lagos crowd as "wicked," presumably because he was a northerner and though notably incorrupt himself, had been permissive in regard to others.

"Their power is finished, and that's that," says popular opinion. The Lagos man-in-the-street—and this probably applies to other areas as well—regards the coup as essentially a purge. The days of "dash," the universal term meaning the gravy train, bribery, corruption, nepotism—this, he says, is all over now, and Nigeria, a cleaner and better place, will ultimately benefit.

The less-pleasant aspects of a military regime, of course, are not yet immediately obvious.

Many "ifs" involved

The ordinary person cannot be expected to worry about the fact that the Army is unlikely to include in its ranks experts in economic and foreign affairs and that a country which can assassinate its leading politicians overnight is unlikely to provide a favorable climate for investment—even if "dash" is done with, and that's doubtful.

There are many other questions also. When, for instance, will the main political parties, which now all hail the new regime, start feeling the itch for power again? How will the Army deal with that situation? Can an Army of 7,000 men control, even with the support of an efficient police force, a country of 55 million people?

And, although there seems no sign of this at the moment, what if the Moslems, including those in the Army, rise up to avenge their lost leaders?

This is of course a victory for the south, and it is known that the military government is already extremely anxious to submerge regional and tribal differences and to move toward a more unitary form of administration. But will the traditionalist north stand for this?

It is true that there had been severe criticism of Sir Abubakar Tafawa Balewa recently. It was suggested that he ought to put his own house in order before dabbling in international affairs. And it was clear that despite his great ability in that field as far as internal affairs were concerned, he was fulfilling his role as "lieutenant" to the Sardauna of Sokoto, for years the real master of Nigeria manipulating affairs behind the scenes in the northern capital.

Yet, even though these matters are considered, many observers question whether they justify this brutal tragedy of a nation at the moment when it was becoming a stable and reasoning force in African and world diplomacy.

> In July 1966, General Ironsi was murdered, and Lieutenant Colonel Gowon, a Northerner, took power with the support of his Hausa troops. Rioting and killing broke out wherever minorities existed within one of the three major regions. This led to official reorganization of the army along regional lines and an unofficial reshuffling of civilian populations. It was all very reminiscent of the partition of India and Pakistan.
>
> During the winter of 1966-67 the polarization of the Hausa and Ibo populations and forces continued and the emotional temperature rose accordingly. In May 1967, the Eastern Region declared its independence as the Republic of Biafra. The central government sought by force to prevent secession and a civil war ensued.
>
> The issue in this struggle can be described as tribalism vs. nationalism or self-determination vs. foreign (i.e. Northern) domination. It bears some resemblance to the situation in the Congo in that Biafra region contains a large share of the nation's mineral (oil) wealth. Unlike the Congo, however, foreign interests and intervention do not seem to be a factor in the struggle.

The Belgian Congo: A Case Study

CHAOS IN THE CONGO

The Belgians, who had prided themselves on the very

good material care they had given their African wards, had given little or no thought to their political evolution. They chose to consider the European master role, in the Congo at least, as a permanent thing. And so it appeared to be, until the late 1950's when the winds of nationalism began to sweep Africa. In 1957 a measure of self-rule was granted to some larger Congolese municipalities. The 1958 All-African Conference at Accra fanned this spark into a violent demand for independence for the Congo. By June 1960 the Congo was independent.

The following excerpts from articles describe the chaos which prevailed in the Congo from 1960 onward.

From Harry R. Rudin, "Chaos in the Congo," *Current History*, February 1961.

Talk of elections and of eventual independence led to the formation of political parties without number, most of them essentially tribal. It was clear that the Belgian government had not made the Congolese aware of any political unity despite the use of French in the schools and despite the large number of Africans living in urban and industrial centers. In Katanga Province the Conakat party, headed by Moise Tshombe, favored a political development of that province separate from the rest of the Congo. The Abako party of the lower Congo was the organ of the tribal group in that region and in border territories. Of all the political parties only one could be regarded as a national party, that of Patrice Lumumba, the *Mouvement National Congolais*, founded in 1958. Its center of power was actually Stanleyville, the capital and Oriental Province and Lumumba's home. This party was the only one with a program for the entire Congo, for which he sought a unitary state rather than a federal one. . . .

While Belgium was putting the date for independence in the far future, at Stanleyville on October 30, Lumumba was demanding "total independence—now, now, now."

The disturbance resulting from his agitation led to his ar
rest and imprisonment.

The local and provincial elections were held in Decem
ber, 1959, and the results were interpreted by nationalist
as a victory for their cause. They demanded "complete
immediate, and unconditional independence" for their
country in January, 1960. The Belgians were not surren
dering to these demands; they had called a round-table
conference of Belgians and Congolese in Brussels on Jan
uary 20. During its month-long sessions Belgian efforts to
tell the Congolese that they were not ready for immediate
self-government and that gradual transition from Belgian
rule to African rule was necessary were shouted down
according to one Belgian official delegate. Unable to keep
African demands within bounds and fearing widespread
violence from the excitable peoples of the Congo if no
definite date were fixed, the government decided to gran
independence on June 30. The 16 resolutions of the con
ference were aimed at effecting the transition. A second
round-table conference met in Brussels from April 26 to
May 16 to provide for economic aid on the theory that
"independence will have its deep significance only if it is
accompanied by prosperity."

In May, the fateful elections were held to choose 137
members of the lower house of parliament. The party of
Lumumba won the largest number of seats in the cham
ber, 33 in all. This support was raised to 40 by means of
an alliance with three minor parties. Tshombe has
claimed that Lumumba won because of the moral and
material support given him in Belgium. The 84 members
of the Senate were to be designated by the provincial as
semblies, 14 from each province. The Senate and the
lower house, sitting together as a constituent assembly
were to draft a constitution for the Republic of the
Congo.

There were difficulties in organizing the new govern
ment. Finally, on June 24, Lumumba was chosen premie
and Kasavubu, who had sought the premiership, wa
elected president. Although the latter's party, the Abako

ad with its 12 seats the third largest representation in he lower chamber, it got only one post in the cabinet of 3 ministries that was created, Lumumba's party got 8 of he ministries, the remaining posts being divided among 2 other parties. A treaty of friendship, assistance, and cooperation with Belgium was signed, but it was never ratified by the two states because of the difficulties that soon arose.

For some time trouble had been simmering within the *orce publique*, where the enlisted men saw themselves getting nothing from independence while African politicians seemed to get everything. They demanded that their Belgian officers be replaced by Congolese. Before Lumumba could arrange the change, a revolt of African enlisted men against their Belgian officers occurred in Thysville, 5 miles from Leopoldville. News of the revolt and frightening rumors of attacks on white women and children threw Belgians in Leopoldville and elsewhere into a panic and led to the hasty flight of thousands from the Congo. Shattered by the flight were the arrangements that had been made for ten thousand Belgians to remain in the Congo to help the new state with essential technical aid. The result was the sudden breakdown of transportation, communications, electric power, and water systems. With the disappearance of their Belgian employers Africans found themselves without jobs and without the means to provide for their families. This was the opposite of what had been expected to come from independence. By early October, of a normal male labor force of 125,-000 in Leopoldville 80,000 men were idle.

To protect their harassed nationals, the Belgian government sent paratroopers from Europe into the Congo on July 8. This move was interpreted as aiming at the reconquest of the Congo. Lumumba turned to the United Nations for help, against the Belgians and against local disorder. The first United Nations troops arrived July 15 under an arrangement that kept the major powers out of the Congo. When these troops declined to drive out the Belgians or to force Katanga (which Tshombe had de-

clared independent) back under his rule, Lumumba
turned against the United Nations and threatened to turn
to the Soviet Union for aid. . . .

THE CONGO'S FIRST YEAR

> *From* Alan P. Merriam, "The Congo's First Year of Independ
> ence," *Current History,* October 1961.

The United Nations faced a continual series of crises
during the first period of the Congo's independence: with
Patrice Lumumba who constantly changed his mind
about the desirability of the United Nations operation,
with Moise Tshombe when the United Nations decided
that it must enter Katanga to make its control effective,
with Belgium which withdrew its troops slowly and with
obvious reluctance and, time and time again, obstructed
the United Nations operation; and with Russian unilateral
action. In late August and early September, it had become
clear that Russia was pursuing a policy of direct assistance
to Lumumba in his "war" against Katanga and Albert Kalonji's Mining State; in response to this crisis, the United
Nations closed all the Congo's airports and radio stations
which effectively blocked Russia's actions. This move
coincided roughly with the joint Lumumba-Kasavubu fir-
ings, with the assumption of control by Mobutu, and with
the expulsion from the Congo of the Russian and Czecho-
slovakian diplomatic representatives. It helped to mark the
end of the first phase of the Congo's independent history.

Period of stalemate

The second phase, which might be called the period of
consolidation, began with Lumumba's loss of control and
ended with his death, announced by the Katanga government on February 13, 1961. During this period of
some five months, a stalemate occurred in the Congo
precipitated primarily by the inaction of the United Nations.

Having achieved some small control of the Congo situation, the United Nations seemed to be at a loss as to

what to do next, and it entered into a period of inactivity during which it made few efforts to reestablish a functioning government. . . .

This stalemate had an extremely important effect on the Congo as a whole, for it gave the political leaders outside Leopoldville a chance to consolidate their lines of power. Thus in Katanga, which had seceded officially on July 11, Tshombe was able to organize his army effectively; to bring in outside mercenaries to lead it; to print his own currency; to attempt to negotiate trade agreements with other countries; and in essence to organize an effective regime out of what had formerly been simply a loosely organized state which had declared itself independent. Although the effectiveness of Kalonji's Mining State or South Kasai has never been too clear, it is obvious that in the period of stalemate Kalonji, too, was given a chance to solidify his secession.

At the same time, the Stanleyville regime headed by Antoine Gizenga began to organize itself. During the period near Christmas of 1960, Stanleyville pro-Lumumba forces raided Bukavu, the capital of Kivu, kidnapped its president (whose fate remains unknown today), reduced the effectiveness of local political leaders such as Anicet Kashamura, and effectively took over control of the Kivu province. Similarly, through the cooperation of Jason Sendwe, Tshombe's chief rival in Katanga, Gizenga's forces, or forces amenable to him, were able to control the northern portion of Katanga and even some of the eastern Kasai.

Thus it was out of the inaction of the United Nations and its preoccupation with its own problems in Leopoldville that the three major lines of power which still exist in the Congo were able to form themselves into more effective blocs. Kasavubu, Mobutu, and Lumumba primarily were engaged among themselves and with the United Nations in the struggle for control of the Leopoldville and Lower Congo area—from which Kasavubu has emerged as the dominant power. Gizenga meanwhile was securing his position in the northeastern part of the Congo. At the same time, Tshombe was strengthening his independent

Katanga, and Kalonji, who more or less had thrown hi
destiny in with that of Tshombe, was at least making hi
position in South Kasai more secure. Had the United Na
tions been asking dynamic action to restore the politi
cal stability of the area, the blocs might never hav
solidified; the time gained by Tshombe, Kalonji, and Gi
zenga was priceless for the furthering of their secessionis
and power ambitions.

The third phase in the Congo's first year of independ
began with the death of Patrice Lumumba and ha
persisted; it can be called the period of movement towarc
control and toward the possible resolution of the Congo's
difficulties. On February 9, 1961, the Katanga government announced that Lumumba had escaped from jail;
on February 10, that it was still searching for him. On
February 11, it attempted to implicate United Nations
Moroccan troops in his escape, and on February 13, it
announced that Lumumba had been killed by "over-zeal-
ous villagers" in an unnamed Katanga town. . . .

UN Intervention

With Lumumba gone, the struggle for power devolved
upon Kasavubu, Mobutu, Gizenga, Tshombe, and Kalonji, and because of the nature of the crisis aroused by his
death the African members of the United Nations were
led to a round of extraordinary activity. Thus on February 14, 1961, Ceylon and the United Arab Republic,
later joined by Liberia, announced they would offer a resolution in the Security Council which called for United
Nations troops to set up a buffer zone between the forces
controlled by Gizenga and those of the other leaders; demanded the immediate departure of all Belgian military
personnel; and called for a commission to investigate
Lumumba's death. . . .

This new attitude toward the Congo on the part of the
African nations resulted in the resolution of February 21,
which gave the United Nations and Hammarskjöld real
authority to intervene in the Congo. It urged that the
United Nations stop civil war, halt military operations,

expel Belgian and other foreign military and political advisers, and carry out an investigation of Lumumba's death. It gave the United Nations authority to keep foreign military and political personnel out of the Congo. It also urged the reconvening of parliament and the reorganization of the Congo army. . . .

KATANGA RESISTS FEDERATION

From Harry R. Rudin, "The Republic of Congo," *Current History*, December 1962.

Efforts were made during 1961 to solve the problem of separatism. In March, political leaders met in Tananarive, where Tshombe of Katanga succeeded in getting the principle of a loose confederation accepted for what might be in the neighborhood of 20 provincial states in the Congo. In April, a conference was held in Coquilhatville to implement this agreement. It failed. Kasavubu, the head of the Congolese government, now favored a centralized state. He turned against Tshombe's federal scheme, and even had him arrested and imprisoned for two months. The task of forming a government was later given to the parliament that had been elected in 1960. It met in July. To the surprise of most observers, Cyrille Adoula was made premier; and Antoine Gizenga, who had got himself recognized as Lumumba's successor and had been working to create a separatist state in Oriental Province, became deputy vice-premier. He was careful, however, in succeeding months not to appear in Leopoldville to perform the functions of his office, preferring to operate from the base he had in Stanleyville with the support he got from a number of foreign governments that recognized him as head of a sovereign state.

Now that a government had been formed, the effort was made to compel Tshombe and Katanga to submit to the central Congolese government. The United Nations and the United States, which had opposed Lumumba's efforts in this direction, gave their support to this cause. Despite the invasions of Katanga in September and in December, 1961, and despite the Kitona agreement that terminated the second invasion, nothing substantial was really achieved because the terms of that agreement were not carried out.

One of the unhappier results was that the United Nations had now become deeply involved in the Congo, where Secretary-General Dag Hammarskjöld was killed while on a mission to make peace with Tshombe. The 18,000 armed men of the United Nations are costing the international organization $10 million a month, far too much for the small budget needed for normal operations. . . .

After the first break in April, Adoula appealed to the United Nations for a tougher mandate to liquidate the secession of Katanga. He demanded the total reintegration of the state into that of the republic of Congo; he wished to do away with Katanga's army, stamps, currency, and flag. In a mood of determination, Adoula persuaded his parliament to deprive Antoine Gizenga of his immunity so that he could be punished for his separatist activities in Oriental Province.

With the final breakdown of talks in late June, the United States and the United Nations decided that the settlement of the issue could be postponed no longer. Adoula and members of the Leopoldville government came out in favor of strong action, while proposing the drafting of a federal constitution to replace the temporary constitutional device of the *loi fondamentale*. On his trip to Europe to win support for the plan that was being developed, U Thant, Acting Secretary-General of the United Nations, stated in England that the Congo crisis had to be finally solved; he said he would try to persuade *Union Minière* to divert revenue from Katanga to the central government. The Secretary-General's patience and sense of tact burst its oriental barriers in Finland, where he referred to Tshombe and his supporters as a bunch of clowns.

President Kennedy had also come to the conviction that strong action was called for. There were rumors that the United States and some allies might compel Tshombe to accept federation; the State Department denounced the

Katangese leader and threatened economic pressure and measures short of war if he persisted in secession. . . . It was the United States that worked out the new plan for dealing with the situation. Belgium and Britain were consulted; both agreed with the goals of federation, shared revenues and merged armed forces, but drew the line at the proposal for economic pressures like the boycott of copper and cobalt or the cessation of all trade. The principle of federation had been accepted by both Adoula and Tshombe, and steps were already taken to draft a constitution with the aid of United Nations experts. The United States insisted on economic and other sanctions to compel acceptance of the plan for settling Congo's difficulties. . . .

After drafting this program for positive action, the United States submitted it on August 9 to U Thant, saying that the next move was up to him and to the United Nations. . . .

EFFORTS TOWARD UNITY

> *From* Harry R. Rudin, "Aftermath in the Congo," *Current History,* December 1963.

The plan provided that the central government and Katanga would have equal shares in the rebel province's revenues from taxes, duties, and mining royalties. The armies of the two regions were to be merged into a single national Congolese army. A monetary council for the control of foreign exchange was to be established. The plan also asked experts appointed by the United Nations to draft a constitution for the united Congo, to replace the Belgian-drafted *loi fondamentale,* which had served as a constitution ever since independence.

Acting under this mandate, legal experts of the United Nations drafted a new constitution. Instead of the six provinces in the Congo it was proposed to have 21, with the central government having a large measure of control. The constitution empowered the president to declare an emergency, even to suspend the constitution. In the sum-

mer of 1962, Katanga was actually divided into two provinces, North Katanga and South Katanga, to weaken
Tshombe's powers.

Adoula accepted the United Nations plan on August
26, 1962. Tshombe waited, however, until September 4,
when he agreed to the principles of the proposal just in
time to avoid a virtual ultimatum from U Thant. The
plan provided for sanctions against Tshombe if he did not
cooperate; consuming nations would be asked to stop their
purchases of Katanga's copper and cobalt, the chief
sources of Katanga's revenues. Should this boycott fail
the United Nations could resort to the use of force to end
Katanga's secession.

U Thant's plan did not have the approval of all members of the United Nations. The Soviet Union and its sat-
ellites had not been consulted when the plan was drafted;
they naturally objected to it, just as they had objected to
the presence of United Nations forces in the Congo.
Great Britain, France, Belgium, and other states objected;
they had no intention of applying force to compel
Tshombe's adherence to the proposals and to the reintegration of Katanga into a united Congolese republic. Several countries, notably the Soviet Union, France, Belgium, South Africa, and others, persistently refused to
pay the contributions assessed by the United Nations for
the cost of United Nations forces in the Congo.

The situation was one that Tshombe felt he could exploit. In preparation for the fight to come, he strengthened
his economic and military position by tightening his control over the Union Minière and its funds, by hiring white
mercenaries, by increasing the size and improving the
training of his army far beyond its numbers and quality in
1960, and by acquiring an air force of 50 planes to overcome his earlier military weakness vis-à-vis the United
Nations.

Disagreement in the United Nations encouraged
Tshombe. He also found comfort in the problems that
confronted Adoula, who had to face serious parliamentary
criticism throughout 1962. . . .

This predicament of Adoula, the division of opinion

mong leading members of the United Nations, and the
ossession of a strong army and air force may well ex-
lain Tshombe's refusal to end Katanga's secession and to
ecome a part of the government in Leopoldville despite
ressure from U Thant and from the United States in
avor of the United Nations plan. Tshombe believed he
ould avoid giving effect to the plan by offering a part of
Katanga's revenue to the financially hard-pressed government of Adoula. It was only natural for Adoula, for U
Thant, and for the United States to come to the convic-
ion that time was running out and that reunification of
he Congo could not be put off any longer. . . .

On the last day of 1962, an ultimatum from United
Nations authorities gave Tshombe two weeks in which to
nd the secession of Katanga. Tshombe replied that he
was willing to return to Elisabethville to negotiate an end
of secession. Robert Gardiner, the United Nations' chief
representative in the Congo, cautioned against the mis-
ake of stopping too short. Contrary to instructions, it is
said, United Nations troops moved against Jadotville instead of waiting in Elisabethville to give Tshombe a
chance to submit to the ultimatum. This military move
resulted in the accidental shooting of two civilians by the
troops. Nonetheless, United Nations Under Secretary
Ralph Bunche gave the green light for further military
operations against Tshombe.

Tshombe called on his people to prepare for total war
and again he talked of adopting a scorched-earth policy.
When Tshombe returned to Elisabethville on January 7,
1963, saying that he was ready to make a peace settlement, Bunche refused to see him and declared that the
time for negotiation of a settlement was over.

By order of U Thant, Tshombe was first placed under
house arrest, then mysteriously released to guide a column of United Nations troops into a peaceful occupation
of the territory between Elisabethville and the Rhodesian
border. Thereupon Tshombe suddenly disappeared again,
to give rise to rumors that he had gone to Kolwezi to prepare for a last-ditch stand. Bridges on the way to Kolwezi were destroyed to hamper the movement of United Na-

tions troops. Tshombe talked of blowing up installation of the Union Minière in Kolwezi, where explosives were already *in situ* for the operation. . . .

Then in mid-January, with that gift he has for sudden and most unexpected decision, Tshombe capitulated and declared himself ready to cooperate with the United Nations. He offered to return to Elisabethville and to work out the terms for ending secession. . . .

The fiscal situation in the Congo has become a matter of serious concern. The 1962 budget provides for expenditures amounting to $362 million and for doubtful revenues amounting to $202 million. Not satisfied with a fifty-fifty split of Katanga's revenues, Adoula insists on getting 65 per cent. Much of the gold that Leopoldville had hoped to capture in Katanga had been sent out of the country; only a small part has been recovered.

Many people in critical positions in the Congo are far from satisfied with the treatment they have been getting. Thousands of teachers in the rural areas have been reported as having received no pay during the last year, and 35,000 of them have gone on strike. In April, 1962, an unsuccessful general strike was called by the country's largest trade union to force politicians to reduce their salaries and other perquisites of office. In May, 1963, 3,000 men in the police force in Leopoldville mutinied for an increase in pay, a move that the government believed to be a conspiracy aiming at its overthrow.

When government workers struck in August in Leopoldville, it was again said that the move aimed to overthrow Adoula. This time the army was called in to halt the demonstrations. During these public protests for higher pay, leaflets were distributed calling for the overthrow of Adoula's regime. The quick and successful rebellion against President Fulbert Youlou in the neighboring Congo Republic (Brazzaville) during the summer of 1963 naturally made Adoula nervous. One writer has said that the corruption within the government in Leopoldville is far worse than that which caused Youlou's ouster across the river. Adoula's numerous political opponents in parliament, in particular the followers of Lumumba ba, take advantage of these expressions of discontent to embarrass the premier.

Despite the settlement made last January with Tshombe, one cannot say that the country is really united. That work remains to be done. Many ancient tribal rivalries were intensified during the war and still plague Leopoldville. The fear persists that Tshombe will seek to regain power in Katanga. Only a small number of his gendarmes have surrendered their arms in accordance with the agreement of last January; and it is said that thousands of them roam about the country living by robbery and other violence. Efforts of the Congolese Army to disarm then have led to a number of bloody clashes. The central government charges that many of the white mercenaries and gendarmes who aided Tshombe are in Angola, where the Portuguese permit them to remain and to train. . . .

REBELLION

From Marvin D. Markowitz and Herbert F. Weiss, "Rebellion in the Congo," *Current History*, April 1965.

But the star of the Adoula government continued to decline, largely because of a growing restiveness among the rural masses. During the struggle for independence, this segment of the population had been militant and radical; the rural masses had greatly contributed to Belgium's surrender of sovereignty. Still, the aftermath of independence was a tremendous disappointment. The white rulers had left, or had become the assistants of Congolese leaders, but the standard of living dropped drastically, the security of life and property disappeared in many parts of the country, and sporadic tribal wars broke out. Congolese political leaders frequently lived in ostentatious splendor, thriving on corruption and nepotism. The army became a praetorian guard renowned for injustices and arbitrary brutality. Under these circumstances, the initial reaction of the rural masses was one of passive withdrawal. Participation in political parties dropped to a zero point and, apart from relatively isolated eruptions of violence (or tribal wars), the mood in the villages reflected a stunned sense of betrayal.

But this rural passivity—which never covered the whole Congo—could not last for long. In addition to disappointed expectations and material hardships, a lawless desperation spread throughout much of the countryside. One of the manifestations of this general condition was the increase of religious movements and traditional African sects. In a word, the situation was ripe for revolution.

Probably the most important event during the Adoula regime was an uprising in the Kwilu area of the former Leopoldville province—the beginning of this revolution. In the fall of 1963, Pierre Mulele, a former minister under Patrice Lumumba and Antoine Gizenga, began to organize the untapped revolutionary potential of the rural masses among his kinsmen in this area. The "Kwilu Rebellion" was characterized by attacks not only against the representatives of the government but also on virtually all aspects of Congolese life which had assimilated European culture. Thus not only district commissioners were attacked, but also the ordinary government clerks; not only the white missionaries, but also the Congolese priests. It was this peasant orientation which distinguished this outbreak from earlier conflicts which were generally confined to city politics and their extension into the countryside, or tribal warfare.

Comparisons have been rather loosely made between the goals and methods of this uprising and Chinese revolutionary doctrines. The fact that Mulele spent some time in China has given such comparisons a certain amount of credibility. However, as one commentator has pointed out, what has been occurring in the Congo is closer to the Boxer Rebellion than to the Chinese Revolution after World War II.

Initially, the Kwilu uprising was not taken very seriously in Leopoldville. Eventually, however, the need for determined action was felt by the Adoula regime, and a crack battalion of the Congo army was sent into the area. Since this pitted a force with the most modern weapons against villagers who for the most part had only bows and arrows and spears, the army scored a few spectacular victories. It managed to hold on to the key towns and to keep the roads open. But this limited success became the basis for gross overestimation—both in the Congo and abroad—of the army's effectiveness.

The second chapter of the revolution began when fighting spread to the eastern Congo. . . . In this instance, the army proved to be almost completely ineffectual and rapidly lost vast areas and several important towns.

Facing this debacle and the departure of the last of the United Nations Force, President Kasavubu demanded Adoula's resignation, and assumed virtually all government authority. Days of great political confusion followed. All major leaders participated in the negotiations over the formation of a new government, including the exiled Katangan leader, Moise Tshombe, and the leaders of the CNL. Although the details of the negotiations remain a mystery, it is evident that Tshombe was the most astute bidder for power. More than others, he succeeded in presenting himself as the last hope for national reconciliation—this despite the enormous handicap of having started off as the chief secessionist leader of the Congo. At any rate, to the astonishment of practically the whole world, Kasavubu named Tshombe as the Congo's new prime minister. . . .

Consequently, Tshombe turned almost exclusively to military force, hiring white mercenaries, including Rhodesians, South Africans, and various adventurers. He received increased military aid from the United States and Belgium. Fighter-bombers contributed by the United States and piloted by anti-Castro Cubans were particularly important, since they terrorized the rebels. This combination of power proved somewhat successful, and the Congo army–mercenary force recaptured many key towns. But, as in the Kwilu, the government troops tended to stick to the main lines of communication, leaving the countryside to the rebels.

Government victories were accompanied for the most part by acts of the most indiscriminate brutality and looting. Prisoners were either shot outright or tortured to death. Hardly any distinction appears to have been made between active rebel soldiers and the civilian population; troops entering towns and villages shot anything that moved. In their relations with the civilian population, discipline in the Congo army was often at a lower ebb than among the rebel soldiers, who demonstrated a degree of idealism and self-restraint. ·

Nonetheless, the rebels executed thousands of Congolese who were identified in their terms with the "old regime." . . .

Knowing that continued military aid to the Tshombe regime would mean the defeat of the uprising, the rebel leaders desperately sought to obtain the departure of the white mercenaries and pilots. However, they were in no position to bargain. On the ground they were losing, and in the diplomatic arena they had almost no support. Out of this desperate predicament they conceived the idea of making the whites in their territory hostages. By becoming hostages, some of the whites obtained slightly better treatment, since the leaders made a special effort to protect them from youth gangs in the hope of exchanging them for political gain. But at the same time, the stresses of the situation made the populace increasingly antiwhite, while the control which the leaders had over their followers became more tentative. These developments naturally made the position of the hostages most precarious.

With their nationals as hostages in rebel-held territory, the Belgian and United States governments faced an agonizing choice. They felt that they could not abandon their citizens. Yet they were reluctant to press for a halt of the advance on Stanleyville, and it is questionable whether Tshombe would have been responsive to such pressure. Still, with every government victory, the lives of the hostages were increasingly threatened. It was in response to this dilemma that the plan for a Belgian-American air drop on Stanleyville was first conceived. An additional political motivation was the conviction, very generally held in Brussels and in Washington, that the fall of Stanleyville would mean the collapse of the rebellion.

The situation was further complicated by the involvement of the Organization of African Unity (OAU), which was seeking a negotiated settlement to the whole Congo problem. Consequently, before launching the attack, the United States agreed to meet a rebel representative in Nairobi under Kenyan President Jomo Kenyatta's sponsorship. By the time the meeting took place, plans for the attack were being implemented; after only one meeting, the United States broke off the negotiations and, with Belgium, launched the attack. Part of the reason for this hasty action was the fact that Congolese army-mercenary columns were already within striking distance of Stanleyville and the lives of the hostages were therefore feared to be in immediate jeopardy.

The attack on Stanleyville encountered considerable resistance, although from a military point of view it was a complete success. True to the warning previously given by the rebel radio, hostages were shot once the attack began. But these killings appear to have resulted from panic rather than in execution of precise orders. Because of the fast action of the Belgian paratroopers, there were only about 100 casualties, with approximately 1500 whites evacuated from the city. . . .

International repercussions were very serious. Most Africans were especially offended. First of all, they felt that the United States had broken off the Nairobi negotiations under Kenyatta's sponsorship in a cavalier manner. Second, they deplored the total lack of Western concern for the death of numerous Africans during the rescue operations. Third, they were upset by the spectacle of Western military intervention in an African civil war upon the formal request of Moise Tshombe, considered by many to be a traitor to African nationalism. Given this atmosphere of resentment and shock, the more radical African states seized the opportunity to give open support to the rebels, while Tshombe became more isolated than ever.

In the aftermath of the most recent upheavals, two conclusions can be drawn. At the grass-roots level, in the vast areas touched by the rebellion, the fall of Stanleyville and the scattering of the rebel leadership has resulted in heightened revolutionary activity without any effective direction. It is most improbable that the countryside under rebel influence can be brought under any kind of control in the near future. In purely local terms, this has probably resulted in uninhibited destruction (especially of those things which can be identified as European in origin) and anarchy.

At the political level, the rebellion has lost its capital but has gained considerable international support, notably among the radical African states and the communist countries, but also among some middle-of-the-road states. A military solution will therefore be difficult to achieve. However, a negotiated settlement is unlikely so long as Tshombe is prime minister.

Nonetheless, since even Belgium and the United States are now reported to be pressing for a political solution, a new prime minister acceptable to all factions may emerge in the not too distant future. . . .

> That prediction proved to be correct. In November 1965, General Joseph Mobutu took control of the government in a bloodless coup, thus preventing a new power struggle between Tshombe and Kasavubu, but not ending a bewildering series of power plays—domestic and foreign—which reflect the Congo's basic weaknesses. One fact that clearly emerges from this is that General Mobutu, or anyone else who would govern the Congo, must be strong.

The Republic of South Africa: Its Problems and Role in Africa's Future

> On the southern tip of Africa the winds of change are being stoutly resisted, and the European has expressed his determination to retain the master role at all costs. Portuguese Angola and Mozambique, the breakaway British Crown Colony of Rhodesia, and the Republic of South Africa are all equally dedicated to the proposition that a white minority must rule.
>
> Quite aside from any moral consideration, this determination adds an element of considerable danger to

the continued political development of Africa. It would be serious enough even if the line between "Black Africa" and "White Africa" could be cleanly drawn—but it cannot be. The British-created Central African Federation has already broken up because its northern members, Nyasaland (Malawi) and Northern Rhodesia (Zambia) feared the political weight of the third member, white-dominated Southern Rhodesia. Not only have the economic advantages of federation been sacrificed to racial fears, but Southern Rhodesia (now Rhodesia) unilaterally declared its independence because the British insisted on maintaining their responsibility there until the African majority was given a meaningful degree of political participation. The outlawing of the illegal Rhodesia regime and the imposition of economic sanctions on it placed Zambia in a very precarious position, surrounded as she is on three sides by white-dominated territories.

The Rhodesian issue created even more extreme partisanship throughout Africa on black versus white lines. Black African nationalists universally identified with the unfranchised Africans in Rhodesia. The Organization of African Unity urged its members to break relations with Great Britain if that country did not succeed in ousting the illegal government of Rhodesia within a two-weeks deadline. When the time ran out and the breakaway regime was still in power, African leaders were faced with the choice of rejecting the recommendation of the OAU or biting the hand which was (quite literally in some cases) feeding them. Thus even the British Commonwealth was put in jeopardy by the racial tensions of southern Africa. After more than a year of futile economic sanctions, Britain called on the UN to supplement her efforts and those of the OAU to end the illegal white regime.

All the lines of tension which beset southern Africa seem to come together in the Republic of South Africa. The future of the Rhodesian situation, the survival of Zambia, the future of South-West Africa, and perhaps the prestige of the UN—all depend in some measure on developments within that republic.

Our treatment of the African state, therefore, is more extensive than that of the other states with which we have dealt because it occupies a unique position relative to the rest of Africa. It is not only larger, older, and wealthier than the other states, but it represents the most extreme example of an African majority completely dominated by a minority of European origin. The situation is complicated by a sharp division between the descendants of British settlers, who have a background of democratic ideals, and the descendants of Dutch settlers (Boers, now called Afrikaners) who advocate white supremacy.

The Dutch East India Company first promoted the establishment of a settlement on the Cape of Good Hope in the seventeenth century, as a necessary way station to the Indies.

During the eighteenth century many Dutch settlers, restless under restrictions of Company rule at Cape Town, began to push into the interior. The Hottentot and Bushman populations inhabiting the nearby countryside were decimated by severe smallpox epidemics and continual fighting with encroaching Europeans. The Afrikaners claim that they moved into a country unpopulated by any Bantu groups and that the migrating Bantu moved in on them in the nineteenth century. Although there remains considerable debate as to exact dates, there can be little doubt that some Bantu people were settled on the Kei River by 1400. Furthermore, there are written records of European–Bantu contact on the South African coast by the mid-sixteenth century, and, most certainly, Bantu groups had crossed into the area southwest of the Fish River before the 1780s when the Dutch began moving into the same fertile area. Since the Bantu were a pastoral people, the competition for the land was keen.

Following the Napoleonic Wars, the British became owners of the Cape Colony and brought with them many ideas of governmental and humanitarian reform alien to the Dutch-settler population, whose intellectual ties with Europe had been broken for 150 years. The British abolished slavery and instituted an organized system of taxation. Although the British at first did not want to extend their authority far into the interior, administrators soon found themselves trying to maintain order and justice for the widely dispersed population.

The immigration of about 5,000 English families in the early 1820s was part of the British policy of Anglicization of her South African territory. This policy, with the language provisions which made English the official tongue of administration and schools, created further resentment between the Dutch settlers and their new government. Just as in the eighteenth century they had escaped regulation by migrating, the Boers now began to move beyond British jurisdiction. During the 1830s and 1840s the "Great Trek" was undertaken by perhaps 10,000 men, women, and children across the Orange and Vaal rivers into Bantu territory.

The Great Trek affected the subsequent history of South Africa in many ways. It withdrew a large part of the Boer population from the Cape, giving British ideas freer reign. It led to the establishment of two Boer republics, the Transvaal and the Orange Free State, in which Boer racial ideas went unchallenged. It constituted additional trespass on Bantu lands. And finally, the tradition of the Great Trek had a profound psychological impact on the Boers themselves. It became a national symbol similar to our own covered-wagon pioneer heritage.

However, the Trek did not end the friction between the British and the Boers. The conflict was amplified by the discovery of gold in Boer territory in 1886. It brought on such a gold rush that the Boers soon found themselves outnumbered by foreigners in their own land. The gold-seekers demanded citizenship in the Boer republics, but the Boers rejected this idea. The quarrel was fanned by the ambitions of the British imperialist Cecil Rhodes, who dreamed of a belt of British territory from "the Cape to Cairo" across Boer, Bantu, and German-held land.

War broke out between the Boer republics and the British in 1899. This so-called Boer War was embarrassing to the British because the odds were so uneven, and yet they had a hard time subduing the Boers. To discourage continued resistance the British rounded up Boer civilians and placed them in guarded compounds, where many of them died of epidemics. To the Afrikaner, the martyrs of the concentration camps are the emotional equivalent of our barefoot soldiers at Valley Forge.

With the war over, the embarrassed British offered very generous terms to the conquered Boers. By 1910 they had established within the British Commonwealth a federal state, the Union of South Africa, by uniting the British colonies of the Cape and Natal with the two Boer republics. The Boer population became a majority with full political rights.

This settlement was never completely acceptable to the Boers. They continued to resent the British presence and influence. Hence, the Afrikaner nationalist movement grew in power as time went on.

From this history of conflict developed an Afrikaner personality alien to anything in the twentieth-century Western world. The Afrikaners believe that they are a chosen people with a mission to fulfill, and onto this seventeenth-century Calvinistic notion have been grafted ideas which are the product of three hundred years of unique experience in Africa.

From the grim frontier situation involving constant hardship and danger of Bantu raids grew an attitude of racial fear—the insecurity of a small white minority holding out against the onslaught of the overwhelming black majority. The fact that the Boer society became dependent on black slavery did nothing to reduce this fear, and intensified the white assumption of superiority.

The Reformed (Boer) Church in South Africa did not modify these tendencies. Rather, its crusading zeal tended to justify Christian conquest of the pagans, equating Christian with white, and pagan with black. This attitude still prevails in the Afrikaner Church.

By combining the attitude of an American Southerner toward the Negro and the attitude of an old-time Western settler toward the American Indian, we come close to understanding the Afrikaner attitude toward the Bantu.

While the Afrikaner has his roots deep in Africa with no other place to call home, the Britisher usually maintains some ties with England and has been accused of divided loyalties. He usually left England in the first place in order to make a better living in Africa. But even the British community was divided in its attitude toward the African populations. British settlers who became farmers quickly allied with the Afrikaner in his competition for land with the African, and the more numerous urban settlers were more interested in doing well than in doing good. They preferred to leave matters of political and social philosophy to the Boers. The imperial government, trying to impose order with a minimum of expense and a limited staff, often left the settlement of interracial disputes in the hands of local settler officials. Only the missionaries working among the African peoples tried to plead the Africans' cause in official circles. Their influence was not sufficient to overcome the more powerful force of Europeanization in South Africa. The average South African of British descent may not approve of Afrikaner policies, but he has conformed more frequently than he has protested.

Since the Union of South Africa was formed, the Afrikaners have been steadily increasing their influence over the less well defined British point of view. In 1948 the Afrikaner Nationalist Party came to power. Ten years later this party came under the control of its most radical element, and by 1961 the long-sought Boer dream of republican status outside of the British Commonwealth was achieved.

The policy of apartheid was introduced after the 1948 victory and spread with the increasing Afrikaner Nationalist power.

Apartheid means different things to different people even in South Africa. The government itself has been fuzzy in outlining its ultimate objectives. The policy has ranged all the way from the complete division of the country into separate "Bantustan" and white states to a mere maintenance of *baaskap*, the Afrikaners' word for white supremacy.

APARTHEID: THE DO'S AND DON'T'S

The following reading puts apartheid in more concrete terms. It provides a catalog of what the African may, but mostly what he may not do in terms of everyday living.

From James Cameron, *The African Revolution*, 1961.

The apartheid laws carry color bar to the final and possible logical conclusion. They mean no vote for the

African, no political standing of any kind, no right to work, to travel, to change his address, no recognized right to protest against anything. They mean the reinforcement of old laws preventing Africans being trained as artisans. They mean the abolition of the Native Representative Council. They mean the Group Areas Act, defining the areas where an African may live. They mean regulations which make illegal and punishable with imprisonment any cohabitation or sexual relations between a white person and anyone even remotely touched with color. They mean the exclusion of Africans from citizens' buses, hotels, restaurants, schools, toilets, booking-offices, even roadside seats. They mean a poll-tax of a pound a head for every adult male and a local tax of ten shillings for a reservation dwelling. To produce this sum the African is compelled to leave the kraal and seek employment in town, mine, or farm, and to do this he must contrive to carry, to be produced on demand, his latest poll-tax receipt; in the Transvaal or Orange Free State a traveling pass; a municipal permit to enter a town; a permit to seek work; a registered copy of his contract; a permit to reside in the town; a pass from his employer to move after dusk. (After the Pass Law riots of March 1960, when seventy-one Africans were shot in the Transvaal and the Cape, the regulations on carrying passes were suspended but only temporarily; five months later the regulations were extended to cover not only men but also women, a measure that was described as declaring bureaucratic war on the Bantu people.)

An African who was born in a town and lived there continuously for fifty years, but then left to reside elsewhere for any period, even two weeks is not entitled, as of right, to return to his birthplace and remain there for more than seventy-two hours. If he does, he is guilty of a criminal offense punishable by a fine not exceeding ten pounds or in default, imprisonment for a period not exceeding two months.

If an African, born in a town, has lived there continuously for fifty years, no African friend is entitled, as of right, to visit him for more than seventy-two hours.

If an African born in a town has lived there continuously for fourteen years and has during that period worked continuously for one employer for nine years, neither his wife nor his dependent daughter is entitled to live with him for more than seventy-two hours.

Whenever the Governor-General (acting on the advice of the Minister of Native Affairs) in his unfettered discretion deems it fit to proclaim so, an African who has been required by Court Order to leave a certain area must do so —nor may any appeal or review stay or suspend such removal, even when it has been established beyond all doubt that the Order was intended for some other person and was served on him in error.

Without a special permit it is unlawful for a white and a nonwhite person to sit down together to a cup of tea in a tearoom anywhere in South Africa.

Unless he has a special permit, an African professor delivering a lecture to a white club—which has invited him to do so—commits a criminal offense.

No African is entitled, as of right, to acquire freehold title to land anywhere in South Africa.

Any policeman is entitled, without warrant, to enter and search by day or night any premises in a town on which he has reason to suspect that an African boy of eighteen years of age is committing the criminal offense of residing with his father without permission.

A white person living in a town who employs an African to do any bricklaying, carpentry, or other skilled work in his home, commits a criminal offense unless special exemption has been obtained from the Ministry of Labour, so also does any African who performs such skilled work, and each is liable to a fine of £100.

If a nonwhite person sits on a bench in a public park set aside for exclusive white use, by way of protest against apartheid, he is liable to a fine of £300, or to three years' imprisonment, or to a whipping not exceeding ten strokes, or to such fine and such imprisonment, or to such fine and such whipping or to such imprisonment and such whipping.

It is unlawful for an African worker to take part in a

strike. If he does he is liable on conviction to a fine o
£500 and/or three years' imprisonment.

APARTHEID: ITS PSYCHOLOGICAL CAUSE AND EFFECT

The following reading describes the fear that prey
on members of both races. The author is writing specifically about conditions in South-West Africa, which i
under the legally dubious domination of the Republic
of South Africa, but the description applies with equa
validity to the Republic itself.

From Allard K. Lowenstein, *Brutal Mandate*, 1962.

Then there are the white men who have no worry tha
their phones are tapped but who sleep with guns under
their pillows and locked gates at the top of their stair-
ways; this one may be worth a million pounds and that
one may sit in Parliament or at the head of his profes-
sion, but their wives tremble when the servants huddle.
Do not be surprised if such men take you aside to inquire
of prospects for starting over again in America or Britain
or Canada or Israel.

The greatest fears of all are the fears of the white man
for the black and of the black man for the white. The
fear of the white man is that he will be swamped and his
civilization drowned in a sea of blacks. So strong is this
fear that it has already overwhelmed some of his noblest
traditions and undermined some of the finest contributions of the civilization he hopes to preserve.

The fear of the black man is less theoretical, an om-
nipresence more personal and perhaps more rational,
since it is rooted in long experience and in the existing
legal code of the country, and is reinforced by a hundred
daily encounters and a thousand permanent contrasts
which do as much to poison the atmosphere as the law
itself.

Perhaps the worst thing about these crossed fears i
that each feeds on the other until communication is neve
free of them and becomes a funnel of misunderstanding

at further nourish them. Thus the black man retreats
to a constant groveling, and the white man sees him
only in the mask of cloying deference that he has forced
him to wear, hears him only through the endless staccato
of "sir" and "baas" that brings subservience to each sentence, knows him only as feudal lord knew faceless serf.

The cleverest black man is the one who learns to lie
most convincingly to the white, the one who remembers
that the master wants to hear only what he wants to hear
and who knows that he wants to hear even that in tones
purged of spirit and of any hint of independence. And
when most black men accommodate to such a tone, the
few who speak with candor must appear to the white not
as men of unusual integrity but as agitators: misleading,
inciting, dangerous, wicked, and theirs shall be the fate of
the bad example.

Such are the customs of the place that minor matters
can irritate or upset the newcomer quite out of proportion. The African who insists on calling you "sir" because
"It is a bad habit" to get out of, "sir"; the post-office window for blacks where the old lady waits endlessly while
the separate line of Europeans is served, replenished, and
served again; the stuttering terror of the African service
station attendant who discovers while putting gasoline in
a car that the gas cap is missing, and knows his employer
will accuse him of stealing it and perhaps fire him if the
driver of the car complains. One wonders if it is possible
to get used to such things; it is essential to get them in
perspective if one is to keep functioning in South Africa.

A DEFENSE OF APARTHEID

> While the policy of apartheid may seem indefensible
> to most of us, it is a mistake to underestimate or to dis-
> count the sincerity with which the Afrikaner justifies
> his position. This defense is written by a lawyer born
> and educated in South Africa.

From Charles A. W. Manning, "In Defense of Apartheid," *Foreign Affairs,* October 1964.

It is not as if it were open to South Africa to do jus
nothing. The situation in which she finds herself is a her
itage from a complicated past. Where the irresponsibl•
foreign onlooker has merely to insist that apartheid i
"morally wrong," the responsible South African has rath
er to ask himself whether there is any less immoral ap•
proach to South Africa's problem. He reads, for instance
in the Tomlinson Commission's report that "a continua
tion of the policy of integration would intensify racia
friction and animosity," and that "the only alternative i
to promote the establishment of separate communities i•
their own separate territories where each will have th•
fullest opportunity for self-expression and development.'
And he remembers how, at the Savoy Hotel dinner i•
1961, Dr. Verwoerd threw down his challenge to a fasci
nated company: "Ladies and Gentlemen, what would yo•
do?" He remembers also how, although the so-called "na
tive question" had been on the agenda for South Africa•
statesmanship since before the turn of the century, it wa
not until 1948 that the country had a government with
the necessary electoral backing to undertake any treat
ment of the question at all. And he notices that, while th•
world's judgment on apartheid is commonly expressed i•
moralistic language, it was, by contrast, upon sociologica
appraisal that the architects of the program based thei
recommendations for the progressive bettering of a give•
state of things which mere condemnation would not cure
Different policies might be adopted tomorrow, but a
present it is separate development that is being tried. T
understand it, one must, of course, examine it in its histor
ical and sociological context; for to study apartheid in th•
abstract would be as inept as to study the policy of de
segregation in the United States in the same restricte
manner.

"Ours," declared George Kennan in referring to th•
defensive nationalism of the American people, "is not th•
imperial frame of mind." At the root of the separate de
velopment program lies the nationalism, equally defen
sive, of the Afrikaner *volk*. It is indeed an error to se•
apartheid as expressive only of an attitude of the whi•

man toward the black. For nationalism as such is not a question of color feeling, and it is nationalism, rather than racialism, that the honest inquirer has basically to comprehend. In the first place the nationalism we are speaking of is not that of all South African white people. Rather it is the nationalism of the Afrikaner *volk,* a majority indeed, but by no means the whole, of the enfranchised population. It is easy for the foreigner to deride a nationalism which he does not share; but nowhere in human history has nationalism ever been destroyed by foreign scorn. Admittedly, Afrikaner nationalism is a form of collective selfishness; but to say this is simply to say that it is an authentic case of nationalism. For what is nationalism anywhere if not collective self-love? What underlies apartheid is at bottom an attitude not toward the black man, but toward the forefathers—and the future—of the Afrikaner people. It is to these that a responsibility is felt, to conserve a cultural heritage in defense of which white men fought against white men from 1899 to 1902.

True, it is not full sovereign independence that is now being conferred on the Transkei [first of the proposed Bantustans to achieve "self-government"]; but today's developments are declaredly no more than a phase in a process, the speed of which it will be partly up to the several Bantu peoples to decide. When, therefore, it is asked, "What is to be the ultimate outcome, what the final pattern, in South Africa?" the very question reveals a lack of understanding of apartheid. Apartheid means the granting of autonomy—the enthronement, that is, of communal wills independent of that of the existing white electorate. Purportedly to give autonomy to others, while at the same time prejudging issues in respect of which their autonomy would be promising them a say, would be somewhat contradictory. The definitive blueprinting of South Africa's future is not being attempted now. There is no way to know what choices the Bantu may make in the situations of tomorrow. It is a liberal fallacy to suppose that those to whom freedom is given will use it only as foreseen by those who gave it.

Apartheid is sometimes referred to as an "ideology";

and, since it is on the face of it inconsistent with Western liberalism, it is seen as in principle wrong. But it is wiser to recognize it as simply an expedient, an exercise in social therapeutics. It is a remedial treatment for a state of things deriving from the past. In part it is, of course, dictated by a passionate concern for the future of a European-type white society, and no doubt that society's right to self-preservation is itself a matter for debate. But it is this, and not the principle of apartheid, which thus is the matter for debate. Concede to the white man a right to preserve his achievement, and some such policy as apartheid may well appear as an inevitable corollary. Deplore the white man's collective self-concern, and you may equally well damn every other example of nationalism, white or black. It is absurd to assume that nationalism is nice, or nasty, according to its color.

It is possible that the Afrikaner, strict legalist that he is, may exaggerate the moral importance of constitutional right. Contrary to what his detractors imply, he shows little disposition to seek his objectives save through the methods of the constitution. What cannot be done constitutionally cannot, in his philosophy, be done. But conversely what can so be done, it is technically his right to do; and he is prone to hold that he is, therefore, right to do it. He has little patience with those who brush his constitutional arguments aside, even censuring his reliance on them—and this in a period when it is from people's disregarding of their constitutions rather than from their using, even manipulating, of them that mankind has probably the more to fear.

It is perhaps propitious that everybody should think of his own political system as about the best there ever could be; but if each wants to impose the principles of his own on all others, the outlook for peace is poor. Honored voices have lately proclaimed the ideal of a world made safe for diversity. What else is this but the very principle of the apartheid program? Just as in the world as a whole there are many societies, each distinctive in its peculiar culture, so also within the confines of geographical South Africa there are more than one or two societies. Tha very self-determination which his fathers fought for is what the Afrikaner now envisages for each of the African peoples still subject to the white man's rule. The philosophy of separate development implies a rejection of the fallacy that wherever a single system of government is in operation, there do the governed compose a single people. Were the critics of South Africa to accept squarely the fact that South Africa comprises more communities than one, their admonitions would be more persuasive and their proposals more to the point. As it is, what many of them keep calling for is something which they might well know to be impossible—the inauguration, namely, of a system in which South Africa's many peoples would resolve themselves unreluctantly into one.

It is this cult of unreality in the assumptions of her critics that has given South Africa her now, alas, almost habitual indifference to what they may choose to say. When, for instance, they affect to see in the Transkei experiment a device for providing a reservoir of cheap labor, they seemingly forget that that is just what the Transkei has traditionally been, and that the granting to it of autonomy, with the creation of thousands of local opportunities both in government and industry, must tend, if anything, to make the territory's manpower less rather than more plentifully available for service in the white man's system. Or again, when they dismiss primary school instruction in the "mother-tongue" as a stratagem for barring the Bantu's access to the cultural resources of the West, they overlook that degree of proficiency in both English and Afrikaans which the Bantu child has concurrently the opportunity to achieve before moving up from one standard to the next. When they hail as a "setback" for the apartheid policy the success of possibly awkward candidates in the Transkei elections, they only show how apparently defective is their conception of what may be expected to occur in free elections. When they complain that the autonomy now being accorded is incomplete, they ignore the object lessons offered by Belgium's precipitate withdrawal from the Congo. And when they question the capability of the Bantustans to stand economically on their own, they neglect to ask themselves whether even Britain's Basutoland will ever be able to do that either.

The philosophy of apartheid is the standpoint of politicians who, having no mandate for effecting the liquidation of so-called white supremacy, must do the best they can, in circumstances where nothing they may realistically contemplate can be expected to win them the approval of the world. It is the philosophy of patriots who, while aware that certain powers could presumably choose to destroy them tomorrow, do not, therefore, feel free to abandon their tasks of today; and who, though charged with despising their African fellow-citizens, have more occasion to condemn their erstwhile Western friends who, for fear of the displeasure of the Afro–Asian "Establishment," can seemingly no longer afford to have eyes and minds of their own.

South Africa knows that it is not she that has lately changed; that never at any time were her peoples a single community or her constitution other than oligarchic, and that it is nevertheless essentially for this that she is now being blamed. And, from the fact that in their reviling of her, critics rely so largely on misconceptions as to what she is doing, she can draw a measure of hope. For perhaps it will not be too long before persons of independent outlook, who as of now are apparently accepting the fashionable evaluation of her policies, will begin to perceive and to appreciate those policies for what they are.

> This closely reasoned presentation is evidence that all South Africans are not completely insensitive to world opinion. Its appeal to nationalism and sociological principles is a far cry from the naked doctrine of white supremacy backed by Old Testament theology, which is still the popular justification of apartheid in the mind of the Afrikaner public.

INDUSTRIALIZATION AND URBAN LIVING COMPLICATE RACIAL PROBLEMS

South Africa offers many examples of the cultural problems arising when large numbers of Africans were recruited from their native homes to work and live in urban centers. At first Africans were needed for farm and domestic labor, but a century ago work opened for them in the mining industry. Because Africans were at first reluctant to leave their homes, a tax was imposed on them which could only be paid if they worked for the European's wages, and gradually these wages drew more Africans to urban centers.

Solving the labor problem created several new ones. Africans moving to the urban areas severely dislocated the economy of the native reserves. The door to the twentieth century was opened to the African, but only a crack, and then held firmly. He was barred from all but unskilled jobs and denied union organization whereby he might bargain for better wages and employment conditions. Most significantly, Africans clustered in towns where they were economically necessary, but socially unwanted. Between 1921 and 1951 the native population in urban areas increased by 23 per cent.

The African population living in urban areas is complex, both ethnically and socially. The young migrant from the country is bewildered by the rush and hostility of the city environment and the inadequacy of his living facilities. He most likely misses the security of his family. New migrants are soon incorporated into barracks with other migrants from their home areas. These "home boys" frequently live twenty-five to a room, but they do have familiar companionship and can provide each other with mutual loan associations and collective defense if one of the number gets into a dispute with someone outside his group. These groups partially fill the role of tribal or kinship relationships, and some migrants never forsake their country ways and are always ill at ease when apart from their close companions.

The majority of men who come to the towns, however, rapidly become urban dwellers. Although they may marry country women, they try to establish their families in the cities. If they are fortunate they may find a flat or house in one of the "locations"—rigidly segregated communities on the outskirts of the European urban areas. Despite severe restriction of their freedom, they may have associations where they participate in sporting, musical, and dancing activities or in religious affairs.

Many younger Africans have never lived outside this environment: their "kraal" is a slum shanty and their "age set" is one of the many gangs roaming the location streets. Often all ties with family in the country have been broken. However harsh the city conditions, these people are ill-equipped to survive in the country. They are the ones who suffer most from the government's policy of returning members of ethnic groups to their "native homeland."

Rapid economic growth in South Africa demands the constant flow of Africans to the cities, and they now outnumber all other groups in every major urban center. But to secure the cities as European strongholds, the government may force Africans to pack up and move back to homeland areas on less than twenty-four hours' notice.

Even though Afrikaners behave as though the rest of the world does not exist, the world cannot be indifferent to events in the Republic of South Africa. It seems inevitable that the strong position taken by the South African government will serve as a rallying point for like-minded white people. White supremacy today draws the Republic of South Africa into closer and closer association with English-dominated Rhodesia and Portuguese-dominated Angola and Mozambique. As the United Nations adds more nonwhite members, the issues before it which involve South Africa, however indirectly, inevitably assume racial overtones. Any state that does not oppose the South African side of the debate will risk censure from the non-Caucasian states. Furthermore, it is unlikely that the communist bloc will overlook chances to fish in South Africa's troubled racial and political waters.

THE AFRICAN NATIONALIST: LUTHULI SPEAKS

With all our attention on the Afrikaner nationalist we tend to lose sight of the fact that there is another kind of nationalism in South Africa today.

In 1960 the Nobel Peace Prize was awarded to the late Albert John Luthuli, a Zulu chief from South Africa, for his efforts to bring much-needed peace between the races of his homeland. The actual presentation of the award was not made until December 1961, because the government of South Africa would not at first permit the chief to leave the country. The following are excerpts from Mr. Luthuli's acceptance speech before the Norwegian parliament.

From *Time,* December 22, 1961.

It is not necessary for me to speak at length about South Africa. It is a museum piece in our time, a hangover from the dark past of mankind, a relic of an age which everywhere else is dead or dying. Here the cult of race superiority and of white supremacy is worshiped like a god. . . . Thus it is that the golden age of Africa's independence is also the dark age of South Africa's decline and retrogression. . . .

To remain neutral, in a situation where the laws of the land virtually criticized God for having created men of color, was the sort of thing I could not, as a Christian, tolerate. . . . How great is the paradox and how much greater the honor that an award in support of peace and the brotherhood of man should come to one who is a citizen of a country where the brotherhood of man is an illegal doctrine.

Outlawed, banned, censured, proscribed, and prohibited; where to work, talk, or campaign for the realization in fact and deed of the brotherhood of man, is hazardous, punished with banishment or confinement without trial or imprisonment; where effective democratic channels to peaceful settlement of the race problem have never existed these 300 years, and where white minority power rests on the most heavily armed and equipped military machine in Africa.

WHY I AM READY TO DIE

> Gradually since 1960, all black African political parties have been banned in South Africa. Where possible, their leaders went underground, but by 1965 all of the prominent African nationalists had been arrested and imprisoned. Faced with police-state opposition to normal political activity, many of the underground groups resorted to plans for sabotage.
>
> Nelson Mandela was a successful lawyer and leader of the oldest African nationalist group, the African National Congress. He, along with many other leaders, was charged with treason and other subversive activities in 1961. During these famous "treason trials" which continued for four years, Mandela made the following speech which dramatically conveys the tragedy of the African nationalist movement in South Africa.
>
> *From* Nelson Mandela, in *Student Action on Apartheid in South Africa,* 1965.

I am the first accused. I hold a Bachelor's Degree in Arts and practiced as an attorney in Johannesburg for a number of years in partnership with Oliver Tambo. I am a convicted prisoner serving five years for leaving the country without a permit and for inciting people to go on strike at the end of May, 1961.

At the outset, I want to say that the suggestion made by the State in its opening that the struggle in South Africa is under the influence of foreigners or communists is wholly incorrect. I have done whatever I did, both as an individual and as a leader of my people because of my experience in South Africa and my own proudly felt African background.

Some of the things so far told to the court are true and some are untrue. I do not, however, deny that I planned sabotage. I did not in a spirit of recklessness, nor because I have any love of violence. I planned it as a result of a calm and sober assessment of the political situation that had arisen after many years of tyranny, exploitation, and oppression of my people by the whites.

I admit immediately that I was one of the persons who

helped to form Umkonto We Sizwe (The Spear of the Nation) and that I played a prominent role in its affairs until I was arrested in August, 1962.

I and the others who started the organization, did so for two reasons. First, we believed that as a result of Government policy, violence by the African people had become inevitable, and that unless responsible leadership was given to canalize and control the feelings of our people, there would be outbreaks of terrorism which would produce an intensity of bitterness and hostility between the various races of this country which is not produced even by war. Second, we felt that without violence there would be no way open to the African people to succeed in their struggle against the principle of white supremacy.

But the violence we chose to adopt was not terrorism. We who formed Umkonto were all members of the African National Congress (ANC) and had behind us the ANC tradition of nonviolence and negotiation as a means of solving political disputes.

Our problem was not whether to fight but how to continue the fight. We of the ANC had always stood for nonracial democracy, and we shrank from any action which might drive the races farther apart than they already were. But the hard facts were that 50 years of nonviolence had brought the African people nothing but more and more repressive legislation, and fewer and fewer rights.

It must not be forgotten that by this time violence had, in fact, become a feature of the South African political scene. How many more Sharpevilles would there be in the history of our country? And how many more Sharpevilles could the country stand with violence and terror becoming the order of the day?

Umkonto was formed in November, 1961. Umkonto was to perform sabotage, and strict instructions were given to its members right from the start that on no account were they to injure or kill people in planning or carrying out operations.

Another of the allegations made by the State is that the

aims and objects of the ANC and the Communist Party are the same. That allegation as to the ANC is false.

The ideological creed of the ANC is, and always has been, the creed of African nationalism. It is not the concept of African nationalism expressed in the cry, "Drive the white man into the sea." The African nationalism for which the ANC stands is the concept of freedom and fulfillment for the African people in their own land.

It is true that there has often been close cooperation between the ANC and the Communist Party. But cooperation is merely proof of a common goal—in this case the removal of white supremacy—and is not proof of a complete community of interests.

It is perhaps difficult for white South Africans, with an ingrained prejudice against communism, to understand why experienced African politicians so readily accept communists as their friends. But to us the reason is obvious. Theoretical differences amongst those fighting against oppression is a luxury we cannot afford at this stage. What is more, for many decades communists were the only political group in South Africa who were prepared to treat Africans as human beings and their equals; who were prepared to eat with us, talk with us, live with us, and work with us. They were the only political group which was prepared to work with the Africans for the attainment of political rights and a stake in society. Because of this, there are many Africans who, today, tend to equate freedom with communism.

It is not only in internal politics that we count communists as amongst those who support our case. Although there is a universal condemnation of apartheid, the communist bloc speaks out against it with a louder voice than most of the white world.

I turn now to my position. I have denied that I am a communist, and I think that in the circumstances I am obliged to state exactly what my political beliefs are.

I have always regarded myself, in the first place, as an African patriot. After all, I was born in Umtata 46 years ago. It is true that I have been influenced by Marxist thought. But this is also true of many leaders of the new independent states. Such widely different persons as Gandhi, Nehru, Nkrumah, and Nasser all acknowledge this fact. We all accept the need for some form of socialism to enable our people to catch up with the advanced countries of this world and to overcome their legacy of extreme poverty. But this does not mean we are Marxists.

I have been influenced in my thinking by both West and East. All this has led me to feel that I should tie myself to no particular system of society other than socialism. I must leave myself free to borrow the best from the West and from the East.

Africans want to be paid a living wage. Africans want to perform work which the government declares them to be capable of. Africans want to be allowed to live where they obtain work, and not be forced out of an area because they were not born there. Africans want to be allowed to own land in places where they work, and not be obliged to live in rented houses which they can never call their own. Africans want to be part of the general population, and not confined to living in their own ghettos.

Above all, we want equal political rights, because without them our disabilities will be permanent. I know this sounds revolutionary to the whites in this country, because the majority of voters will be Africans. This makes the white man fear democracy.

This then is what the ANC is fighting for. Their struggle is a truly national one. It is a struggle of the African people inspired by their own suffering and their own experience. It is a struggle for the right to live.

During my lifetime I have dedicated myself to this struggle of the African people. I have fought against white domination, and I have fought against black domination. I have cherished the ideal of a democratic and free society in which all persons live together in harmony and with equal opportunities. It is an ideal which I hope to live for and to see realized. But if need be, my Lord, it is an ideal for which I am prepared to die.

A REPORT TO THE UNITED NATIONS

With more than thirty-nine African countries in the United Nations it can be assumed that the explosive South African situation will continue to come up for consideration frequently before various branches of the world organization. The United Nations has already moved to boycott the shipment of munitions and military supplies to South Africa.

The following two selections contain proposals made in the United Nations and the United States' reaction to them. First are excepts from a report to the Secretary-General by a group of experts. The South African government refused to make any official comment on it.

This report not only contains a hearty condemnation of the racial policy of South Africa but outlines possible approaches, both cooperative and coercive, to the problem.

United Nations and regional organization pressure

94. The case for economic sanctions against South Africa has often been stated in the United Nations and on 6 November, 1962 the resolution (A/RES/1761 (XVIII)), calling for sanctions, was passed by a majority of more than two-thirds in the General Assembly. We have also taken into account the resolution adopted in Addis Ababa by the African Heads of State on 25 May, 1963, which decided to concert and coordinate their efforts to put an end to the South African Government's policy of *apartheid,* including measures of sanction; and appealed to all States, and more particularly to those which have traditional relations and cooperate with the Government of South Africa, to apply the United Nations resolution of the African Foreign Ministers at their meeting held in Lagos in February, 1962, in which *inter alia* they decided to recommend to the Organization of African unity: "That it should renew its appeal to all States to apply strictly the economic, diplomatic, political and military sanctions already decided upon by the United Nations

General Assembly and Security Council; That it should address a special appeal to the major trading partners of the Government of South Africa to desist from the encouragement they were giving to *apartheid* through their investments and their trade relations with the Pretoria Government; That it should decide to take all necessary steps to deny the right of overflight, landing, and docking, and all other facilities to aircraft and ships coming from or bound for South Africa."

95. These resolutions provide ample proof, if such is necessary, of the determination of all African States to pursue the cause of South African emancipation and to make sacrifices in that cause.

Uselessness of United Nations action, unless—

96. But while many African and other States have responded to the call of the General Assembly for sanctions, the hard fact remains that the South African economy is not seriously affected by the sanctions so far undertaken. Even if full sanctions were imposed by all the States whose representatives voted for the resolution of the General Assembly, the effect on the economy of South Africa would still be entirely inadequate. It is on the trading relations of South Africa with a few main trading partners that the strength of its economy rests. Nearly 40 per cent of South Africa's exports go to the United Kingdom and the United States, and nearly 50 per cent of her imports are drawn from these two countries. As Mr. Eric Louw pointed out in referring to the vote in the General Assembly in 1962, "The nations not supporting sanctions absorb 79.6 per cent of South Africa's exports and send her 63.7 per cent of her imports."

97. Without the cooperation of the main trading partners of South Africa, no move to impose sanctions can be effective. . . .

The case for sanctions

104. As to the argument that sanctions should not be imposed because they would harm the non-White population of South Africa, it should be noted that the African leaders have vigorously rejected any such contention. As Oliver Tambo of the African National Congress said when he was making his statement in the United Nations on 29 October, 1963: "This is a type of pity and paternalism which hurts us even more than sanctions would hurt us."

105. It is true that sanctions would cause hardship to all sections of the population, particularly if they had to be long maintained, but for the supporters of *apartheid* to use this argument to oppose sanctions would lay them open to a charge of hypocrisy.

106. Secondly, it is clear that if sanctions are to be effective they must be put into effect with the cooperation of South Africa's principal trading partners, particularly the United Kingdom and the United States. . . .

Recommendations

110. With these considerations in view we recommend that use should be made of the interval before a final reply is required from the South African Government on the proposal for a National Convention to enable an expert examination to be made of the economic and strategic aspects of sanctions. There seems to us to be an urgent need for a further practical and technical study of the "logistics" of sanctions by experts in the economic and strategic field, particularly in international trade and transport. [This was made in March 1965.]

The purpose of sanctions

111. It is obviously of great importance to keep constantly in mind the purpose of sanctions. That purpose is not to cripple the South African economy, but to save it.

If the decision to impose sanctions is universal then the threat of sanctions will be compelling. The period of imposition will be reduced thus lessening hardship, and indeed if the threat is universal and complete the actual imposition of sanctions might in fact become unnecessary.

Conclusions

112. Our conclusion is that it can only be by United Nations action, in the form of a unanimous decision of the Security Council, that the weapon of sanctions can be rapidly effective. Only if action is agreed and complete can the threat of sanctions achieve its purpose. Only by this drastic means can material loss and trade dislocation and hardship to many innocent people both in South Africa and elsewhere be avoided.

UNITED STATES POLICY

In view of the statements in the preceding report that coercive action by the United Nations would be meaningless without the support of the United States, Ambassador Adlai Stevenson's statement of United States policy in reply to the report is of great significance. In December 1966, Ambassador Arthur Goldberg reiterated this stand.

Adlai Stevenson's statement

From United States Mission to the United Nations, Press Release, June 16, 1964.

The United States has consistently held that the ultimate solution in South Africa must be worked out by the peoples of South Africa themselves, worked out on the basis of a free and equal exchange of views between all segments of the population, worked out on the basis of give and take.

The first link in such consultation must be the establishment of communication. We would hope the South African Government for its part would respond favorably to such a concept, would cooperate with the United Nations, and would seek such assistance, both within and outside the United Nations.

We also see merit in the concept of a special training and educational program for South Africans to be established under the auspices of the United Nations. Such a program would afford to those South Africans who have chosen to leave their country, or who have little access to higher education within their country, a chance to pursue their studies elsewhere. The United States is prepared to examine opportunities to contribute to such a program, both financially and in terms of scholarship and other facilities at American educational institutions. . . .

Much has been said here in the Council and elsewhere on the question of sanctions. My Government continues to believe that the situation in South Africa, though charged with somber and dangerous implications, does not today provide a basis under the Charter for the application by the Security Council of coercive measures. Nor can we support the concept of an ultimatum to the South African Government which could be interpreted as threatening the application of coercive measures in the situation now prevailing, since in our view the Charter clearly does not empower the Security Council to apply coercive measures in such a situation.

However, [a] group of experts has suggested that a study of sanctions be undertaken. My Government has given this proposal serious and prolonged consideration, and would be prepared to support the initiation of a properly designed study and to participate in it. But, and let me be explicit, our willingness to see such a study go forward under certain circumstances or our willingness to participate in such a study represents in no way an advance commitment on the part of my Government to support at any specific time the application under the Charter of coercive measures with regard to the South African situation or any other situation, nor should this position be interpreted as relating to our view of the situation in South Africa today or what it may become tomorrow. . . .

PART VI

The Future of Africa

With events moving so rapidly in Africa, it is difficult to project future trends. The best we can do is to list some of the directions which events may take, cite some examples, and discuss the forces which are at work to produce the different situations.

Balkanization

One possible direction which African nationalism could take is toward further political fragmentation—Balkanization.

Uganda in East Africa offers a classic example of the nineteenth-century disregard of ethnic divisions in the establishment of colonial political units. European missionaries, Catholic and Protestant, preceded the colonial power in Uganda by some thirty years. They entered an area of considerable political upheaval where several African kingdoms were fighting for expansion, and added fuel to the warfare by creating further divisions between Catholics and Protestants. When the British organized the thirteen major tribal groups into the Protectorate of Uganda, they froze the competition for power between the various kingdoms.

The kingdom which has most consciously protected its separate identity is Buganda. The Baganda were twice as numerous as any other single tribe and had a well-organized hierarchical political system when the British arrived. The present Kabaka (king) is the thirty-fifth member of his dynasty to rule the Baganda.

In 1953, the Baganda, fearing that the British planned to federate Uganda with white-settler-dominated Kenya and Tanganyika, demanded independence for Buganda from the Protectorate of Uganda. The British resisted the prospect of secession by this wealthy and populous kingdom and responded to the resulting disturbance by exiling the Kabaka. The era of bad feeling which followed was dissolved in the Namirembe Conference of 1955, when the British granted a privileged share in the Protectorate government to Buganda, allowing her separate representatives on the Legislative Council. Furthermore, the Kabaka was reinstated as a constitutional monarch.

As the following readings illustrate, the recognition of a state within a state has not aided the creation of an integrated nation. Under Prime Minister Milton Obote, however, who is not a Baganda, political unity was increased, although the Kabaka remained as head of Buganda within the Ugandan federation.

UGANDAN POLITICS AFTER ONE YEAR

After a year of independence a journalist assessed the success of Prime Minister Obote in meeting the challenge of creating a Ugandan nationalism.

From *The Christian Science Monitor*, October 3, 1963.

Uganda celebrates the first anniversary of its independence this month, and now—like other young African countries with a British connection—it proposes to install an African head of state in place of the Queen's Governor-General in the national capital. Ugandans intend, nevertheless, to remain within the Commonwealth. Both Ugandans and Britons will take all this in their stride; but alongside this constitutional development has gone a remarkable step toward a Ugandan national consciousness, thanks largely to the shrewdness and singleness of purpose of Prime Minister Milton Obote.

Fledgling Uganda was faced twelve months ago with an internal conflict between African conservatism and African radicalism that many thought would indefinitely hamper healthy political growth. Mr. Obote was the quiet representative of radicalism, and the Kabaka (or king) of Buganda the champion of conservatism. Such a conflict is found elsewhere in Africa; but in Uganda, the scales seemed inordinately weighted in favor of conservatism because of the strength and size of the kingdom of Buganda within Uganda and of the loyalty which the Kabaka seemed able to command among his people.

Mr. Obote, however, has played an astute political game during his premiership. To begin with, he apparently decided not to challenge the Kabaka head on. When he took office some five months before independence, Mr. Obote invited the Kabaka's party, the Kabaka Yekka, into coalition with his own Uganda People's Congress (UPC). This seemed to assure to the Kabaka significant influence at the center of federal power when Britain gave up sovereignty later in the year. But national prestige soon prevailed over regional interest, and six of the Kabaka Yekka members in the federal legislature—including two cabinet ministers—have since transferred their allegiance to Mr. Obote's UPC. The latter now has an overall majority in the house, regardless of the coalition arrangement.

The Kabaka has simultaneously discovered that with three lesser kingdoms within Uganda enjoying similar status to his, Buganda finds it hard to call the tune. Further, the Kabaka has made the mistake of unwisely pressing a territorial claim against one of the other kingdoms despite every indication that a vote in the claimed territory would go against him.

Thus Mr. Obote has done far better than many had dreamed possible to prevent Buganda separatism from wrecking Uganda's national unity. And such is the Prime Minister's flair for seeing the difference between the semblance and the substance of power, that it would not be surprising if he allowed the Kabaka to become Uganda's first President. The job is largely a ceremonial one.

SETTLEMENT OF THE LOST COUNTIES DISPUTE

This report was written one year later, in November 1964.

From "Milton's Paradise Regained," *The Economist,* November 7, 1964.

This most unusual and choice African state boasts four kings. Two of these kings, the Omukama of Bunyoro and the Kabaka of Buganda, faced each other on Wednesday for a final settlement by referendum of the 70-year-old quarrel over "the lost counties of Bunyoro." It has been accepted by all except those Baganda who are blinded by tribal loyalty that the result will be a return of the counties to Bunyoro.

For years the disputed ownership of the "lost" Buyaga and Bugangazzi counties has been seen as the main stumbling block to Ugandan unity. The prime minister, Mr. Milton Obote, has now adroitly demolished this obstacle. Before independence he rejected the conscientious British offer to try to settle it; after *uhuru,* he gave the area a cooling-off period with a two-year moratorium written into the constitution. He seems to have enjoyed watching the Kabaka make himself uncomfortable by setting up an encampment of ex-servicemen on the Bunyoro border. Mr. Obote was able to dictate the voting qualifications in the referendum, and he had little doubt that Uganda's judges would rule (as they did) that the Kabaka's 9,000 ex-service newcomers were not qualified to vote.

In the middle of the moratorium period, Mr. Obote shocked some of his own supporters by making the Kabaka president of Uganda. When some northern Ugandans accused him of handing over far too much power to the Baganda, he replied that there would be no unity until the million Baganda had been drawn out of their separatist shell. An early state in this process had to be the transmutation of the Kabaka, the prime symbol of separatism, into Sir Edward Mutesa, the first national president. A year's experience has proved him right.

In the last three months, however, the Baganda have retreated some way back into their shell. The Kabaka Yekka section of Mr. Obote's coalition government moved to the opposition benches in August when the "lost counties" referendum was announced, leaving the prime minister just short of a two-thirds majority. This shift was probably inevitable; what is important is the number of Baganda leaders who find that they can no longer fit into the tribal pattern. Nearly half the original Kabaka Yekka members of the national assembly have stayed with the government, and Buganda is still well represented in the cabinet.

The question now is whether the militant northerners in the cabinet will persuade Mr. Obote to follow up this central government victory over Buganda, or whether the prime minister will now give the subject a rest. The second course is likelier, both because it fits Mr. Obote's character, and because it is time he concentrated on economics.

> The author of this article misjudged. Either the Prime Minister did decide to follow up his victory over the Baganda or the Kabaka Yekka's growing strength forced his hand. In the spring of 1966, Mr. Obote moved to break the power of the Kabaka and the Baganda. In May, fighting broke out in Kampala, the Kabaka's palace was burned, and the ruler whom the Baganda regard as almost divine barely escaped with his life. Mr. Obote then assumed the title of President as well as Prime Minister and powers which were close to dictatorial. In June 1967, Mr. Obote decreed the abolition of the kingdom of Buganda.
>
> Whether or not this strong-man approach will serve to unite Uganda in spite of the hostile emotions it has aroused among the Baganda remains to be seen.

Pan-Africanism

Many experiments with union are being tried in Africa. In 1961 the British Trust Territory of the Southern Cameroons voted to break its colonial ties to Nigeria and join the former French Trust Territory of the Cameroun to create the Federal Republic of the Cameroun. While reuniting peoples of similar ethnic and linguistic background, the union has merged peoples of two different traditions of colonial policy and European languages.

The impulse to African unity has been strong throughout the history of the Pan-African meetings and the nationalist movements of the twentieth century. The founding of the Organization for African Unity (OAU) in May 1963 at Addis Ababa was preceded by a variety of formal political unions and organizations for cooperation between African states. The following readings are excerpts from a study of the OAU by a prominent political scientist, Norman Padelford. His discussion of the background for an African organization includes statements of representative points of view of African leaders.

DIVERSE PATHS TO UNITY

From Norman Padelford, "The Organization of African Unity," *International Organization,* Summer 1964.

The forces contributing to Pan-Africanism and the forces tending toward economic, political, or social fragmentation are an inherent part of the cultural and political background underlying the Addis Ababa agreement and its subsequent implementation—the search for "an African personality," a sense of "African community." Independence has brought statements from many African leaders of a common aspiration for a "united Africa." The background of colonial status, shared in one way or another by nearly all, gave meaning to the aspiration which had its intellectual birth in the series of Pan-African congresses held at intervals from 1900 on. At the same time, this centrally focused ideal has been countered by the centrifugal force of rival personal ambitions and interests as various leaders have grasped political power and felt the urge to stimulate popular support for their regimes or to enhance the position of states. The various groupings of African states formed since 1958 have served to focus and sharpen these rival interests.

The leaders of Ghana and Guinea, in particular, have urged that a close union of states be formed with a centralized executive, a consultative assembly, planning and development ministries, and an African high command. They also have pressed for an African armed force with power to "intervene" in troubled situations. President Nkrumah has pressed hard along these lines for a number of reasons. Among them are the sense of destiny which he feels as the leader of the first country of tropical Africa to achieve independence, his conviction that it is good politics to be the forefront of such a movement, and Ghana's need for access to the raw materials and markets of other countries. The case for the centralist approach has been put by Ghanaian Ambassador Alex Quaison-Sackey in this wise: "If the destiny of Africa as a whole is the common cause of each individual state . . . then we [can] . . . make common cause against the vast economic and social problems confronting the whole continent . . . [and] the African Personality will be realized."

The thirteen countries of West and Equatorial Africa forming the Brazzaville grouping have been disposed to move more slowly toward exclusively African measures. While not rejecting a loose association of states, they have preferred to maintain their ties with France and the European Common Market and to develop the regional African and Malagasy Organization for Economic Cooperation with headquarters at Yaounde in Cameroon. Because of the defense ties which some of these states have retained with France, they have been accused by some of the more radical African leaders of being "victims of neocolonialism" and not being "genuinely independent." This has produced resentments as have attempts, such as that in Gabon, to overthrow their governments.

The states forming the Monrovia Group, often operating under Nigerian leadership, have strongly favored a gradualist policy on unity and preferred functional cooperation unification. They have frequently tended to counterweight the more radical elements. Many of the members of this grouping have preferred an emphasis on pluralism, consultative rather than executive organs, and stress upon the forming of a development bank, a private investment guarantee fund, and stepped-up activities in the field of education, labor, and social welfare before political union.

The leaders of the East African countries joined in the regional Pan-African Freedom Movement of East, Central, and South Africa (PAFMECSA) have, with the principal exception of Milton Obote of Uganda who has made common cause with Nkrumah, generally favored a relatively loose association of states and functional cooperation while praising the theme of African unity. In forming their movement in 1962, Jomo Kenyatta, Julius Nyerere, and Milton Obote affirmed their "hope that our action will help to accelerate the efforts already being made by our brothers throughout the continent to achieve African unity." An apparent further step in this direction was taken in the spring of 1964 when the presidents of Tanganyika and Zanzibar signed articles of union for their countries.

In addition to the differing outlooks of the members of these groupings there are, of course, other factors, both domestic and external, environmental as well as human, that have influenced the policies of states. These include a reluctance on the part of young leaders who have struggled for freedom to sacrifice independence for an uncertain supranational order in which others might come to dominate their destiny or achieve advantages at the cost of their people and resources. Fears of a new African-initiated imperialism have been conjured up. Boundary disputes such as the Morocco–Algeria conflict in 1963 and the recurrent fighting on the Ethiopian and Kenyan frontiers of Somalia, have also impeded unity.

Cultural and religious differences have to some extent invaded the sphere of cooperation, but these have on the whole figured less prominently than outsiders had predicted they would, especially along the Arab–Negro and Islam–Christian–Pagan cleavages. The split associated with Israel has been a factor; Arab emissaries have criticized the use of Israeli technical assistance and trade which not a few of the less developed countries have found invaluable in their development. The attitude of some has been expressed by Julius Nyerere of Tanganyika when he said: "We do not want our friends to choose our enemies for us," and Tom Mboya has said:

> We also think we can play a more useful part in trying to remove difficulties and misunderstandings between nations which are our friends, rather than in intensifying hatreds which existed before we came to nationhood. We hope that both Israel and the Arab states will give us an opportunity of helping them resolve this problem. . . . Neither of them should ask us or expect us to hate the other.

No less significant are the weak national regimes in a number of states and the transportation and communication difficulties that beset Africans. The fact that "it is five hours from Dakar to Paris but a week to Addis Ababa or Nairobi" is a common problem throughout the continent. Compounding the difficulties are the many tongues (over 800) spoken among the Africans aside from English, French, Portuguese, and Spanish.

These are but some of the complications that beset the trial to unity. Others include the unremitting efforts of outside powers to maintain and increase their own national interests in Africa and the effects which the competition and conflicts among these powers have in pulling and hauling the African countries this way and that. Notwithstanding sturdy efforts to avoid being drawn into the Cold War, the African states are continually being pressed in one direction or another by virtue of their friendships and dispositions toward one way of life or the advantages being offered by one power or another. These are unavoidable, but they do affect the strivings for unity. . . .

THE 1963 ADDIS ABABA SUMMIT CONFERENCE

As the leaders arrived at Addis Ababa for the summit meeting, a new atmosphere began to manifest itself. The spirit of caution and dispute gave way to a sense of exhilaration and confidence as, one after the other, the heads of state or government, or their deputies, deplaned.

Speaking directly to the main issue in his welcoming address, Emperor Haile Selassie called for immediate action on a charter of African unity. . . .

Pointing to experience elsewhere, the Emperor came out forthrightly for the gradualist approach:

> The union which we seek can only come gradually, as the day-to-day progress which we achieve carries us slowly but inexorably along this course. We have before us the examples of the United States of America and Union of Soviet Socialist Republics. We must remember how long these required to achieve their union. When a solid foundation is laid, if the mason is able and his materials good, a strong house can be built.

Coming to the point of his argument the Emperor urged:

> Let us here and now agree upon the basic instrument that will constitute the foundation for the future growth in peace and harmony and oneness of this continent. Let us not put off, to later consideration and study, the single act, the one decision which must emerge from this gathering if it is to have a real meaning. This conference cannot close without adopting a single African charter. If we fail this, we will have shirked our responsibility to Africa and to the peoples we lead.

The declarations contained in the subsequent addresses by the heads of state ranged over a broad terrain. . . .

In a speech infused with a deep philosophical spirit, President Leopold Senghor of Senegal aligned himself with the positions of Haile Selassie and Habib Bourguiba:

> What binds Africans together arises from culture—it is that community of culture which I call African-ness. . . . Though its nature is material and technical, it is on spiritual energy that we must call. We must forge together a common soul. That means we must begin by rejecting all fanaticism. . . . The aim we assign . . . to our action [must be] bringing each and every African to full worth. . . . The important thing is that we make a developed man, because he has consciously cultivated in himself, in body and soul, all the virtues of African-ness.

Among other specific steps, Senghor appealed for the creation of an African common market as a means of transforming weakness into strength. Another who spoke for the middle way was Ahmadou Ahidjo of Cameroon.

> The organization that we can give to African unity has to be a highly flexible one. It seems to us that any rigid form of institution would be premature at this stage. And so, for the moment, let us have neither Federation nor Confederation.

Many speakers stressed the importance of uniting in order to ensure that territories that are still dependent may be given support to realize their ambitions for independence too. Among those emphasizing this point of view was President Fulbert Youlou of the Congo (Brazzaville), who urged that the leaders join in proclaiming a "Monroe Doctrine" for Africa. For example, that Africa was no longer open for colonization or interference by non-African powers, and that a time limit be fixed for the independence of all territories.

The most anxiously awaited speech was that of President Kwame Nkrumah of Ghana. His book entitled *Africa Must Unite* had been published shortly before the meeting and was being circulated among the delegates. In keeping with his beliefs he urged the leaders, in a political phrase used before, to "seek ye first the political kingdom and all things will be added to it." He stressed in the first place the need for unity in the distribution of scarce resources to escape poverty and to develop heavy industry at the same pace as agriculture. Only by achieving a continental economy could there be economic development and satisfaction of needs. This, he insisted, could be attained only by planning on a continental basis. Second, he insisted that economic and social development depended upon political unity and could occur only within it. The United States and the Soviet Union, he argued, "were the political decisions of revolutionary peoples before they became mighty realities of social power and material wealth." Third, he argued the necessity of delivering the progress which the newly nationalistic elites had been led to hope for, lest "resentment which overthrew colonialism be mobilized against us," possibly a presentiment of the unrest that has been manifest in his own state. Fourth, he urged the nations to adopt a unified military and defense strategy with an African army. Finally, he emphasized that Africa had to adopt a common foreign policy to give political direction to its efforts to protect and develop the continent.

In presenting his proposals for an African charter, Nkrumah followed the reasoning of his book that "without necessarily sacrificing our sovereignties, we can forge a political union." This qualified tone perhaps came from Nkrumah's awareness that the tide of opinion was running against him and he may have employed this as a device for saving what he could. Or possibly the spirit of compromise evoked by Haile Selassie and others made him realize that whatever came from the Conference would have to represent a melding of different viewpoints. Whatever the reason Nkrumah presented his proposals but did not press them hard. And when the Conference ended with the adoption of essentially the Ethiopian plan, he joined in praising the results.

THE OAU IN THEORY AND PRACTICE

> Diallo Telli, the Administrative Secretary General of the OAU, summarized the purpose and direction of the organization.
>
> *From* Diallo Telli, "The Organization of African Unity in Historical Perspective," *African Forum,* Fall 1965.

In looking at the OAU as a going concern against the background of the history of Pan-Africanism, we might start by spelling out what the organization is and is not. First, the organization is not a supranational body. It is strictly an intergovernmental body with the limited purpose of fostering cooperation among the member states. Second, the charter of the OAU is not a constituent act of the peoples of Africa, but rather an agreement freely entered into by governments. The contractual charter of the organization is further emphasized by the recognition of the sovereign equality of states. The signatories have, however, recognized in the preamble that the creation of the organization is a "response to the aspiration of our peoples for brotherhood and solidarity in a large unity transcending ethnic and national differences." . . .

There is no doubt, therefore, that the conscious building of African unity is the primary objective of the organization, and as the years go by this task is bound to assume prominence. At this juncture of the history of Africa, the anticolonial fight, in actual fact, seems the first order of things. This should be considered, however, as a passing phase. When the colonial battle is at last won, the building of African unity will inevitably force itself to the forefront.

The defense of the sovereignty, territorial integrity, and independence of member states is one of the more specific purposes of the organization. It is to be noted, however, that the charter does not provide for a collective security arrangement in the sense that member states are not under any legal obligation to come to the assistance of another member state if aggression is committed against it. All that the charter requires of member states is that to achieve this objective they should coordinate and harmonize their policies in defense matters.

To guide the relationships of member governments with one another, the charter lays down certain principles, which member states have solemnly pledged to respect. A few of these are well-accepted principles which have evolved over the years in traditional law, the League of Nations, and the United Nations. Such principles as noninterference in the internal affairs of states, respect for the sovereignty and territorial integrity of states, and the peaceful settlement of disputes fall within this category. But a number of concepts have been elevated to the level of principles to guide the African states. These include the unreserved condemnation of political assassination in all its forms; absolute dedication to the total emancipation of African territories still dependent; and affirmation of the policy of nonalignment with regard to all blocs.

The condemnation of political assassination is, of course, tied up with the principles of noninterference in the internal affairs of member states. Why this aspect was singled out and laid down as a principle could be explained only in terms of the topicality of the problem as it prevailed then. But special note should be taken of the fact that dedication to the total emancipation of the continent is written not only as an objective, for whose achievement member states are dedicated to strive, but significantly also a fundamental tenet of the charter to guide the daily action of African countries. This shows the depth of anticolonial feeling in Africa and the realization that Africa would not become master of its destiny until its total emancipation. This recognition has always been evident, in varying degrees, during the evolution of Pan-Africanism.

Nonalignment has also been written into the charter as a positive principle to guide the external policy of African government. Thus a concept that could have been at best elaborated into a policy is elevated to the level of a principle. The significance of this can hardly be overemphasized. It was born out of a deep conviction that if Africa is to contribute to the maintenance of peace it can do so only by effectively insulating itself from the cold war. There is also a sincere belief that the essentials of the cold war have nothing to do with present problems.

Membership under the Charter of African Unity is a right for all independent African states. No qualification such as one would find in the United Nations Charter, that the prospective member should be peace-loving, is a condition for membership in the OAU. The unqualified and unrestrictive nature of membership has made it possible for all independent African countries to join the OAU. If, on the other hand, membership were contingent on adherence to a certain official ideology, or a political-economic system, the OAU would not be the all-inclusive organization that it is. At any rate, whether one considers the absence of a political and economic ideology as a blessing or an inherent defect, the fact remains that this lack is a phenomenon of Pan-Africanism. . . .

Reading through the charter, one is bound to be impressed by the generalities of some of its clauses. Some concepts and guarantees which one would expect to find in a legal instrument of this nature are missing. There is, for example, no "domestic jurisdiction" clause. Whether financial contribution to the running of the secretariat is obligatory or not is not emphatically stated. The whole question of sanction is altogether left out. The status of all decisions of the assembly and the council are far from being clear. Unless one looks at these conspicuous absences and ambiguities with an understanding that the entire undertaking is not a supranational organization, one might find it difficult to comprehend their total significance.

On the other hand, the lack of precision in some of these clauses might be a blessing in disguise. For one thing, it makes the charter a highly flexible instrument, capable of responding to the needs of the circumstances. The first two years in the life of the organization can be characterized as years of institution building. A complete network of rules and regulations, conventions for immunities and privileges, and headquarter agreements had to be worked out to enable the organization to function as an entity. This phase has now been completed.

Although the last two years have not been without their political difficulties, the member governments have found in the OAU a suitable diplomatic platform where constructive discussions could take place and where mechanisms could be evolved for the settlement of intra-African disputes. The Algeria–Morocco conflict was the baptismal test for the organization. It is a source of pride to all Africans that this conflict has been effectively contained through diplomatic initiatives within the OAU. In the meantime, the source of the conflict is being studied with a view to a solution by a special *ad hoc* commission. Likewise, the Somalia–Ethiopia and the Kenya–Somalia border problems have been effectively brought under the continuous scrutiny of the Council of Ministers. Although the problems are far from being solved, an effective ceasefire and a withdrawal of troops from the border area have been effected by diplomatic initiatives within the OAU. Two years ago, following an army mutiny in Tanganyika, effective military assistance was given to Tanzania under an OAU umbrella.

The usefulness of the organization as an instrument of constructive diplomacy, and its ability to respond to situations and emergencies, can be attested by the fact that over a span of less than two years the Council of Ministers has held five extraordinary sessions. At two of these sessions, the Council of Ministers considered the Congo problem in the light of recent events. Although none of us could be so presumptuous as to suggest that a solution is in the offing for the Congo problem, African governments have let it be known at every appropriate occasion that the Congo problem is an African problem and that its solution should be sought within the purely African diplomatic framework and in complete isolation from the cold war.

It is not very uncommon these days to hear pessimistic speculations about the future of the OAU. It is said that the organization is crumbling because such-and-such disputes have broken out, because such-and-such governments do not see eye to eye on a number of problems. But is it not because we had anticipated the possibilities of frictions and problems that we built this edifice, the OAU? Not to have anticipated such an eventuality would have been to consider Africans less or more than human. The frequency of conflicts and misunderstandings among African countries, and to a lesser extent the inability to work out hard and fast solutions to problems, could not be the sole criteria for judging the failure of the organization. Life is more complicated than that. Diplomatic solutions could not be stripped down to such a bare minimum. A long-term view has to be adopted; and in the final analysis, a more objective criterion would be to think of what would have happened if there had been no OAU. . . .

Adapting Modern Political and Economic Concepts

The development of a stable political system within each state poses another set of questions: What do African leaders envision the relationship between government and the goals of society to be? What do they mean by democracy? To what extent do they advocate political opposition to the party in control of the government?

In the United States, representative government elected by the adult population has been inextricably linked with private ownership of property and the free-enterprise system. In Africa, the lack of industrial development, the unevenness of resources, and the almost total absence of indigenous capital contrast sharply with the people's desire for greater social and economic equality. African leaders work toward the development of ideologies and programs which will be most beneficial in the African context. The result necessitates a new definition of terms such as democracy and socialism.

THE ROLE OF OPPOSITION PARTIES

Tom Mboya, now minister for Economic Planning and Development, is one of the key political figures in Kenya. Here he speaks of the role of a responsible opposition.

From James Duffy and Robert A. Manners, eds., *Africa Speaks,* 1961.

Too often people think of democracy in terms of British, French, or American parliamentary and institutional patterns. Such people reckon that Africa must therefore import a blueprint of similar institutions and all the paraphernalia that go with it. This attitude often tends to overlook the fact that in developing their institutions, Europe and America were influenced by the set of circumstances and conditions in which they were operating and developing. Without departing from the basic principle of individual political and civil freedoms, Africa must be free, during the period of consolidation, to determine what pattern of institutions would be suitable in running a democratic government in Africa. Critics of Africa have sometimes declared that democracy would not work because of illiteracy and because opposition parties are not yet in existence. Illiteracy is no bar to democracy—it may call for a departure from some of the patterns of institutions used elsewhere, but this does not mean democracy is abandoned. Opposition parties must develop not because the textbooks say so but rather as a normal and natural process of the individual freedom of speech and freedom to criticize government and the right of a people to return a government of their choice by use of the ballot box. Thus, in practice, when a country has just won its independence most of its effective leadership will have worked together as a team in the nationalist struggle and the new government will have pledged itself to serve the people's most urgent social and economic needs. Such a situation can only leave room for a very weak and small opposition often with less impressive leadership, at least in the initial period. Unless a split occurs in the ranks of the new nationalist government, this situation may continue for ten or even more years. This does not mean the abandonment of democracy, but it is a situation which calls for great vigilance on the part of the people in respect to their individual freedoms. The party in power has a heavy burden while the small and weak opposition must not be tempted to use violence or undemocratic means to compensate for her weakness or for her frustration when she fails to make herself heard on national issues.

A DEFENSE OF ONE-PARTY DEMOCRACY

> Julius Nyerere, President of Tanzania, has long been an advocate of one-party democracy in Africa. A classic statement of his philosophy appears below.

From Julius Nyerere, in *Symposium on Africa,* 1960.

Within the next decade at the outside, Africa will be free from colonialism. The challenge she faces is to consolidate her freedom after it has been won. To do that Africa must maintain the moral principles on which she has based her fight. She must be able to judge issues on their own merit, without being slavishly committed to alignment with this or that power bloc in the world. She must herself contribute to world understanding, for it is obvious that the newly emerging nations of our continent have a vested interest in world peace, without which their vital development programs would be disrupted.

Apart from such material considerations, it is clear that Africa's strength is a moral strength. I suggest that the world today needs a champion for democracy and personal freedom, a champion who must be free from ties of history, or ties of alliance, which might embarrass her stand. Today it seems that Africa is in the best position to take that role—to speak to the world from moral strength, in fact, to continue in the world the moral struggle in which she has already engaged herself on the African continent. To my thinking, no other continent, as a continent, has either the common sentiment or the unblemished moral standing which is Africa's.

But if Africa is to take up this challenge, she must maintain the highest democratic standards within her own territories. The slogan of the African agitator like myself —"Africa Must Be Free"—must not be confined to the idea of freedom from foreign rule. If it is going to be worthy of the sacrifice that our people are making, it must mean freedom for the individual man and woman on the African continent. It must mean freedom from every form of oppression, indignity, intimidation or exploitation, whether by fellow citizens, by foreign government, or by any government of free Africa. It must include the right of the individual citizens, regularly and through the ballot box, I emphasize *and through the ballot box,* and without intimidation, to reelect or to replace the government of his own country. It must also include the freedom of the governments to govern without fear of attempts being made to replace them by means other than the ballot box.

The African claims that his fight is for democratic rights. There are many, both in Africa and elsewhere, and I am sure in this country and in this audience probably, who believe in the sincerity of that claim. There are others who question whether, in fact, the African can really understand and practice democracy. Democracy is believed to be such a difficult thing to understand or to practice. It would be naive to think that the African Nationalists themselves do not sometimes question whether, once having established democratic institutions in their own countries, it will be possible to use those institutions to maintain full democratic rights. But I have often wondered whether the people who question either the sincerity of the African's belief in democracy, or his ability to establish and safeguard democratic rights, are clear in their own minds as to what the essentials of democracy really are.

I have very often heard doubts expressed about the possibility of maintaining freedom in Africa, but I have been struck by one thing that most of the doubters and critics have in common: they have not bothered to define the essentials of the democracy of which they are speaking. They have usually confined their idea of it to certain democratic institutions or forms which have been developed in particular countries as the result of local circumstances and national characteristics peculiar to those countries. For instance—and my friend, Duncan, I see is looking at me there—the British critic when he speaks of democracy has a picture in his own mind of what democracy should be. This picture—certainly the picture which appears in the criticism he offers—includes the Parliament buildings, beautiful ones; it includes a party in power within those Parliament buildings; and another party, within those same imposing buildings, not yet actually in power but with hopes of getting in power if and when their turn comes to win a general election, and in the meantime enjoying the title of Her Majesty's Official Opposition. In other words, to the Briton, democracy is an institution consisting of a debating house in which one group is for the motion, another group against the motion, and each group is quite distinct from the other. Similarly, the American has his own picture of democracy. To my thinking, each is confusing the machinery, or structure, with the essence of democracy. Each is in fact saying, and some have in actual fact been saying in so many words, "Can you imagine an African country where you have one party governing and another party in opposition?" To such critics an organized and officially recognized opposition has become almost the essence of democracy.

I am certain I may be oversimplifying the basis of the criticisms and doubts, but that is certainly the way in which most people argue when they question Africa's ability to maintain a democratic form of government. They assume that if a country is governed by one party, that government cannot be democratic. In doing so, I suggest they ignore three important factors.

The first is this:—and I have said this so often I now sound monotonous to myself repeating it—That a country's struggle for freedom from foreign domination is a

patriotic struggle; it leaves no room for difference. Th
issue, at that stage, is a simple one, and one which unite
all elements in the country. As a result you find, not onl
in Africa but in other parts of the world which face ;
similar challenge, the growth, not of a political party, bu
of a nationalist movement. It is this nationalist movemen
which fights for and achieves independence; it therefor
inevitably forms the first government of an independen
state. It would surely be ridiculous to expect that a coun
try should voluntarily divide itself for the sake of con
forming to a particular expression of democracy whicl
happens to be seen in terms of a Government party and
an Opposition party, and to expect the country to do thi:
in midstream, during a struggle which calls for the com
plete unity of all its people. Democracy has been defined
—and the person who defined democracy in that way i:
so popular I do not have to name him—as a governmen
of the people, by the people, for the people. Surely, if a
Government is freely elected by the people, there can be
nothing undemocratic about it just because nearly all the
people, rather than only one of them happen to have
elected it into power. This appears to be one of those
self-evident truths.

Indeed, it appears natural that young nations whicl
emerge as a result of a nationalist movement having
united their people, will be governed at first by a nation
alist government as distinct from a party government. N
one should therefore jump to the conclusion that thi:
means such a country is not democratic, or does not in
tend to be democratic.

. . . In my opinion there are two basic essentials o
democracy. The first of these is the freedom and the
well-being of the individual. The second is the method by
which the government of a country is chosen; the method
must ensure that the government is freely chosen by the
people. If you have a country where the system of the
government respects and upholds the freedom of the indi
vidual, I would say here is one essential of democracy
And I don't care whether it's one party or twenty parties
provided the government of that country can be replaced

without assassination, if the people go to the ballot box freely and regularly, and reelect their government, or replace it with another, then as far as I am concerned, the two basic essentials of democracy are there, whether you have twenty parties or one party.

The third factor which is conveniently forgotten by the critics of African democracy is the history of Africa. I shall try to show, late, in the course of this talk, that in traditional African society the African was never and never thought of himself as a cog in a machine. He was a free individual in his own society. But his conception of government was personal, not institutional. When government was mentioned, the African thought of the chief—a person, not a building. Unlike the Briton, he did not picture a grand building in which a debate was taking place in a very organized manner.

. . . When I say that Africa today seems to be in the best position to champion personal freedom and well-being and the democracy which must preserve that freedom and well-being, I am not basing my claim solely on the moral strength which is hers because of her history. There is another, though less lofty, reason. In the world today there is a conflict between the advocates of the freedom of the individual and those who champion the primacy of the State. When one examines the differences between the ideologies of the Eastern and Western Powers, I think one can reduce them generally to this very conflict. The West seems to have exaggerated its idea of freedom beyond the point where freedom becomes license; to have accepted a society in which, provided a man does not—or a woman for that matter—too obviously steal or murder, he can defend any form of self-indulgence by calling it Freedom of the Individual. The Communist world, to my mind, largely I think, as a reaction against this exaggeration, has swung like a pendulum to the other extreme. The individual in a Communist society is secondary to something called the State. Here, then, I think is the problem: Where does society, or the State, draw the boundary of its rights and obligations; and where does the individual? It is a problem which has not yet been solved by either side in a way that can be accepted by the other.

In primitive African society this question of the limits of responsibility as between the individual and the society in which he lives was not very clearly defined. The traditional African community was a small one, and the African could not think of himself apart from that community in which he lived. He was an individual: he had his wife, or wives, and children, so he belonged to a family. But the family merged into a larger "blood" family, which itself merged into a clan or tribe. Thus he saw himself all the time as a member of a community, but he saw no struggle in that traditional community—he saw no struggle between his own interests and those of his community, for his community to him was an extension of his family. He might have seen a conflict between himself and another individual member of the same community, but with the community itself, he saw no struggle. He never felt himself to be a cog in a machine. There could not be this all-embracing, all-powerful modern concept of a society which could use a person as a cog.

That traditional community is still visible in Africa today; in a sense it is one of our problems. Having come into contact with a civilization which has overemphasized the Freedom of the Individual, we are in fact faced with one of the big problems of Africa in the modern world. Our problem is just this: How to get the benefits of European society—benefits which have been brought about by an organization of society based on an exaggerated idea of the rights of the individual—and yet retain the African's own structure of society in which the individual is a member of a kind of fellowship.

Let me put this another way. One of the complaints of the European employer in Africa, and that point was put by one of the speakers here, is that the African is paid a wage to which he has agreed and then complains that it is not enough after all—usually because he does not use his wage merely upon himself and his family, but also upon other individuals who lay claim upon his wage. This is a fact. But one must not think that the African is therefore a natural communist. He is not. To him, the wage is his wage; the property is his property; but his brother's need is his brother's need and he cannot ignore that need. He has not yet learned to ask the question "Am I my brother's keeper?" That he does not yet ask. The African is not communistic either in his thinking or in his traditional way of life. He is, if I may borrow the expression—I have heard it used in India—the African is not communistic, he is "communitary," in thinking and in his way of living. He is not a member of a commune, some artificial unit of human beings; he is a member of a genuine community or brotherhood.

Today, when there is this conflict between East and West—and I have said that I think this conflict is basically one between the rights of the individual and the rights of the State—Western Europe, which has had a much longer experience of its own pattern of society, is becoming self-critical. Africa is, in this sense, fortunate in that there is still to be found on our continent a form of organization of society which fundamentally solves that conflict between the individual and society. It should be possible, therefore, for Africa to use both her own basic structure and the self-criticism of Western Europe in order to evolve from them a form of society which can satisfy both sides.

ELECTIONS IN A ONE-PARTY STATE

> The following is a journalistic account of Tanzania's recent elections. It shows how vigorous campaigning was encouraged despite a single-party system.

> From *Time,* October 8, 1965.

Elections in a one-party state are usually about as exciting as guessing how many beans in a bottle. As one-party Tanzania went to the polls last week, however, the roar in the foreground sounded strangely like politicians fighting for votes. For six weeks, candidates had been crisscrossing the nation, walking as far as 30 miles to appear under banyan trees at isolated village rallies. Even President Julius Nyerere felt constrained to stump through the countryside with his new Polaroid camera, aweing prospective voters by handing out pictures he had just taken of them.

Such tactics quickly earned Nyerere the title of "the god with the magic eye," also brought in observers from such distant monolithic states as Russia and Hungary to watch Nyerere's Tanganyika African National Union (TANU) party pull off a far more impressive feat: free, contested elections.

Nyerere himself ran unopposed for his second term as President, but 107 seats of Parliament were also at stake last week. Rather than go through the farce of running a single slate, TANU had put up two candidates for every seat except those held by six top party officials. TANU gave each opponent equal support, paired them off in daily joint appearances and assigned three referees to supervise each match. Then the party stood aside and let the candidates fight it out.

The results were surprising. Forced to return to their districts for the first time in five years, many Congressmen found themselves accused of ignoring the home folks, breaking previous campaign promises for new roads and wells, and living it up in Dar es Salaam. Voters who showed up at one rally greeted their Congressman with such prolonged boos that he went home and shot himself, "accidentally," in the hand. Another was haunted by the local witch-doctor, who went so far as to put a bloodstained coffin containing a strangled chicken outside the polling booth on election day.

All told, it was a bad week for officeholders. Only 16 members of the current Parliament managed to get themselves reelected, and among the losers were nine ranking party officials, including Finance Minister Paul Bomani, who had invoked the wrath of the electorate by raising income taxes. One of the biggest winners, hard-working Health Minister Derek Bryceson, carried his Dar es Salaam district by a resounding 30,000 votes.

AFRICAN SOCIALISM

Coming out of independent Africa is a great deal of talk about "African socialism." The following readings examine this economic and social doctrine. The first discusses the uniqueness of African socialism and the disagreements among African leaders concerning its nature.

From Ruth Schacter Morgenthau, "African Socialism: Declaration of Ideological Independence," *Africa Report*, May 1963.

What is the specifically African feature of this socialism? On this most spokesmen agree. It is the solidarity of the kinship group, most evident at the local level. President Julius Nyerere of Tanganyika has explained, "[The African] is not a member of a 'commune'—some artificial unit of human beings—he is of a genuine community, or brotherhood." ("Will Democracy Work in Africa?" by Julius Nyerere, *Africa Report*, February 1960, p. 4.) This solidarity was very important to the nationalist political parties which achieved independence. Most Africans still live at least in part within the subsistence economy, and from this sector came the bulk of the contributions to party finances in the form of free transport, gasoline, housing, food, work, and other volunteer services. These contributions did the job done by hired professionals in political parties in industrialized countries.

The postindependence task, as most African leaders see it, is to preserve the sense of community found in the extended family, spread it throughout the whole society, and harness it to development. To describe this task, Julius Nyerere and Sekou Touré, on opposite sides of the continent and educated respectively in the use of Catholic and Marxist political vocabularies, nevertheless coined similar words. Nyerere spoke of the "communitary" society; Toure, of the *"communaucratique"* society. (Nyerere, *op. cit.*, p. 4; *"L'Expérience guinéenne et l'unité africaine,"* by Sekou Touré, *Présence Africaine,* Paris, 1959, p. 394.) Extending this "sense of community" to the national level poses serious problems. The solidarity of a village is based on kinship; so are the communal claims to the land. In contrast, cooperatives must be based on contract and employees must be selected on merit. In a modern system, recruitment based on kinship is nepotism. Here lies one of the main points of controversy. Are the actual institutions of kinship or only its spirit to be preserved? Can anything more than the spirit of village solidarity be infused into the new economic institutions?

In most French-speaking countries, the new governments encouraged *investissement humain* programs, in which villagers gave their time to build or improve roads, bridges, meeting halls, schools, infirmaries, and mosques. They planted communal fields to produce agricultural crops and to replace food being imported in return for precious foreign exchange. The initial enthusiasm for *investissement humain* wore off, however, as it became increasingly clear that more planning would be needed to produce effective results. Many governments have tried to encourage producer cooperatives at the village level, some along the lines of Israeli *kibbutzim*. . . .

Points of disagreement

African spokesmen of socialism disagree on many points. To some, like Senghor, the village is the source from which African society will be transformed; it is almost a mystical entity whose institutions must be preserved. Others believe that, while the spirit of communal cooperation found in some villages and most kinship groups must be the inspiration for the new African society, the traditional institutions are doomed.

There is a difference, too, in the role assigned to the individual within the state. Senghor, and those who share his debt to Emmanuel Mounier's *personnalisme*, developed in the immediate postwar period in the French Catholic review *Esprit*, emphasize that society exists for the individual and not the reverse. At the same time, they claim the individual can fulfill himself only through service to society. This is a difference at the level of theory, since, in practice, the Senegalese Government, like those of Mali, Guinea, Ghana, and most other African states, uses repressive techniques readily: jails opposition party leaders or potential ones, discovers plots against the security of the state, compels papers to print only favorable comments, and demands uncritical loyalty from civil servants and others who enjoy state patronage.

Guinean and Malian leaders couple the ideas of individualism and selfishness. Sekou Touré warns his followers against *"aventures personnelles."* In both states, intellectuals are warned not to think they count more than anyone else in the party; all are urged to be vigilant lest there emerge a privileged class. Nkrumah has something similar in mind when he attacks "a new ruling class of self-seekers and careerists." (Kwame Nkrumah, "Dawn Broadcast," April 8, 1961.) . . .

There is disagreement also on the role the state should have in economic development. Where individual land ownership does not exist, as in most of Guinea and Mali, the governments are taking steps to maintain the communal bases of land ownership. But where individual African landholders emerged under colonial rule, there are no signs governments intend to eliminate them. All proponents of African socialism say that the government must have a considerable part in economic planning and that there must be state enterprises, but there is disagreement about the extent. Ghana and Senegal do not discourage the growth of their existing indigenous entrepreneurial classes; but Mali and Guinea, where such groups do not exist, discourage their formation and assume that the government will take on most of the risks and responsibilities for development. At the same time, all welcome foreign capital from government or private sources, although there are variations in controls and conditions.

Ideas and reality

The terms of discussion of African socialism change with experiment, experience, and testing. Ghana, for example, started from relatively little official emphasis on socialism; there were only a few references to it in Nkrumah's autobiography (published in 1957) and in the early CPP literature. When the international price of cocoa fell after the late 1950's, the Ghana Government had to ask people to pull in belts and pay more direct and indirect taxes, and discussion of socialism became more widespread. Guinea, on the other hand, started with the clear objective of building a socialist economy and set about doing it with some Soviet help. It set up a government monopoly to handle export and import trade and sharply curtailed the role of African middlemen. These measures, and several other factors, had disastrous results for Guinea's economy, however, and Guinean leaders have now reversed their policy. Controls over export and import trade have been reduced and traders have been freed to compete.

The African setting gives content to the discussions of African socialism. This is what Sekou Touré meant when he said: "To understand both the language of Africa and its true content we must seek to find in its words, expressions, formulations, not the abstract character of a dialectic, but the substance and reality of the life they express." ("Africa's Future and the World," by Sekou Touré, *Foreign Affairs,* October 1962, p. 142.)

> In this selection we take a look at socialism in Guinea, one of Africa's more leftist states. This is followed by a realistic appraisal of probable trends.

From Walter H. Drew, "How Socialist *Are* African Economies?" *Africa Report,* May 1963.

With independence, Guinea—encouraged by the severity of French policy at the time—nationalized or, more often, simply closed down foreign banks, trading houses, and commercial buildings in Conakry. But the less visible (since they were not located in the capital) and economically much more important Western concessions producing bauxite, alumina, and iron ore were treated very circumspectly. . . .

Despite the strong commitment of the Touré government to the creation of a socialist state, and the socialist thrust of the original development plan, it was recognized that these foreign economic enclaves provide major revenues to the government budget and much of the foreign exchange for Guinea's import bill. Indeed, even during the high-water mark of Soviet Bloc influence in Guinea, most of Guinea's exports went to the West and most of its imports came from the West.

Since 1961, Guinea has markedly attenuated its socialist program, at least in the economic sphere, and has adopted one measure after another calculated to *increase* local foreign commercial activity, especially in extractive and processing industries. Within its new and more pragmatic policy, Guinea is concentrating on negotiating the most profitable possible arrangement.

Most other African countries, whether avowedly socialist or not, share the Guinea dilemma—how to reconcile the political necessity of curtailing local foreign enterprise thriving amid relative poverty and unproductiveness with the minimal economic objective of maintaining living standards at pre-independence levels. Too sharp a drop in personal income, which an abrupt eviction of the foreign business presence is likely to entail, may lead to an overthrow of the regime. Too cozy an attitude toward the foreign business presence is equally dangerous, since the relatively poor African population, even if its living standard is improving, will not notice its own modest betterment as much as the continuing prosperity of the foreign business community and the visible enrichment of cooperative African leaders. . . .

Probable trends

As African countries move toward greater economic nationalism or regionalism, they will probably strengthen and extend central government controls over more and more aspects of economic life. Extensive regulatory controls are not a special aspect of socialist states, but are common to the United States and all other developed countries. Because many regulatory measures which are commonplace in the West appear novel in the less developed African context, they demand ideological justification in order to win local acceptance. At the present early stage of decolonization, regulatory innovations are justified most easily in terms of a revolutionary program to eradicate remnants of colonial influence and to release latent African productivity for the benefit of Africans. This ideological rationale ought to be read as a governmental slogan justifying pragmatic but increasingly regulatory economic development policies and should not be assumed to have any necessary connection with rigorous, classical socialism.

> The most obvious fact of African economics is the extreme poverty in which most of the people live. Political stability without economic viability is unlikely, if not impossible.

UNEQUAL DISTRIBUTION OF AGRICULTURAL RESOURCES

From William A. Hance, *African Economic Development*, 1958.

It is all too often assumed that Africa suffers from lack of population when in reality very considerable areas are overpopulated. Most of the desert, discontinuous belts in the Sudan of West Africa and in the humid tropical regions along the Guinea Coast, the Victoria plateau and many of the highlands of East Africa, Ruanda-Urundi and adjacent parts of the Belgian Congo, and Nyasaland show evidences of strain. Increasing rates of natural growth threaten to place other areas in the same category. These densely populated regions contain some of the most serious actual and potential problem centers of Africa. They may appear to cover a relatively small part of the total area, but the numbers of people involved are a far higher percentage of the total population.

On the other hand, areas such as the two Rhodesias, the Congo Basin, and French Equatorial Africa could probably develop more rapidly if they had larger populations. In these areas, a low density has necessitated a wasteful system of migrant labor, limited the development of a domestic market, made more difficult the construction of transport and public utilities, and led to serious problems occasioned by excessive migration of able-bodied males from the farming communities.

There are, however, certain real advantages in a relatively low population. When labor is plentiful and cheap, the temptation is strong to use it poorly. One sees Africans in these areas cutting grass lawns with knives, mining with pick axes, and building roads by hand. Where labor is scarce, more attention is given to the productivity of the individual African, labor-saving equipment is employed, and there is greater possibility of eventually achieving a standard well above the peasant level. Certainly it is far easier to set ambitious goals in areas like the Congo than it is in southern Nigeria, where an increasing population constantly presses against the available resources.

The output of food in Africa is not adequate to meet the needs of the present population; the rate of expansion of food production in the postwar years has not been adequate; large areas that should and could be surplus food producers are becoming more important deficit areas. Unless agricultural supplies expand more rapidly, advances in other fields will be increasingly impeded, as will the organic growth of the economies involved.

Contributing to the serious dimensions of this problem, in addition to all the physical difficulties and the pressure of population on the land already noted, have been an overemphasis on cash cropping in some areas and an excessive migration of men from tribal areas in others. In the Rhodesias, for example, from 40 to 70 per cent of the males are absent from many rural areas, resulting in a deterioration in the systems of cultivation, an unbalanced diet in the home community, and an inadequate supply of domestically produced food in the mining centers. Greater attention must be given almost everywhere to indigenous agricultural development. . . .

Many factors contribute to the urgency of tropical Africa's agricultural situation. Among the more important are the following:

1. In many areas, misuse of the land—the continent's

most valuable resource—threatens permanent loss, or will saddle future generations with enormous costs for regeneration. Overgrazing, destruction of vegetation by fire, overcropping, and improper rotational practices, including emphasis on a single crop, are important examples of misuse. Degradation of the soil and vegetation, outright erosion, and reduction of available water, are the consequences.

2. The ravages of plant and animal pests and diseases plague many areas, while human disease takes a terrible toll in life and energy.

3. Even areas with nondestructive practices require agricultural improvement, because most Africans have an improperly balanced, if not inadequate, diet. The African continent stands out with undesirable prominence on the maps depicting areas of human starvation.

4. In large areas, the population is growing with such rapidity, or has already reached such densities, that the land is, or soon will be, incapable of supporting it. As medical knowledge improves, the fear arises that population growth will outstrip the development and adoption of improved agricultural techniques, so that the fertility of man will surpass the fertility of the soil.

5. In some regions, excessive migration of men to seek employment in mining, agriculture, and industry has led to deterioration in farming practices and in dietary standards in the home communities, while at the same time creating food-supply problems in the mining and industrial centers.

6. Overemphasis on cash crops has been carried to extremes in some areas. This is not only harmful to the food supply but causes more rapid soil deterioration.

7. No effective economic advance is likely to be achieved in any country unless greater output per worker is achieved. In some territories increased productivity may be achieved by building up mining and industry. But opportunities along these lines are quite limited in many regions, and any improvement in the economic standard must come primarily in agriculture, whether grazing or tillage.

8. The continent's ability to export, to meet the demands of other areas, and to pay for the imports it requires, is obviously reduced by many of these factors. . . .

[Vast] areas of Africa [are] now characterized by low production for commercial return, [and there exist] . . . only small islands of intensified activity. . . . In Liberia, three economic points are dominant—the Harbel Plantation, Monrovia, the Bomi Hills—while the vast bulk of the interior is little touched. In Madagascar, producing areas are only a fraction of the total surface. Even in the relatively advanced Federation, most of Northern Rhodesia and the lower parts of Southern Rhodesia are not concerned with commercial production.

The high percentage of area with low productivity under present techniques is explained by two main factors: the physical deficiencies of the area—particularly the permanent or seasonal aridity—and deficiencies of indigenous farming methods. Even if the most modern techniques could be applied, however, the larger part of the continent would still have a low productivity capacity.

THE VOLTA RIVER PROJECT

Central to the process of transition from a subsistence economy to an exchange economy is investment in equipment and training. Capital accumulation is a problem common to all developing countries. There are, however, some special facets of the problem as it exists in Africa.

African-owned business, what little there is of it, has very limited access to foreign sources of capital, which more often finds its way into European-owned African enterprises. Domestic sources of capital such as banks and savings societies are limited in numbers and wealth, so African governments are looked to for funds necessary for the expansion of African business.

But African governments, like those of India and China, have capital problems of their own. Beyond the needs of private business are the needs of government to finance dams, power plants, and roads. The government must then do one or more of the following: tax citizens more heavily and restrict luxury imports, tax foreign-owned enterprises on a scale comparable to that of their home country, or look for increased foreign aid.

Another way is to use unemployed people and rural workers with spare time in government capital building projects. Ghana has sought to do this in community development programs. Outside the African continent, China, India, and Israel have all experimented extensively with this means of developing a sound economy.

Another interesting approach to the problem is under way in Ghana. The Volta River project is being financed by foreign capital: loans from governments and investment by foreign companies.

From U.S. Department of State, Publication 7556 (July 1963).

One of Ghana's major development activities is the vast Volta River project. In December 1961 the U.S. Government announced that it had decided to join Ghana, the United Kingdom, the International Bank for Reconstruction and Development (IBRD), and U.S. private industry in financing the Volta River project. This involves the construction of a dam, powerplant, and transmission grid, to be owned and operated by the Government of Ghana through its Volta River Authority (VRA), and the construction of an aluminum smelter, to be owned and operated by the Volta Aluminum Company, Ltd. (VALCO), which is owned by two private American companies. . . .

The total cost of the dam and the hydroelectric installation is estimated to be $196 million. One-half of the financing is being provided by loans from IBRD ($47 million), AID ($27 million), Export-Import Bank ($10 million), and the U.K. ($14 million). The Government of Ghana is providing the other half.

The aluminum smelter will be constructed and owned by VALCO, which in turn is owned by Kaiser Aluminum and Chemical Corporation (90 percent) and Reynolds Metals Company (10 percent). The construction of the smelter is scheduled to begin in 1965. The two owners will invest $32 million in VALCO. In addition, they have obligated themselves to put up $22 million to provide for any overrun costs. This total investment of up to $54 million has been covered by an AID political and convertibility risk guaranty. The Export-Import Bank has loaned $110 million (of which AID has taken a 50 percent participation) to VALCO to cover U.S. procurement of goods and services for the construction of the smelter.

SELF-HELP IN AFRICA

> An all-African approach to the problem of capital accumulation is described in the following article about the African Development Bank.

From *The Economist,* November 21, 1964.

A good augury for African unity has been the smooth and unpolemical launching of the African Development Bank. At the bank's first meeting in Lagos earlier this month, representatives from thirty African countries decided without much trouble where the bank should be and who should be its president and its directors. The result was a quiet compromise between the claims of black and Arab Africa.

Not even the sensitive question of where the bank's headquarters should be held up the discussions. Kenya, Sudan and Cameroon had each at one time made claims for their own capitals, but at the Lagos meeting they stepped down in favor of the Ivory Coast's luscious capital, Abidjan. It was all part of the compromise. Since the bank's presidency went to the distinguished Sudanese economist Sayed Mahmoun Beheiry (Sudan is the nearest thing to an Arab country that the black Africans will easily accept), the headquarters had to be south of the Sahara. Since the president is French-speaking, the signs pointed to a francophonic capital.

But the significant point about Abidjan is that it is in Africa. The African bank had thus emphatically shown that it is not going the same way as its nearest equivalent, the Inter-American Development Bank whose headquarters are not in Latin America, but in Washington. Membership in the ADB is limited to sovereign African states, and it is planned eventually to include them all. Its capital resources are to be entirely African; its special operations to be financed from whatever sources are available. The Inter-American bank has, so far, only one special fund, and that financed by the United States.

The idea for an African Development Bank grew out of the specific shortcomings in existing financial arrangements, both for the supply of credit from outside Africa and, conversely, for Africa's capacity to attract and make the best use of funds. Loans from the World Bank, the United Nations Special Fund and from similar sources are made only to governments; they are restricted to large schemes and are subject to guarantees from the recipient governments. The ADB, on the other hand, will lend to private firms as well as governments or corporations, and its loan will not be restricted by the size of the scheme or, necessarily, by the precondition of a government guarantee.

Basically, the idea is that the bank should act as a catalyst for investment, both public and private, from inside and outside the continent. Hitherto, a notorious factor slowing down both aid and investment has been the paucity of properly presented projects drawn up in "bankable" form. The ADB will be equipped to do this, notably on behalf of projects in its smaller members' territories. The bank is empowered to provide its own technical assistance, ranging from surveys of a country's economy, preparation of loan requests, and training of personnel to the granting of credits or equity investments.

How seriously the ADB takes its pan-Africanism is shown in its articles, which enjoin it to give special priority to schemes which "by their nature or scope concern several members" or which "make the economies of its members increasingly complementary." It will thus work to overcome the economic balkanization and lack of intercountry infrastructure which is possibly the biggest single obstacle to development.

Will the bank now get quickly down to business or will

it founder amid infighting, inertia, or squabbling over priorities? A good sign is the choice of president—Mr. Beheiry, the man who set up the Sudan's own development bank. Ever since the idea of the bank was first adopted by the All African People's Conference in 1960, he has been not only its champion but has insisted, after an initially lukewarm response from Western governments, that the bank should be exclusively African. He is a firm upholder of the tenet that one must help oneself before being helped.

Better yet, the bank, which has been expertly and enthusiastically midwifed by the United Nations Economic Commission for Africa has a carefully built in set of safeguards against disputes and anomalies. Capital stock subscriptions are calculated according to the "economic potential" of members: each member has 625 basic votes plus an additional vote for every $10,000 subscribed. This arrangement gives the United Arab Republic the biggest single voice, with Algeria and Nigeria next. The bank is controlled by a board of governors, a board of directors and a president. The authorized capital is at present $250 million.

The agreement establishing the bank makes a distinction between ordinary and special operations: the former are to be financed from ordinary capital resources, that is, from within Africa. For special development projects, the whole world is open, with particular scope for bankers' consortia. The interest of private bankers was underlined by the presence in Lagos of representatives from such banks as the Midland, Barclays, Banque Lambert, Chase Manhattan, Rothschild, and half a dozen others.

A possible first venture, and one typical of what the ADB can and should do, might be to establish an integrated telecommunications scheme. A comparatively cheap and easy revolution that would link West Africa's ports to each other by telephone might lead to West Africa establishing its own shipping lines conference. This is the sort of project for which private non-African funds would be readily forthcoming, and which has long needed something like the ADB to get it going.

A PROGRESS REPORT ON ECONOMIC DEVELOPMENT

The foregoing readings have sketched Africa's economic potentials—its limitations and its assets. To see just how much of this potential was actually realized, we turn to *The New York Times'* summary of Africa's economic progress for the year 1966.

From Brendan Jones, "Review of Economic Conditions in Africa," *The New York Times,* January 27, 1967.

Africa seemed last year to be like a new planet that was still cooling off. Fresh political upheavals, together with tensions of the unresolved issue of Rhodesia, continued to obscure Africa's future. But on the firmer ground of economic development, most African countries managed to maintain some progress.

In many countries the rate of development appeared to be slackening. Obstacles in the form of basic limitations as well as financial difficulties and shortages of capital and technical skills were beginning to slow the drive for economic independence.

But at the same time, opportunities for overcoming these obstacles were being offered by a new movement for regional economic cooperation. This project, in which groups of countries would pool their resources and development efforts, is being organized by the United Nations Economic Commission for Africa at its headquarters here [Addis Ababa, Ethiopia].

Meanwhile, a new sense of economic realism appears to be growing among African leaders. The realistic approach is showing itself in a greater concentration on fundamental development of primary land and human resources. Earlier ambitious plans for large-scale industrialization have been deferred except as possibilities under regional development.

New emphasis now is being put on modernization and diversification of agriculture, processing industries to add value to export crops, and on health, housing, and technical training. African development, in effect, is becoming an exercise in the art of the possible.

This trend is not universal throughout developing Africa, but it is gaining as more and more leaders realize that economic progress cannot be forced. In several African countries there already are enough inefficient and even idle industrial plants to prove the point.

Generally, major events in Africa last year also served to spur the leaders of the African-ruled nations into turning more attention to problems closer to home. On the issues of Rhodesia, apartheid in South Africa, and lingering colonialism elsewhere on the continent, black and brown Africa has suffered at least a temporary setback. . . .

For the moment, therefore, a stalemate has set in in the confrontation between African-ruled nations and the white-ruled southern bloc. This does not mean an end of the struggle to liberate the south, but the lull is providing a reminder for many leaders that independent Africa must direct more energies to building its own strength.

Apart from the general need for more effective economic development, there are also the tasks of preserving Nigerian unity and reconstructing Ghana's weakened economy. . . .

Most Nigerian leaders recognize the economic advantages of maintaining some form of nationhood. Nigeria, with her more than 56 million people, is Africa's most populous country. Simply on the basis of her size as a market, the country's economic potentials are among the best in Africa. . . .

The revolt that overthrew Kwame Nkrumah last February was widely applauded as a forward step for Africa as well as Ghana. But the oppressive and wasteful Nkrumah regime left a staggering external debt of some $785-million, which the Ghanaian people must now repay.

Ghana's new government has been working effectively to revive an economy that was close to collapse before the February revolt. Arrangements for repayment of the Nkrumah debts are being worked out, but it is estimated that it will be at least two years before Ghana can begin to make new economic progress. . . .

For a great part of Africa, the new movement toward regional cooperation can be the means of overcoming the low economic vitality that presently is slowing development.

The basic cause of the lag is the small size and small population of most African countries. Of the 38 African-ruled nations, 24 have populations of less than 5 million.

In many of these, the economies depend on one or two cash crops that are vulnerable to drought and sharp falls in prices. They are handicapped further by low income, a lack of skills, and a subsistence agriculture.

All these conditions make market and investment potentials of these countries—and others with larger populations—low at best. For some, the possibilities of attracting private capital are practically zero, and what progress has been made is the result almost entirely of foreign aid.

In the moves to remedy this basic African weakness, the United Nations Economic Commission here is promoting the formation of four new regional groupings of African countries—northern, western, central and eastern.

The objective is to encourage, initially, economic cooperation of the member countries for regional integration. This would lead, for example, to agreements under which individual countries would become the center of new industries to supply the entire region's needs in tires, cement, electrical equipment, steel, and like items. In short, the regional market would be the basis for development that is now impossible in any one country.

By a similar process of economic integration in other areas—agriculture, transportation, and ports, for example—the regions could develop into customs unions or common markets.

Efforts at such regional development are not new in Africa, but their success has been limited by rivalries and frictions among member countries of various groupings.

One example is the East Africa Common Services Organization, a customs, postal, and transportation union of Kenya, Uganda, and Tanzania, which has recently tended to disintegrate.

This economic union, with a combined population of more than 26 million, was formed originally to suit the requirements of colonial regimes. Although the member countries recently have been introducing new tariff barriers, they have also been studying a plan for reorganizing the union to fit their needs as independent countries.

The plan of the United Nations commissioner for much larger regional unions in Africa is the most ambitious yet undertaken. Preparatory conferences by countries in each of the four regions were held last year and in each case consideration of coordinated development in various fields is now in process.

So far, the East African regional group has progressed the furthest toward formal agreements. Nine countries of the region met in late 1965 in Lusaka, Zambia, to discuss integration, chiefly through coordination of industrial development. Last May, a provisional treaty of association was signed here by seven of the group—Zambia, Kenya, Tanzania, Ethiopia, Malawi, Burundi, and Mauritius.

Progress also has been made by the northern region, which includes Algeria, Libya, Morocco, Tunisia, the Sudan, and Egypt. In view of the present political harmony generally among these countries, their efforts at regional cooperation are expected to develop fairly rapidly.

Political frictions, however, are still a major obstacle in the way of the regional development plans. Political unity, particularly since the last summit conference here of the Organization [of] African Unity in November, seems, in fact, to have reached a new low. . . .

Despite their quarrels, African heads of state are more aware than ever that their own political future may depend on how effectively they push ahead with economic development. This urgent need, it is held, will force either a patching up of differences or at least playing down of them at economic conferences.

Ready to assist in the new efforts at regional cooperation is the new African Development Bank, which has its headquarters in Abidjan, the Ivory Coast. The bank, with an authorized capital of $250-million subscribed by African countries, was organized in 1964, specifically to aid multinational projects or, in effect, regional development.

Last year, initial proposals for regional projects were being studied by the bank, but so far it appears that few of these have been worked out in sufficient detail to make them feasible or "bankable" undertakings.

A regional approach to development is still a novel one in Africa. But with technical help by the development bank and the United Nations commission, it is expected that some regional projects, possibly in transportation and communications, will begin to take form this year.

Despite the general lag in African development, evidences of rising living standards have continued to grow in many countries.

While the pace may not be so rapid as Africans would wish, steady improvement is evident in agricultural techniques, health, education, and some new industry.

Although there is much to be done in advancing diet and child-care standards, many of the new generation of Africans are developing sturdier bodies and a brighter-eyed way of looking at their world. The number of children attending new schools continues to grow.

Africans also are displaying considerable aptitude in adopting new farming techniques, and many are successfully opening new farmlands and raising new and better crops. More Africans also are becoming wage-earners in industry, commerce, and transportation.

In many African cities, a new kind of building boom is under way. It is different from the boom of earlier independence years, which produced mainly prestige symbols in large new public buildings. In the new boom, more banks, office blocks, shops, and houses are being built.

But Africans' biggest and continuous need is for more technical and managerial skills. The shortage of these is acute at all levels. The rate at which more technical training centers and engineering schools are established promises soon to become more important for development than the inflow of capital.

According to one United Nations commission official here, if it were possible to give Africa all of the technical assistance service now provided for the entire world by the United Nations and the United States, it would still be far short of filling African needs.

This may not be an optimistic view, but it is a realistic appraisal of the tremendous effort that still is necessary for creating a stronger Africa.

The United States and Africa

Since the advent of African nationalism in the late 1940s, American interest in that continent has sharpened. Traditionally, the United States has sympathized with the national aspirations of colonial people. We have, however, often counseled more patience in these affairs than was shown by our own revolutionary forefathers.

Immediately after World War II we lent our support to the founding of Indonesia on the ashes of the Dutch East Indies. As the Cold War developed and we made NATO the foundation of our foreign policy, our sympathies for African independence were compromised by what we considered to be the necessity of not offending our NATO allies, most of whom were colonial powers.

The Cold War further clouded our attitude toward emerging states. While John Foster Dulles was Secretary of State under President Eisenhower, the neutralism espoused by many new Asian and African states was regarded officially by the United States as a form of hostility and the next thing to being in the Moscow–Peking orbit.

The 1960s brought a much more forceful stand on behalf of African nationalism. This shift in emphasis, away from NATO commitments, can be seen primarily in our efforts through the UN to end the Katanga secession in the Congo (contrary to Belgian interest) and our support of a UN resolution against Portuguese colonial policy in Angola. In support of this resolution, the United States reaffirmed the "inalienable right of the Angolan people to self-determination and independence" and urged Portugal "in particular to set up freely elected and representative political institutions with a view to transfer of power to the people of Angola."

In UN debate the United States has also opposed the Republic of South Africa's refusal to recognize UN authority in South-West Africa and urged the abandonment of its apartheid policy. The United States reiterated its belief that "in the partnership of races" and not in their separation lies "man's best hope for a peaceful and successful society." But the support given to the European-dominated countries in southern Africa by extensive American investment there causes many of the African nations to be skeptical of United States policy statements about apartheid. Unless American foreign policy is bolder in support of the African nationalisms in southern Africa, her political effectiveness elsewhere in Africa will be limited.

We are tempted to believe that because we are so generous with foreign aid our leadership in all matters should be eagerly accepted. But we must reckon with the determination of African leaders to resist foreign pressures and chart their own courses. We must realize that there is a limit to the United States' power to influence the course of events. To make friends is not the same as influencing people.

AMERICAN ECONOMIC AID TO AFRICA

Since 1961, when the Agency for International Development (AID) was created and linked administratively to the Department of State, assistance to Africa has been related more closely to American foreign policy objectives.

From U.S. Department of State, "U.S. Economic Aid to Africa, 1950–64," *Africa Report,* December 1964.

[It] can be said that eight basic principles govern all U.S. assistance programs:

1.   Economic development is a long-term process. AID assistance should relate to development criteria, and serve development rather than political purposes.

2.   Comprehensive planning is a prerequisite for economic development, and African governments should be encouraged to produce realistic national development plans. . . .

3.   . . . AID programs are geared to vigorous self-help efforts by local governments. By "self-help," AID means development efforts which can be effectively taken

by an African country without foreign assistance—such as land reform, development planning, tax reform, restriction of luxury imports, community development, road improvement, and establishment of savings institutions. . . .

4. In view of the U.S. balance-of-payments problems, it is AID policy to spend dollars for American goods and services to the greatest extent consistent with sound foreign assistance objectives. (In fact, about 80 per cent of AID funds were spent in the United States last year.)

5. In general . . . AID prefers to fund capital assistance projects through loans on relatively soft terms but repayable in dollars.

6. To use most efficiently all U.S. resources available, AID often cooperates with other United States agencies and private institutions in joint projects. The use of PL-480 food surpluses under the administration of the Department of Agriculture is the best known example. Surplus foods granted to an African government for emergency relief are often administered by voluntary agencies such as CARE or the Red Cross. AID is also cooperating with the Peace Corps in many countries by providing equipment or advisory services to supplement Peace Corps volunteers. In the educational field, ASPAU, African Students Program of American Universities, exemplifies this kind of cooperative effort.

7. It is the established policy of the United States Government and of AID to foster, encourage, and promote participation by private enterprise in foreign economic development. Under an investment survey program, AID may participate with private business in up to 50 per cent of the cost of approved surveys which explore the feasibility of specific private investments. . . . AID grants investment guarantees against the specific risks of inconvertibility of foreign currency, expropriation or confiscation, or loss due to war, revolution, or insurrection. . . . Private contractors are often employed by AID, at the request of African governments, to survey possibilities for investment, conduct feasibility studies, and promote investment opportunities abroad.

8. . . . AID is placing increasing emphasis on regional

assistance. As the role of the Organization of African Unity, the UN Economic Commission for Africa (ECA), and regional economic groupings is strengthened, the United States will relate more of its economic assistance programs to these collective institutions.

MISSIONARIES, STUDENTS, AND THE PEACE CORPS

> Americans also have a much more personal interest in Africa which must be weighed here.
>
> From Rupert Emerson, "The Character of American Interests in Africa," *The United States and Africa*, 1958.

Strategic and economic considerations are an important part of the American interest in Africa, but they are far from constituting the whole of it. Another major sphere of contact between Africans and Americans is the impressive missionary work which has been undertaken by American churches, with notable results not only in the direct religious impact but also in education and medical services. Since Catholic missions in Africa are staffed primarily from Europe, less than 10 per cent of American Catholic missionaries overseas are functioning in that continent. American Protestant churches, on the other hand, are currently concentrating 30 per cent of their overseas missionary activity in Africa, where the number of American missionaries has increased fourfold in the last three decades. The most striking increases have occurred in West Africa, the Belgian Congo, Tanganyika, the Central African Federation, and Ethiopia.

The stepping up of American missionary activity in Africa has been accompanied by a highly significant reverse movement of persons: the appearance in this country of larger numbers of Africans. Some of these are official visitors, here for one or another purposes, including meetings of the United Nations, but in the long view the most important group is the body of African students who have come to complete their higher education. These are the men who are likely to be numbered among the leaders of the new Africa when they return, and the effect which their American experience has upon them may be of decisive consequence in the attitudes they adopt toward the development of their own countries and toward the world at large. To name only two who have risen to the highest place in the political life of their countries, both Prime Minister Nkrumah of Ghana and Prime Minister Azikiwe of the Eastern Region of Nigeria are products of American universities.

A distinctive element in the relations between the United States and Africa is contributed by the 20,-000,000 Negro Americans . . . [they] inevitably watch Africa's development with a vivid and undisguised interest which is strongly reflected in the Negro press and Negro colleges. "From the ranks of our own Negro fellow-citizens," *The New York Times* recently suggested, "we can find men and women who can play useful roles in building bridges between the United States and Africa." But Americans must also be keenly aware that the way in which the Negroes are treated here has a great bearing on the esteem or disesteem with which Asians and Africans view the United States. Vice-President Nixon was well justified in pointing out in his report to the President when he returned from Ghana's ceremonies that every instance of prejudice in this country is blown up abroad and results in irreparable damage to the cause of freedom: "We cannot talk equality to the people of Africa and Asia and practice inequality in the United States."

> The Peace Corps, America's bold experiment in international goodwill, seems to relate more than any other agency to the condition of the people of the developing nations.
> The following selection, written by a Peace Corps teacher in Tanzania, could explain why this may be so.

From Leonard Levitt, *An African Season*, 1966.

We sat down, Mr. Biboko, Mr. Ngubile, Mike, and I, as an old woman came and brought us a bowl of pombe [local beer]. The old men began coming over to us, *Oog-*

onile, ndaga [greetings], sitting down and drinking from our bowl.

Then another group of old men, some with turbans wrapped around their heads like Bwana Mbulu's, sat down. They started speaking to Mr. Ngubile and Mr. Biboko in Kinyakusa, and Mr. Biboko told us that they were thanking us for having come to Tanganyika to help them. Some of them had been in Tukuyu, he said, and they had enjoyed it very much.

Then one old man started speaking very rapidly, nodding his head and becoming very excited, as they all nodded their heads to his words. Mr. Biboko explained that the old man was saying how happy he was to see us here drinking together with all of them. Because he had seen the British before who would never mix with them, who would never speak to them, and he had thought that all white men were like that. Now seeing us here, he knew it was not true.

Suddenly he stopped speaking and smiled at us, this old man. It seemed to make him so happy just seeing us here enjoying ourselves with them, sitting there together on the ground drinking from the bowl. I looked around me at the others, and they were also smiling, these old men without any teeth, they looked almost like babies in a way with their bare gums. They seemed so friendly, so pleased to have us sitting there with them, so happy it was enough to make me happy.

> But for the Peace Corpsman, breaking down the stereotype of the aloof white man is an incidental part of his activity. He is there with a specific job to do: engineering, advising farmers, organizing community self-help projects, and in Mr. Levitt's case, teaching in a small village in Tanzania.

I went to class for the first time and the boys all stood stiffly at attention as I walked in the door.

Good morning, class, I said.

Good morning, sir, they said in chorus.

Be seated, I said. The only sound now the scraping of

chairs along the floor as they fitted themselves under their desks.

They sat there in white shirts and white shorts, their bare feet sticking out from under their desks, looking up at me with big black eyes, more than forty of them in that tiny classroom. Some of them were big boys, who looked older than I. Others were so small that they couldn't have been more than ten or eleven years old.

I began telling them something about myself and where I came from, America. There was not a sound in the room. I could feel their big eyes on me, but no noise, nothing, and I wondered if they could understand. Then I said how happy I was to be here in Tanganyika, and especially at Ndumulu School, the way Mike had at the tea party, and they smiled, showing big white teeth. They could understand. . . .

I would go to 7A and struggle through the attendance register of their Swahili names, every name that I pronounced incorrectly sending the boys into fits of laughter, while I stood there and smiled wryly—what else can you do?

Into math and then English, and I would go to 6A for science and then P.C. with the 8's and that would take us up to twelve o'clock, when we broke for lunch—unless there was a staff meeting, which could begin at any time, and we would leave the boys sitting there to work on their own.

And—in a word—these kids were bright. But more than just bright, they were eager. They would sit there at attention, staring at me with their big eyes, without making a sound. And at first I would think it was that they didn't understand me or that they weren't paying attention, but every time I would say a new word or write something on the board, I would see them taking out their notebooks and scribbling in them without saying a word.

And after a while they began to ask questions, What was that I had said, sir, or Would I please write that word on the board, sir. Could you use it in a sentence, sir?

No, they weren't afraid to speak up, these kids, and they would ask good sensible questions about the lesson we had just had. Like about quadrilaterals, where I told them that a square, a rectangle, a parallelogram, were all special kinds of quadrilaterals. And one of them asked, But then isn't a square also a special kind of rectangle? and I'd say, Yes, that's exactly right, why is it special? And they'd say right off, Because the sides are all equal. And then someone else would have his hand up, What about a parallelogram, then, what would you call that if its sides were equal, wouldn't that also be a special kind of parallelogram?

Yes, questions like that—good questions—which made me know that they had really understood. And the bell might ring and I would begin to walk out the door, but some hands would still be up so I'd take another question or two, and that would only cause more hands to go up.

And some who hadn't gotten it in class would begin stopping by my house. Could I explain to them just once more about the square and the rectangle? Or could I correct an extra composition that they had done, or some extra sums?

At night you could walk by the classrooms and see them studying, forty of them, bent over their desks, scribbling by the shadowy light of a pressure lamp hanging from the ceiling. And the Standard 8's would study until late into the night, as their exam for secondary school was at the end of the year—except that only one-third of them would pass as they didn't have enough places for them all, since there were so few secondary schools and even fewer teachers. And if they failed their exam, what could they do, as there were no jobs for them? Only go back to their villages.

But bright and eager as they were, these boys, they just didn't know anything. Not that they were stupid or dull or that they couldn't learn, no, nothing like that—just look how quickly they had picked up the math. And in fact their English was not so bad at all, certainly good enough to understand what I was saying most of the time, and remember they had begun to speak English in grade four, which was only three years ago.

No, it was nothing like that, it was just—well, in math they were so slow, they would spend ten minutes doing one long-division problem, and they could never finish even the easiest of tests on time. And I began to discover that many of these boys—and this was grade seven— could not do fundamentals like fractions or multiply correctly, or would add eight and five and get fourteen.

But more than that—it wasn't merely math—they just didn't seem to have any conception of things. Take science, for example. I brought them to the house once to demonstrate that water has more than one form, showing them the fridge, taking out a tray of ice, telling them to touch the ice cubes. Warily, they stuck out their fingers . . . and jumped back with squeals. Standing there, licking their fingers, stupefied—how could anything be so cold?—with no idea at all what it was they had touched. And then, as the ice in the tray melted . . . the disbelief in their faces as they watched it trickle into water. Pouring it into a glass now and letting them take a sip. They were looking at each other, laughing and smiling—those great white teeth—it really was water . . . all the while casting furtive, sidelong glances at me as though they weren't completely sure it hadn't all been some kind of trick.

Or when I happened to show them a picture one day, something I had cut out of some magazine, of two sailors standing on the bridge of a ship in a harbor, the sun shining on the water, the skyline of New York in the background. They had no idea what it was all about. Not the skyline—of course, they couldn't be expected to know what skyscrapers look like—but they didn't even know these men were on a ship. They didn't know that it was a ship, they didn't notice that these were uniforms that the men were wearing. They just stared blankly, shaking their heads.

And how easy it would be to say, Well, they just don't know anything, they must be stupid or dull. But no, that wasn't it at all. It was just that when you got hold of these boys—even here in Standard 7—you were practically dealing with a clean slate. A real *tabula rasa*. As if they knew literally nothing about anything. And in English it wasn't hard, they had textbooks for that, and I would give them exercises to do each night and one or two compositions a week, since they were so enthusiastic. And in math about twenty sums a night, because they just needed drill and more drill.

But it was this other field, science and general knowledge, that was so hard. First, there was only one book—for the teacher—which described how to do experiments, and some of them you couldn't do because there wasn't any material for them. So I did what I could, about one experiment a week maybe, with another way to discuss hypothesis, explanation, observation and conclusion, which I had taught them for lab sheets.

And on the other days I would bring in pictures I had cut out of magazines—any kind of pictures, like advertisements or landscapes. Once it was a picture of a man and a girl in heavy ski sweaters, against a snowy mountain background. The snow there . . . what was it? Something like rain, like water—another form of water maybe? Was it like anything they had ever seen before?

Yes, someone said, like those ice cubes from the fridge.

And did they think it was cold there? Yes, of course, look how cold the ice cubes had been. How else could they tell? What else was there in the picture that told them?

The clothes, one of them said.

Yes, the heavy ski sweater—look how warm those clothes were that they were wearing.

Was there any place in Tanganyika where there was snow?

Of course they knew that, Kilimanjaro, so it must be cold up there, too. And I read them a passage from a book about Rebmann, the German who had discovered Kilimanjaro, the first man to climb to the top, describing the Chagga, the tribe that lived on the slopes of the mountain. How they had told him about something white on top of the mountain and how they were all afraid to climb up to the top because of the cold. And how Rebmann, who had reached the top, had collected some snow and brought it down to a lower altitude.

And what did they think had happened to the snow?

It had melted.

Could they think of anything else that had melted this way? Yes, those ice cubes.

Africa and the United Nations

The following reading discusses the increasing prominence of African issues in the United Nations since 1948, the positions which African states have taken on some of these issues, and the role of the African bloc in the organization.

A FORUM FOR THE NEWLY EMERGING NATIONS

From Catherine Hoskyns, "The African States and the United Nations 1958–64," *International Affairs*, July 1964.

It is clear that the United Nations plays a key role in the implementation of the foreign policy of the African states. It will be a long time before the OAU (even if its organization grows in strength, and this is by no means certain) can put into the field even such a force as the United Nations mustered for the Congo operation, and until that time the United Nations is the only organization which the African states can hope to persuade to act for them. At the same time, the occasional conferences of African and Asian states give nothing like the steady and regular platform for the views and preoccupations of the African leaders that is provided by the sessions of the United Nations and its various agencies. In addition, especially as the majority of African states cannot afford to set up embassies in all countries, the United Nations provides an extremely useful center where they can keep in touch with each other and with the rest of the world. The African states have shown in practice that they will call on the United Nations when they feel themselves attacked by states outside Africa, as in the cases of the Congo and of Bizerte, and when they need to rally the rest of the world, as in the case of their campaign against South Africa. It has yet to be shown whether they will call on the United Nations to mediate in intracontinental troubles, and the border dispute between Morocco and Algeria, where African rather than United Nations mediators were called in, suggests that they may not.

The period since 1958 has seen the United Nations marked by an increasing preoccupation with African questions, and by a growth in African influence commensurate with the fact that at the beginning of 1964 there were 34 African members compared with the eight which were independent when the African group was first formed. Though the Congo operation is still the only case where one can point to direct United Nations action as a consequence of African pressure, there seems little doubt that African activity has led both to a concentration of international attention on the situation in the colonial territories and to the growing isolation of South Africa and Portugal in the world community. One of the most obvious of the achievements of the African states has undoubtedly been to accelerate discussion on and feeling over questions of human rights and self-determination, and the contrast between 1958, when a very mild resolution on Algeria was defeated in the General Assembly, and 1963, when the Security Council adopted unanimously a call for an arms boycott against South Africa, is striking. Perhaps the most important role of the African states in all this has been to act as a lobby within the Afro–Asian group and tó push the Asians into more effective action. . . .

Criticisms of African activity in the United Nations

In general, these criticisms have centered on three points; that in their dealings at the United Nations the African states are only interested in their own affairs and play no part in the general work of the Organization; that they have double standards regarding both the actions of the rest of the world and the actions of the Soviet Union and the West; and that their actions are in fact distorting the purpose of the United Nations by forcing it into activity for which it was never intended.

For the first of these criticisms there was, particularly in the early days, considerable justification. In 1958 and 1959, when the African group was struggling to establish itself and the African states were trying desperately to arouse interest in African questions, they had no time to consider any other issue. At the same time, because there were so few of them, the African states felt that even if they had a point of view they had very little chance of influencing decisions taken on questions outside their direct sphere of influence. But since 1960, this criticism has been losing its force, and there have been indications that the African states, fortified by their increase in numbers, are beginning to feel that they do have a role to play at least in the big cold-war issues and in attempting to prevent a direct East–West confrontation.

The whole question of disarmament and testing is perhaps a good example of this. African interest in this subject was aroused in 1959 by the French decision to use the Sahara as a testing ground, and since then the African group has carried on an active campaign to get Africa declared a nuclear-free zone. But recently the concern of the African states has gone much wider than this, and they have taken an increasing interest in discussions on general disarmament and in efforts to find some common ground between the Soviet Union and the United States on this issue. By all accounts, the three African states at the Disarmament Commission—Ethiopia, Nigeria, and the UAR—have taken their position very seriously, and there seems to have been some general discussion among the African states as to what line should be pursued. It was also noticeable that the resolutions at the May, 1963 OAU conference dealt with the disarmament issue as a whole and not with its specifically African aspect. This same kind of concern was shown during the Cuba crisis in October, 1962, when it was on a resolution presented by Ghana and the UAR that the Afro–Asian states appealed to U Thant to mediate between the United States and the Soviet Union.

The position at the moment would seem to be, therefore, that though the African states put their main effort into getting action on purely African questions, they are increasingly realizing that their numbers now permit them to have a say in the more general issues which affect Africa and the other continents of the world. To date the action which they have taken on these issues has been by no means extreme, and has tended to support moderate and constructive solutions.

The accusation that the African states have a double standard, both as regards the Afro–Asian states and the rest of the world and vis-à-vis the Soviet Union and the West, is one that is frequently made, particularly in the American press. On the first point, critics instance the case of Goa and point out that when Portugal brought the question of the Indian take-over of Goa before the Security Council, the African and Asian representatives refused to countenance any criticism of Indian actions, even though on the face of it these constituted flagrant violation of the Charter. The African answer to this criticism is that by continuing to hold a colony on the Indian land-mass, and by refusing any attempt to negotiate, the Portuguese were in fact committing an aggression and India had the right to act the way she did. Though this argument has no legal standing in terms of the Charter, it has a certain logic and the case of Goa alone seems hardly sufficient to support a general charge of a double standard. On the other side, it should be remembered that the African states did not give unqualified support in the West Irian case to Indonesia (a state with which most of them had very close links and which had supported them on all important issues) but instead backed up the efforts being made to bring about negotiation and compromise and a solution through the United Nations. In general, therefore, it would seem that in this particular respect the African states are no better and no worse than any other group of states at the United Nations. The temptation in New York, as elsewhere, is for all states to apply quite different standards when judging their own actions or those of their allies, and if the African states fall short of the ideal so do most of the rest.

On the second point, there are persistent complaints in the Western press that the African states go to extreme lengths to condemn every aspect of Western colonialism, but have nothing to say about the situation in Eastern Europe or about China's actions in Tibet and elsewhere. Though it is certainly true that the African states spend the vast proportion of their time in attacking the Western colonial powers and that they are prepared to ally themselves with the Communist states in order to do so, the reasons for this attitude are surely obvious. In the first place Western colonialism is something which they have experienced first-hand and which is of direct concern to them; most Africans have very little knowledge of how the Soviet Union has acted in Eastern Europe and feel in any case that it is not for them to take the initiative in such a question. Second, since their first concern is to get action over African questions, which in all cases involve the West, they cannot at the same time afford to alienate the Communist powers whose support is vital. Third, whereas it is clear that pressure through the United Nations has some chance of getting action over the countries colonized by the West, it equally clearly has little chance of achieving action in Eastern Europe. That this is so is in fact a back-handed compliment to the West, and one which, in private at least, most African politicians will freely acknowledge.

The existence, even to this extent, of a double standard does not, however, prevent the African states from opposing the Soviet Union when they feel it necessary. Thus in 1960 they made it quite clear that they were not prepared to support the Soviet demand that Mr. Hammarskjöld should be dismissed (even though they were very disturbed by his actions in the Congo) or the demand for a *troika* in the Secretariat (even though at a superficial level this would have given them more power). As a result, the Soviet Union was forced to climb down and the measures were defeated. Quite often when it appears that the African states are voting with the Soviet Union it is in fact the other way round, and the Soviet Union is following a lead given by the African states. In general too, a close look at the proceedings of the United Nations shows that in spite of the fact that most of the invective of the African states is reserved for the West, they are, in reality, in most cases much closer to the Western position than they are to any other, and much more influenced by Western tactics than they are by those of the Soviet bloc.

The third criticism, that the actions of the African states are distorting the United Nations itself, is much more difficult to discuss, if only because there are no fixed criteria by which to judge what the United Nations is or should be. The main complaint which people have in this context seems, however, to be that because Africa has come to independence in such a divided state, the African states have far more votes than either their financial or power position would warrant, and are, therefore, tempted to push through resolutions for which in the end they will not have to take the responsibility. It is clear, however, that those who drafted the Charter were well aware of this possibility, and that it was in order to guard against it that while all states were given equal vote in the General Assembly, the Great Powers were given the veto in the Security Council. Thus, though the African states may by their numerical strength be able to get unwise recommendations through the General Assembly, the Great Powers have an opportunity to veto these before any really effective action can be taken.

But in the end criticisms of this kind usually boil down to complaints that African states, particularly over the Congo question and in the current debate over southern Africa, are persistently forcing the United Nations into breaches of Article 2 (7) of the Charter, which prohibits the United Nations from intervening in the domestic affairs of a country unless there is a threat or breach of the peace or an aggression.

Though it is true that in baldly declaring that the secession of Katanga must end, the final resolution passed by the Security Council on the Congo situation did seem somewhat at odds with the Charter, it is also true that this resolution was supported, or allowed to go through on an abstention, by the United States and all other members of the Security Council. If this resolution was therefore a "distortion," those countries which had the power to veto and did not use it were as responsible as the African states.

Over the issue of southern Africa, there has certainly been an increasing move to consider that the questions of human rights and self-determination do in fact merit more than talk at the United Nations, and the persistent breaches of the human rights provisions in the Charter may in circumstances impose a qualification on Article 2 (7). But . . . this trend began long before the African states became active, and it cannot therefore be wholly attributed to them. The question now at issue at the United Nations is whether South Africa's persistent breach of the human rights provisions in the Charter, and consistent refusal to obey any injunctions of the Organization, do in themselves constitute a threat to the peace. If they do, the United Nations has every right to take further action under the Charter; if they do not, then the Organization must be content for the moment with passing resolutions. Since the final decision on this will lie with the Western states in the Security Council, it can hardly be said (whichever way it goes) that the African states are distorting the processes of the United Nations. In this context it is perhaps worth pointing out that the Charter of the United Nations is not an entirely rigid document, and if the general trend in world opinion is toward a more flexible interpretation of Article 2 (7), then it is no distortion for the proceedings of the United Nations to reflect this change.

On all these questions it would seem, therefore, that the attitude of the African states at the United Nations is very similar to that of the other states, and that they are no more self-centered, prejudiced, and irresponsible than the rest of the world community. Perhaps the main reason why they attract more criticism is because they use the United Nations more, but for that they can hardly be blamed.

UNITED NATIONS ECONOMIC AID

The Food and Agriculture Organization (FAO), the Economic Commission for Africa (ECA), the International Bank for Reconstruction and Development (IBRD), the International Monetary Fund, UNESCO, UNICEF, and the Special Fund, are just some of the United Nations agencies which participate in programs in Africa. They provide the very tangible help of investment surveys, capital loans, and technical assistance in the form of expert personnel and equipment. Examples of two specific programs follow.

The United Nations Special Fund was created in 1958 by the General Assembly to assist emerging countries in assessing their physical resources and to train people so they can make better use of them. The funds are not designed to finance development projects, but rather to make grants which will make possible preinvestment surveys.

UNITED NATIONS SPECIAL FUND GRANTS TO AFRICAN COUNTRIES AS OF JUNE 1960

Country	Purpose	Amount
	(in thousands of dollars)	
Ethiopia	River development	930.1
Ghana	Flood-plan survey	345.0
Guinea	General development survey	425.0
Libya	Technological training	1,057.8
Morocco	Engineering School	751.5
Morocco	Area-survey (Rif)	702.8
Nigeria	Dam-site survey	735.0
Togoland	Land-and-water-use survey	700.0
Tunisia	Agricultural research	897.2
Uganda	Aerial geophysical survey	313.5
	Total	6,857.9

Eradication of disease and malnutrition, and providing intensive programs in the fields of public health, nutrition, family and child care, and education are the main African objectives of another UN agency, the United Nations Children's Fund (UNICEF). UNICEF's projects are continent-wide; in 1964, it was involved in 170 different ones in Africa. UNICEF programs are administered by the host country, which on the average matches $2.50 for every dollar provided by UNICEF.

An Overview

To summarize ideas and problems presented in this book, we conclude with a speech made by Robert C. Good, Director, Office of Research and Analysis for African Affairs, U.S. Department of State. Since this article was written in 1962, Nyasaland has become the independent state of Malawi; Northern Rhodesia is now independent Zambia; and Nkrumah has been ousted as Ghana's president. But the issues which he outlines in his section on southern Africa are even more crucial since Rhodesia experimented with unilateral and illegal independence, rather than accede to Britain's demands for an electoral system that would allow full participation to Rhodesia's African population. Otherwise, the issues which Mr. Good discusses will be subject to intense debate in Africa for years to come.

"AFRICA'S UNFINISHED STRUGGLE FOR FREEDOM"

From Robert C. Good, "Africa's Unfinished Struggle for Freedom: The Real Issues," U.S. Department of State Bulletin, December 10, 1962.

The real issues involved in Africa's unfinished struggle for freedom are found in several different, though related, areas. I would identify them as follows:

1. The establishment of a new basis of relations with the former colonial power.
2. The building of the new state.
3. The creation of a new system of states in independent Africa.

4.   The relationship of Africa to the East–West struggle.

5.   The problem of expanding the rights of the populations in the southern third of Africa.

In each of these areas, as we shall see, the issue is known by millions of people only as a slogan. My intention is to examine the content of these slogans to see what about them is real—and in what ways, as all slogans must, they oversimplify and conceal reality.

Relations with the former colonial power

The issue here is often described as "the threat of neocolonialism." Ghana's President Kwame Nkrumah has described neocolonialism as "the practice of granting a sort of independence by the metropolitan power, with the concealed intention of making the liberated country a client state and controlling it effectively by means other than political ones."

There is, of course, a basis for such fears. Many new states become independent almost fully dependent upon foreign skills. The Congo is often cited as an extreme example. In 1959, only one year before independence, there was not a single Congolese doctor, lawyer, engineer, or commissioned officer in the entire country. In the army no Congolese held a rank above warrant officer. At independence there were only sixteen to twenty university graduates in the whole country. The Congo, as one journalist put it, grasped the twentieth century with Belgian hands.

Ironically, independence brings with it still greater reliance on external skills. The new state inaugurates programs—the expansion of services, economic development, literacy drives—that depend for their fulfillment on importing more and more talent.

Under these circumstances it is not to be wondered that many new states fear domination from those upon whom they are so dependent. Many have attempted to protect and consolidate their political freedom—to overcome the threat of neocolonialism—in two ways: first, by rapidly "Africanizing" their government services and, second, by attempting to diversify their dependence on the outside world. These, it seems to me, are perfectly normal objectives. They must, of course, be pursued with care if they are to contribute to the consolidation of freedom. If the new state Africanizes too quickly, technical proficiency will decline and with it the capacity to serve the people well. If the new state attempts to diversify its dependence on external resources precipitately, it is likely to disrupt traditional marketing and financial arrangements before it has found equally profitable substitutes.

Actually, the objective of the new state in ordering its relations with the former colonial power is not simply to cut all existing ties, on the assumption that the more ties it cuts the freer it is. The objective is to mobilize all available resources in order to develop as rapidly as possible its capacity to serve its people.

For this, extensive external help its vital, as all African leaders have acknowledged. Ghana is an interesting case in point, precisely because its President, more perhaps than any other leader in Africa, has warned against the dangers of neocolonialism. When I was in Accra in 1960, there were more British civil servants in the Ghanaian Government than there had been prior to independence. It was only last year that President Nkrumah appointed a Ghanaian to be head of his army. Prior to that the Chief of Staff had been a British general. Yet no one could accuse Ghana of subservience to any foreign master in determining its domestic and foreign policies.

Taking the process of decolonization as a whole, it is truly extraordinary how effective and how cordial has been the transition to independence in, to date, twenty-nine African countries. I am not unaware of the exceptions, but the rule is impressive. Equally impressive has been the extensive and indispensable assistance to these new states extended by the former colonial powers. Even more remarkable is the fact that this assistance has been given without the donor dominating the policies of the recipient.

State building

The consolidation of freedom implies of course more than the development of mutually beneficial relations with the former metropolitan power. It also involves, as has already been suggested, the task of state building. Here two slogans are frequently invoked by African leaders: "African democracy" and "African socialism." I want to say a word about each.

All of the new states are engaged in a desperate struggle to become nations. The familiar sequence of political development has been foreshortened—in a sense, even reversed. First comes nationalism, an emotional-intellectual ferment among a small elite. Then comes independence, precipitately and for many new states without a national struggle of any significance. Only last comes what should have been prior to or at least concurrent with the first two stages—the long and difficult task of building something like a national society to go with the newly won legal status of nationhood.

In the Congo, for example, there are some two hundred tribal groups, over seventy dialects, and no vivid consciousness (except among a small elite) of what it means to be a Congolese. The problem is capsuled in a line taken from the introduction of Prime Minister Cyrille Adoula to a mass meeting in Stanleyville: "Adoula is a great nationalist, and he will explain nationalism to you."

A prominent Nigerian nationalist had these problems in mind when he observed that a Greek and a Briton had more in common than a Sokoto and an Ijaw villager in Nigeria; for the Greek and Briton, he explained, enjoy a common Greco–Roman culture and share the same religion, Christianity, while the Sokoto and Ijaw have widely variant native cultures and quite different religions, Islam and Christianity.

Moreover, these new states have had little apprenticeship in the arts of politics. In many cases their political infrastructure—parties and political systems—are still rudimentary. Political skills designed to represent and conciliate diverse interests cannot be developed overnight.

Given these limitations it is a moot question as to whether the governments of many new states can satisfy the requirements of democracy. Of course democracy is fashionable and everyone today is a democrat—whether a "basic democrat," or a "guided democrat," or a "people's democrat," or an "African democrat." Our analysis might be helped if we looked behind the slogan to identify the two basic requirements of a viable political system regardless of its forms or its institutional structures or the way in which it describes itself.

First, sufficient power must be accumulated at the center to make the writ of the government effective. . . . But the accumulation and consolidation of power in the hands of the leaders is not enough. The second requirement is that there also be established channels for the effective communication and representation of the essential interests of the various groups that make up the national community. The balance between orderly cohesion and diversified expression may be weighted very differently in different situations, and the institutions incorporating that balance may be equally varied. But unless each principle is acknowledged, the freedom of the new state will be both bitter and brittle.

We have been talking about the problem of political development—the creation of a sense of nationhood and the building of political institutions. There is also the problem of economic development. For this, the byword in Africa today is "African socialism." Like other slogans it is both useful and troublesome.

The problem confronting most new African states is not only the relative poverty of physical resources but the lack of human skills and the absence of attitudes essential to economic advancement. "African socialism" is a useful term for it suggests that economic development cannot be engineered from the outside, cannot automatically be induced by huge inputs of foreign capital and foreign skills —necessary as these adjuncts may be.

This is what Mr. Eugene Black, the recently retired head of the International Bank, had in mind when he said that "the road to a self-sustaining growth must be built by the poor society itself." I am reminded of a line from the

French scholar Raymond Aron. "What is called economic development, above all in its first phase," he wrote of tropical Africa, "is a social and human mutation; it is a transformation of the attitude of the population." Not so much for ideological reasons but by sheer necessity, governments in the underdeveloped countries become the engines of change, laboriously cajoling and pressuring a change-resistant society.

The term "African socialism" is also deficient. It suggests a doctrine for the development of economic institutions when in fact the approach of most African governments is appropriately pragmatic. Even President Nkrumah, who has preached the doctrine of African socialism with sustained eloquence, practices in fact a mixed economy based on pragmatic, not doctrinaire, considerations. Cocoa is the staple of his foreign exchange. It is grown by private cocoa farmers. It is marketed by a government corporation. In Ghana state enterprise coexists with cooperatives and private enterprise. Nothing symbolizes this pragmatic mixture more dramatically than Ghana's Volta River project, a public power project financed partly by the Ghana Government and partly by private foreign investors and industries.

Creating a new system of states

We have talked about Africa's unfinished struggle for freedom as it involves establishing relations with the former colonial power and meeting the problems of state building. There is also the search for appropriate relations among the new African states themselves. The byword here is "pan-African unity." Again the slogan is useful. It points to an important reality. But it also helps to conceal a reality.

There is much that unites these new African states. A sense of unity derives from their common colonial experiences and their common postcolonial aspirations. It is the fight to end all imperialism. It is the attempt to nourish those roots of individual or cultural uniqueness that have continued to live in the subsoil of "negritude" or "Africanism" or "Arabism," despite the working of the topsoil by a foreign culture. It is the effort to gain greater access to the economic levers of power—skills, productivity, and capital—so that the new state will more and more be in charge of its own destiny.

Pan-Africanism is a force in Africa today, and he who does not reckon with it does not fully understand Africa. But the slogan "pan-African unity"—again like all slogans—is as mischievous as it is useful, for while pointing to that which unites Africa, it conceals much that divides Africa.

It is worth remembering that we are dealing with an enormous continent—one through which history has flowed for millennia in a great variety of channels. Only a small segment of that history deals with the impact on Africa of the West European cultures. In many instances that impact took place only fifty to seventy-five years ago and was preceded by a number of alien incursions. Gamal Abdel Nasser tells us that the curse he learned as a boy, "O, Almighty God, may disaster take the English," derived from an earlier epithet, "O God, the Self-Revealing! Annihilate the Turk!" Before both the European and the Turk in Africa there were the Arabs themselves. In the late fifteenth century the sailors of Prince Henry the Navigator, sailing northward after rounding the Cape of Good Hope, discovered Arab settlements along the continent's east coast. They derived from settlers who had come from Oman in the first century A.D. to trade for ivory, ore, and slaves. And before the Romans the Phoenicians and Greeks. Indeed—an ominous foreboding— there are ancient maps that indicate the claim of Cathay to suzerainty along sections of the east coast of Africa.

But the principal historical currents and eddies were formed by Africa's own innumerable tribes, separated (as one would expect in a vast continental expanse) by ethnic and linguistic differences, by geography, and by the mutual fear of conquest and pillage. Only in the last few minutes of the day of Africa's history did Western imperialism impose on tribal Africa a set of arbitrary geographical frames, "like a great steel grid," in Margery Perham's image, set "over the amorphous cellular tissue" of isolated and often hostile communities.

Western imperialism at one and the same time further divided Africa—French-speaking Africa, English-speaking Africa, Portuguese-speaking Africa—and helped to create larger unities than had existed before. These are Africa's new states, the controversial legacy of Europe to contemporary Africa.

These new states are a paradox. They stand in the way of Africa's aspiration after greater unity and as such are condemned by Africans as illicit colonial constructions. But let anyone attempt to subdivide one of these new states, as Tshombe attempted in pronouncing the secession of Katanga in July 1960, and what Africans regard as the illicit colonial construction becomes an entity enshrined in law and right reason.

This paradox is not surprising. It expresses both Africa's aspiration and Africa's reality. The important thing is not to ignore one at the expense of the other. The consolidation of Africa's freedom may well depend on the evolution of forms of cooperation and association transcending Africa's new states. But these new states will not easily be written off. Having assumed the rights of sovereignty, each new state has also inherited the obligations of sovereignty, to organize the policy, to assert its authority, and to contribute to the welfare of the community within its boundaries. The new states have also assumed the obligations of membership in international society. Differences between them are many and often profound—as one would expect in a complex and vast system of states. These differences must be adjusted and accommodated according to the rules of the game, or the hope of pan-African unity will stand in jeopardy—and with it Africa's new-found freedom.

If border disputes or tribal animosities, both of which are chronic in Africa, give way to spiraling arms races, the stage will be set for renewed great-power intervention. This brings us to the next area in which Africa's struggle for freedom must be analyzed.

Africa and the East-West struggle

"Keep the cold war out of Africa" is the slogan. Africa is preoccupied with its national birth. The problems vexing the superpowers in their contest with one another are of little importance. When a citizen of the Ivory Coast was asked how concerned were the people of Abidjan with the situation in Berlin, he replied: just as concerned as were the people of Berlin about the situation in Abidjan.

Most of the new states do not measure the issues of international politics with cold-war calipers. The meaningful choices are not between the "free world" and the "Communist world," nor between Western democracy and Eastern authoritarianism, nor between the economic systems of East or West. Insofar as these options are incorporated into issues inviting a choice between one or the other of the two opposing blocs, most of the new states are neutral. And if the cold war is conceived as the development of spheres of influence by East or West, all of the new states want to "keep the cold war out."

This is nothing to be dismayed at. A neutral Africa is in no sense inimical to our interests. Rather than regimes that lean precariously to the left or right, we seek in Africa governments that stand up straight on their own feet.

We should be concerned only that the phrase "keep the cold war out of Africa" is understood precisely. It means no cold-war alliance systems in Africa. It does not mean that Africa is magically impervious to great-power designs and efforts at subversion. Make no mistake about it, the Communist bloc is in Africa and must be reckoned with. If the experiences of Eastern Europe, Korea, Vietnam, and Cuba teach us anything at all, it is that the bloc's ultimate objectives are antithetical to the freedom of states that fall under bloc control. Already this danger has become apparent to more than one African leader.

At the same time we ought to recognize that the bloc's opportunities for penetration are frequently in direct proportion to the failure of the West to fulfill its responsibilities. This brings me to the final area in which Africa struggles to fulfill its freedom, the problem of white-settled Africa and the challenge to expand the rights, including the political freedoms, of the African populations of these areas.

The southern third of Africa

We are talking here about everything south of Tanganyika and the Congo—an area populated by some 35 million black Africans and approximately 3.5 million whites. The shorthand slogans for treating the problems of this area are many. It is a zone of "white privilege and black grievance" where justice demands "one man, one vote" and "political self-determination."

It is not my part to suggest timetables and policies. Rather I want to identify the forces at work and underscore the monumental importance of likely developments throughout the area. As you deliberate about the problem of freedom in this theater, here are some things you might wish to know.

1. The size of the white population differs in the several countries. Its percentage of the total population is a rough indicator of the intractability of the problem. I will list the major areas: . . . Rhodesia: 215,000 whites out of 3 million, or 7 per cent; Angola: 190,000 whites out of 4.5 million, or 4 per cent; Mozambique: 75,000 whites out of 6.3 million, or 1 per cent; South Africa: 3 million whites out of 14.5 million, or 21 per cent.

2. The areas differ from one another politically. . . . Rhodesia has been a self-governing colony since 1923. Its government is still firmly in control of the white settlers. The Portuguese areas of Angola and Mozambique are viewed as provinces of Portugal and are answerable directly to Lisbon. South Africa, of course, is an independent country.

3. The areas differ markedly in their approach to relations between the races. The Portuguese profess no racial bias. They seek to establish a state in which ultimately racial distinctions will be meaningless. (In actual fact only about 30,000 black Africans have achieved status as the

equals of educated whites in Angola and only about 6,000 in Mozambique.) The British settlers of . . . Rhodesia have set partnership between the races as their goal and envisage a situation which the African community will gradually achieve a position of political equality with that of the white community. The Afrikaners of South Africa preach apartheid—the total separation of the white and nonwhite communities.

4. In all of these areas the white settlers have deep roots, frequently going back generations. In all of these areas the white community has been solely responsible for the development of the country and today represents the great preponderance of skills necessary to maintain both the government and the economy at their present levels.

What of the future?

Now what of the future? Clearly we are headed for a period of extremely difficult transition. The question is not whether the black majority will one day gain political control in most if not all of this area. The question is only when and under what conditions. I have no idea how long the process will take. The pace will be different for different areas. And development in one area will have a profound impact on developments in neighboring areas.

What I wish to leave in your minds is the notion—I believe it is irrefutable—that the course of events in Africa's southern third could have the most serious consequences throughout Africa and the world. There are three possibilities which I hope you will ponder.

The first would be a confrontation of white and black communities characterized by mounting violence. The possibility of escalation into racial war embroiling all of Africa, whether emotionally or actually, does not need emphasis, nor does the likely effect such an eventuality would have on Africa's relations to the West.

The second possibility would involve an acute and expanding chaotic situation resulting from the precipitate flight of white settlers—chaos of such dimensions as to make the Congo look like a Sunday School picnic.

The third possibility, which might materialize out of either of the two just mentioned, would be a rapid penetration of the area by communism.

If these ominous developments are to be avoided, we shall need more than slogans to guide us, even though the slogans—"one man, one vote" and the like—indicate one of the requirements for expanding justice. At stake, of course, is not only justice (for majority and minorities alike) but the requirements of minimal order. If all parties concerned—the white regimes and black leadership, the metropoles, the independent African states, and interested Western powers—respond vigorously and simultaneously to the requirements of expanding justice and furthering orderly change, then this final act in the drama of Africa's emergency will conclude, not without agony and not without bloodshed, but with Africa at relative peace and prepared to move forward in cooperation with friendly states to further consolidate the freedom of its people.

I cannot say what the chances are that this will happen. I know only that the stakes are very, very high.

BIBLIOGRAPHY OF SOURCES

BASCOM, WILLIAM R., and HERSKOVITS, MELVILLE J.
Continuity and Change in African Cultures. University of Chicago Press, 1959.

BAUER, LUDWIG
Leopold the Unloved, as cited in T. Walter Wallbank, *Contemporary Africa: Continent in Transition.* Princeton, N.J.: Van Nostrand, 1956.

CAMERON, JAMES
The African Revolution. New York: Random House, 1961.

CARDOSO, A. J. ALFARO
Angola Your Neighbor (Johannesburg, 1950), as quoted in T. Walter Wallbank, *Contemporary Africa: Continent in Transition.* Princeton, N.J.: Van Nostrand, 1956.

CHURCHILL, RHONA
White Man's God. New York: Morrow, 1962.

COUGHLAN, ROBERT
"Black Magic: Vital Force in Africa's New Nations,"

Life, April 21, 1961, as condensed in *Reader's Digest,* September 1961.

DAVIDSON, BASIL
>   *Black Mother.* Boston: Little, Brown, 1961.

>   *The Lost Cities of Africa.* Boston: Little, Brown, 1959.

DREW, WALTER H.
>   "How Socialist *Are* African Economies?" *Africa Report,* May 1963.

DUFFY, JAMES
>   *Portuguese Africa.* Cambridge, Mass.: Harvard University Press, 1959.

DUFFY, JAMES, and MANNERS, ROBERT A., eds.
>   *Africa Speaks.* Princeton, N.J.: Van Nostrand, 1961.

EMERSON, RUPERT
>   "The Character of American Interests in Africa," *The United States and Africa.* New York: The American Assembly, Columbia University, 1958.

FAGE, J. D.
>   "States of the Guinea Forest," in Roland Oliver, ed., *The Dawn of African History.* London: Oxford University Press, 1961.

FITZGERALD, WALTER
>   *Africa: A Social, Economic and Political Geography of Its Major Regions.* New York: Dutton, 1957.

GOOD, ROBERT C.
>   "Africa's Unfinished Struggle for Freedom: The Real Issues," U.S. Department of State Bulletin, December 10, 1962.

GORER, GEOFFREY
>   *Africa Dances.* New York: Norton, 1962.

GREEN, M. M.
>   *Ibo Village Affairs.* New York: Praeger, 1964.

GUNTHER, JOHN
>   *Meet the Congo and Its Neighbors.* New York: Harper, 1959.

HANCE, WILLIAM A.
African Economic Development. New York: Harper, 1958. Published for the Council on Foreign Relations.

HARRIS, RICHARD
"Nigeria: Crisis & Compromise," *Africa Report,* 10 (March 1965), no. 3.

HEMPSTONE, SMITH
Africa—Angry Young Giant. New York: Praeger, 1961.

HODGKIN, THOMAS
Nationalism in Colonial Africa. New York University Press, 1957.

HOEBEL, ADAMSON E.
Man in the Primitive World. New York: McGraw-Hill, 1958.

HOSKYNS, CATHERINE
"The African States and the United Nations 1958–64," *International Affairs,* 40 (July 1964).

JONES, BRENDAN
"Review of Economic Conditions in Africa," *The New York Times,* January 27, 1967.

KENYATTA, JOMO
"The Gentlemen of the Jungle," in Peggy Rutherford, ed., *African Voices.* New York: Grosset & Dunlap, n.d.

KIMBLE, GEORGE H. T.
Tropical Africa. New York: Twentieth Century Fund, 1960.

LAMACCHIA, FRANK R.
"African Economies: Basic Characteristics and Prospects," American Academy of Political and Social Science, *Annals,* Vol. 298 (March 1955).

LEVITT, LEONARD
An African Season. New York: Simon & Schuster, 1966.

LLEWELLYN, RICHARD
A Man in a Mirror, New York: Doubleday, 1961.

LOWENKOPF, MARTIN

In *Africa Report,* 6 (December 1961), no. 11.

LOWENSTEIN, ALLARD K.

Brutal Mandate. New York: Macmillan, 1962.

LUMUMBA, PATRICE

"The Independence of the Congo," in James Duffy and Robert A. Manners, eds., *Africa Speaks.* Princeton, N.J.: Van Nostrand, 1961.

MANDELA, NELSON

"Why I Am Ready to Die," in *Student Action on Apartheid in South Africa.* Philadelphia: U.S. National Association, 1965.

MANNING, CHARLES A. W.

"In Defense of Apartheid," *Foreign Affairs,* October 1964.

MARKOWITZ, MARVIN D., and WEISS, HERBERT F.

"Rebellion in the Congo," *Current History,* April 1965.

MARSH, ZOE, and KINGSNORTH, G. W.

An Introduction to the History of East Africa. Cambridge University Press, 1957.

MATHEWS, RICHARD

"A Visit to the Rebels of Angola," *The Reporter,* September 28, 1961.

MBOYA, TOM

"Vision of Africa," in James Duffy and Robert A. Manners, eds., *Africa Speaks.* Princeton, N.J.: Van Nostrand, 1961.

MEAD, MARGARET

Cultural Patterns and Technical Change. New York: Mentor, 1957.

MERRIAM, ALAN P.

Congo: Background of Conflict. Northwestern University Press, 1961.

"The Congo's First Year of Independence," *Current History,* October 1961.

MEYERS, ALBERT J.
"A Firsthand Story of Today's Hottest War," *U.S. News & World Report*, August 28, 1961.

MORGENTHAU, RUTH SCHACTER
"African Socialism: Declaration of Ideological Independence," *Africa Report*, May 1963.

MURDOCK, GEORGE P.
Africa: Its Peoples and Their Culture. New York: McGraw-Hill, 1959.

NYERERE, JULIUS
In *Symposium on Africa*, Wellesley (Mass.) College, Barnetter Miller Foundation, 1960.

OTTENBERG, SIMON, and OTTENBERG, PHOEBE
Cultures and Societies in Africa. New York: Random House, 1960.

PADELFORD, NORMAN
"The Organization of African Unity," *International Organization*, 18 (Summer 1964).

REED, DAVID
"Jomo Kenyatta, Africa's Man of Mystery," *Reader's Digest*, December 1961.

ROSS, EMORY and ROSS, MYRTA
Africa Disturbed. New York: Friendship Press, 1959.

RUDIN, HARRY R.
"Aftermath in the Congo," *Current History*, December 1963.

"Chaos in the Congo," *Current History*, February 1961.

"History of European Relations with Africa," in Calvin W. Stillman, ed., *Africa in the Modern World*. University of Chicago Press, 1955.

"The Republic of Congo," *Current History*, December 1962.

RUTHERFORD, PEGGY, ed.
African Voices. New York: Grosset & Dunlap, n.d. By permission of the Faith Press, Ltd.

SERVICE, ELMAN R.
A Profile of Primitive Culture. New York: Harper, 1958.
per, 1958.

SITHOLE, NADBANINGI
African Nationalism. New York: Oxford University
Press, 1959.

STEVENSON, ADLAI
In the Security Council, June 16, 1964, United States
Mission to the United Nations, Press Release No.
4415.

TELLI, DIALLO
"The Organization of African Unity in Historic
Perspective," African Forum, 1 (Fall 1965), no. 2.

TOURE, SEKOU
"Africa's Destiny," in James Duffy and Robert A.
Manners, eds., Africa Speaks. Princeton, N.J.: Van
Nostrand, 1961.

UNITED NATIONS
Food and Agricultural Organization (FAO), The
State of Food and Agriculture, 1958.

UNESCO Courier, September 1960.

U.S. DEPARTMENT OF STATE, AGENCY FOR INTERNATIONAL DE-
VELOPMENT
Publication 7556 (July 1963).

"U.S. Economic Aid to Africa, 1950–64," Africa Report, December 1964.

WALLBANK, WALTER T.
Contemporary Africa: Continent in Transition.
Princeton, N.J.: Van Nostrand, 1956.

WALLERSTEIN, IMMANUEL
Africa: The Politics of Independence. New York:
Random House, 1961.

INDEX

DATE DUE